TRANSCENDENTALISM AND ITS LEGACY

Transcendentalism and Its Legacy

Edited by Myron Simon
and
Thornton H. Parsons

ANN ARBOR
The University of Michigan Press

Second Printing, 1967
Copyright © by The University of Michigan 1966
All rights reserved
Library of Congress Catalog Card No. 66—17020
Published in the United States of America by
The University of Michigan Press and simultaneously
in Rexdale, Canada, by Ambassador Books Limited
Manufactured in the United States of America

Acknowledgment is made to the following publishers and individuals for permission to quote copyrighted material.

From *The Poems of Emily Dickinson,* edited by Thomas H. Johnson. Reprinted by permission of the publishers and the Trustees of Amherst College from Thomas H. Johnson, Editor, *The Poems of Emily Dickinson,* Cambridge, Mass.: The Belknap Press of Harvard University Press, Copyright, 1951, 1955, by The President and Fellows of Harvard College.

From *The Poems of Emily Dickinson,* edited by Thomas H. Johnson, by permission of Little, Brown and Company as follows:
For No. 910, Copyright 1929, 1957 © by Mary L. Hampson.
For No. 281, Copyright 1935, 1963 © by Martha Dickinson Bianchi.

Sherman Paul, "The Identities of John Jay Chapman"
Reprinted from *Journal of English and Germanic Philology* (*JEGP*) by permission of The University of Illinois Press and Sherman Paul.

Ruth Nivison and the literary estate of Edwin Arlington Robinson, for excerpts from *Selected Letters of Edwin Arlington Robinson,* edited by Ridgely Torrence.

These essays are dedicated to
Austin Warren

Preface

"I am *Defeated* all the time; yet to Victory I am born." The first half of this statement is intelligible to modern readers taught by Eliot how to carry the somber obsession with cultural malaise and by Baudelaire how to move zestlessly through urban grayness and despair. One part of the legacy of New England Transcendentalism is a rich and graceful warning to secularists against the sin and folly of projecting a personal sense of inadequacy upon the whole creation, and it may be our own little or bad faith that is reflected in any feeling that the warning is naïve.

The subtly negative sophistication that kept our critics from a proper evaluation of Frost and Cummings earlier in this century caused them to neglect or, even worse, to treat condescendingly the New England idealists of the nineteenth century whose first principle was to publish joy and health.

Uneasiness about the legacy cannot be explained simply as the age's bias of sensibility, however. The chief Transcendentalists should, like Hawthorne and James, attract only readers as acute as themselves; instead, they seem to speak personally to all kinds of men—engage even bog-trotting John Field in philosophic discussion—and so have excited every conceivable response. If they have been unfortunate in their commentators, with few manifest exceptions, they appear consciously to have taken that risk; for they did not choose to minimize the chances of misunderstanding by limiting or specializing their discourse, in the manner of Peirce. Hence, they have required—of each succeeding generation—critics no less generous than themselves and, at the same time, no less fastidious in their discriminations.

A movement that resisted definition at the start has been pervasive enough to have influenced subsequent movements as disjunct as Naturalism and Neo-Humanism and to have affected writers as opposed in their loyalties as Irving Babbitt and Eugene O'Neill. Thus, modern students have inherited questions of influence and meaning contemporary with the Transcendentalists themselves and the even larger obscurities of incremental influence and meaning created by time's translation of a live movement into memory and tradition. On the one hand, what was the "formula" of transcendence in Emerson's "Nature," how just has it been to ascribe ingenuousness to Emerson, how extensive is the indebtedness of New England Transcendentalism to French Eclecticism, how valid is the old charge that Thoreau is indistinguishable from Emerson, how is Emersonian doctrine relevant to the poetry of Emily Dickinson? On the other, what precisely is the Transcendentalist current in Santayana, Chapman, Babbitt and More, and O'Neill; in what special way has Transcendentalism diverted recent American philosophical thought from European emphases?

Both kinds of questions are comprehended within the legacy of Transcendentalism, and to engage them come the contributors to this volume.

In a collaboration of this kind, the editors incur many obligations of gratitude. None of ours is greater or more happily paid than the one owed to Doris Parsons, whose scrupulous attentions to accuracy and style in the preparation of the manuscript are reflected on every page.

Contents

PART ONE
Revaluations

I, Eye, Ay—Emerson's Early Essay "Nature": Thoughts on the Machinery of Transcendence

By Kenneth Burke

I

AN ENEMY MIGHT want to rate this early essay of Emerson's as hardly other than a Happiness Pill. But I admit: I find it so charming, I'd be willing to defend it even on that level, it is so buoyant.

Also, we need not confine our speculations to the one essay. I shall try to make clear what I take to be its salient traits, as considered in itself. But I also hope that what I say about it can be considered from the standpoint of symbolic action in general. Since Emersonian "transcendentalism" was quite accurately named, I shall discuss the work from the standpoint of "transcendence."

Though dialectical transcendence and dramatic catharsis have many areas in which the jurisdictions covered by the two terms overlap, there are also terministic situations in which they widely differ. And the simplicity of the procedures embodied in Emerson's essay is exceptionally useful in this regard, as a way to bring out the contrast between transcendence and catharsis.

Catharsis involves fundamentally purgation by the imitation of victimage. If imaginative devices are found whereby members of rival factions can weep together, and if weeping is a surrogate of orgiastic release, then a play that produced in the audience a unitary tragic response regardless of personal discord would be in effect a transformed variant of an original collective orgy (such as the Dionysian rites out of which Greek tragedy developed). Here would be our paradigm for catharsis.

But transcendence is a rival kind of medicine. Despite the area of overlap, the distinction between the two is clear enough at the extremes. And Emerson's brand of transcendentalism is a thorough example of the difference.

There are traces of victimage even here. Similarly, in the Platonic dialogue, there are traces of victimage, insofar as some speakers are sacrificed for the good of the dialogue as a whole (sacrificed in the sense of being proved wrong—yet their errors were a necessary part of the ultimate truths in which the dialogue, ideally, culminates). A similar "cathartic" element is indicated here in references to what has been called Hegel's "logonomical purgatory."

Though transcendence as we shall deal with it is a sheerly symbolic operation (quite as with catharsis by victimage), the process has an *institutional* base as well —and I can indicate my meaning quickly.

In the appendix to the revised edition of my *Attitudes Toward History*, there is an article, "The Seven Offices." It aims to decide how many, and how few, categories are needed to designate the functions that people perform for one another. The first six are:

> govern (rule)
> serve (provide for materially)
> defend
> teach
> entertain
> cure

But one further function still had to be dealt with. For a while, I thought of "console." After a person has been governed, provided for materially, defended, taught, and entertained, but has gone beyond the point where he can be cured, there is nothing left to do for him but attempt to console him, as do the churches. But the priestly function could not be confined to consolation. A priesthood also assists in the processes of rule, insofar as promises of reward in the afterlife are matched by threats of punishment, though Gilbert Murray has pointed out that threats of punishment also have a consoling effect, insofar as we can tell ourselves that our unjust enemy must eventually suffer for his misdeeds—and revenge is sweet. But, in any case, I suddenly realized that, regardless of whether a priesthood is promising rewards in the afterlife or threatening punishment, or even if the priesthood is discussing some other realm without reference to ultimate reward or punishment, a realm HERE is being talked about *in terms of* a realm ELSEWHERE—and there is a terminology designed to *bridge* these disparate realms. So, for my seventh office, I chose the term:

pontificate; that is, to "make a bridge."

Viewed as a sheerly terministic, or symbolic, function, that's what transcendence is: the building of a *terministic bridge* whereby one realm is *transcended* by being viewed *in terms of* a realm "beyond" it. Once you consider this process purely from the standpoint of *symbolic functions,* you will see that it is by no means confined to such "tender-minded" modes of expression as we find in the explicit transcendentalism of an Emerson.

Transcendence, as we shall see, is best got by processes of dialectic (quite as catharsis is best got through drama). And in borrowing so much from Hegel's dialectic, even so "tough-minded" a nomenclature as that of Karl Marx inevitably retained transcendental traces (as when conditions *here and now* are seen *in terms of* a broad historic sweep that quite *transcends* them, and thus imparts to them a kind of "ulterior" meaning).

II

The discussion of catharsis centers in speculations on the way in which an audience is purged by somewhat identifying itself with the excesses of the tragic hero. There are two main meanings of *hubris:* "pride" and "excess." (Both translations fit Coriolanus superbly. He is arrogant—and in his arrogance he embodies with great intensity a moral tension of society as we know it, the distinction between the privileged and the underprivileged.)

We must also consider a non-Aristotelian kind of catharsis, as with the Crocean stress upon the cathartic nature of sheer expression, the relief of getting things said (of turning brute impressions into articulate expression). Perhaps the most effective instance of such gratification in *Coriolanus* is the way in which the play reduces to a clear narrative line the bundle of overlapping complexities among the motives of individual, family, class, and nation.

In many ways, drama and dialectic are alike. Both exemplify competitive cooperation. Out of conflict within the work, there arises a unitary view transcending the partial views of the participants. At least, this is the dialectic of the ideal Platonic dialogue. Both drama and dialectic treat of persons and their characteristic thoughts. But whereas drama stresses the *persons* who have the *thoughts,* and the dialectic of a Platonic dialogue stresses the *thoughts* held by the *persons,* in both forms the element of personality figures.

However, dialectic can dispense with the formal division into cooperatively competing voices. The thoughts or ideas can still be vibrant with personality, as they so obviously are in the essays of Emerson. Yet we think of them as various aspects of the same but somewhat inconsistent personality, rather than as distinct *characters* in various degrees of agreement and disagreement, as in a Platonic dialogue.

Though the Hegelian dialectic lays much greater stress than Emerson's upon the cooperative *competition* (as with Hegel's pattern whereby antitheses become resolved in a synthesis that is the thesis out of which will arise a new antithesis, etc.), Emerson had his variant in his doctrine of "Compensation." (The scheme amounted to this: show how evils will have good results, but play down the reciprocal possibility whereby good might have evil results. "There is no penalty to virtue, no penalty to wisdom; they are proper additions to being." In brief, work up a dialectic that would rule out an ironic concept such as Veblen's "trained incapacity," or the French proverbial formula, "the defects of its qualities.")

All told, however, at their extremes there is a notable difference between tragic catharsis and dialectical transcendence—and the Emerson essay serves as a delightful illustration of this difference. To be sure, the essay is a bit innocuous; but it is charmingly so. It has a kind of exaltation, thanks in large part to Emerson's profuse mixing of his ideas with ingratiating imagery. And we can readily understand why he was so enthusiastic about Whitman, before a more quizzical look at Whitman's poetic evangelism led him to see that it was beckoning "Come hither" to much more than a highly respectable vendor of uplift such as Emerson had bargained for. Both approached the conflicts of the century in terms that allowed for a joyous transcendental translation. To apply in a twisted way (and thereby twisting a twist) Rimbaud's demand for a poetics based on the "reasoned derangement of the senses," we might say that Emerson was as idealistically able as Whitman to look upon some traveling salesmen and see a band of angels. There can be transcendence upwards (as when Coleridge studies the constitution of Church and State "according to the idea of each"). There can be transcendence downwards (as when, thinking of a Church, one speaks of it in terms of the sewer upon which a Church is necessarily built). And there can be a fluctuating between the two. (Cf. in E. M. Forster's novel, *A Passage to India,* the wavering as to whether India is a "muddle" or a "mystery.")

III

Emerson's essay is definitely an idealistic exercise in transcendence up. (There is also a down implicit in such a pattern—but as we proceed, we'll see how it differs from the angry or Beatnik downs.)

Since both tragic catharsis and dialectical transcendence involve *formal development,* by the same token both modes give us kinds of *transformation.*

In tragic catharsis (or, more generally, dramatic catharsis—for there are corresponding processes in comedy), the principle of transformation comes to a focus in *victimage.* The tragic pleasure requires a *symbolic sacrifice*—or, if you will, a *goat.* And the same is obviously true of the comic pleasure.

In dialectical transcendence, the principle of transformation operates in terms of a "beyond." It is like our seventh office, the "priestly" function, in that it pontificates, or "builds a bridge" between disparate realms. And insofar as things here and now are treated in terms of a "beyond," they thereby become infused or inspirited by the addition of a *new or further dimension.*

The Emerson essay is a delightful example of such a terministic process. But before we deal with it in particular, further preparatory considerations are in order, since they bear directly upon the distinction between tragic catharsis and dialectical transcendence. They concern Friedrich Nietzsche's *The Birth of Tragedy.* Though the histories of philosophy usually stress Plato's quarrels with the Sophists, Nietzsche was exercised rather with the difference between the Socratic medicine (as interpreted by Plato) and the medicine of the tragic playwrights. Celebrating the cult of tragedy, the cult of the kill, resolution in terms of extreme victimage, Nietzsche attacked Socrates for being a *reformer* whose policies implied the *death* of tragedy.

You might recommend a cause by tragic dignification (by depicting people of worth who are willing to die for it). Or (along the lines of Aristotle's *Rhetoric*) you might recommend it by showing the advantages to be gained if the cause (or policy) prevails (that is, you might argue in terms of expediency). Or there are the resources of dialectical transcendence (by seeing things in terms of some "higher" dimension, with the spirit of which all becomes infused). In Nietzsche's case the situation was further complicated by the fact that, even while attacking Plato, Nietzsche attributed to Plato a large measure of tragic dignification, owing to the stress that Nietzsche placed upon the figure of the "dying Socrates" who willingly sacrificed himself as a way of bearing witness to the virtues of the Socratic (Platonic, dialectical) method.

Essentially, the dialectical operations in the Emerson essay are to be built around the traditional One-Many (unity-diversity) pair. Emerson states it succinctly: "ascent from particular to general"; for if we say "furniture" instead of "tables, chairs, and carpets," we spontaneously speak of the more general term as in some way "higher." The process is completed when one has arrived at "highly" generalized terms like "entities" or "beings"—whereupon all that is left is a further step to something like "Pure Being," or the One, or First, or Ultimate, or some such. When we arrive at this stage, the overall term-of-terms or title-of-titles is so comprehensive it is simultaneously nowhere and everywhere. Hence, mystics can select just about anything, no matter how lowly and tangible, to stand for it (for instance, the enigmatic role of the wasp, as seen by Mrs. Moore and imagined by Professor Godbole, in *A Passage to India*). Dialectical transcendence depends upon these quite pedestrian resources of terminology.

In the case of Emerson's essay, the underlying structure is as simple as this: the everyday world, all about us here and now, is to be interpreted as a *diversity* of *means* for carrying out a *unitary purpose* (or, if you will, the *principle* of purpose) that is situated in an ultimate realm *beyond* the here and now. The world's variety of things is thus to be interpreted *in terms of* a transcendent unifier (that infuses them all with its single spirit). And by this mode of interpretation all the world becomes viewed as a set of *instrumentalities*. (Emerson more resonantly calls them "commodities.") For we should bear it in mind that Emerson's brand of transcendentalism was but a short step ahead of out-and-out pragmatism, which would retain an unmistakable theological tinge in William James, and furtive traces even in Dewey. I have in mind the ambiguity whereby, when Dewey pleads that people use their "capacities" to the fullest, he secretly means their "*good* capacities." He thus schemes to make a quasi-technical term serve a moralistic purpose—money being a kind of universal purpose (since it can serve for an almost endless variety of purchases); whereas one might ask, "Give our lives *meaning*," or "Give our lives *purpose*," you are more likely to hear the pragmatic reduction, "*Give us jobs*."

It is well to keep such developments in mind when we read the Emerson essay. While affirming much the kind of moralistic utilitarianism that one finds in the Discourses of Epictetus, and with hankerings after the kind of moralistic "Progress" that one finds in Bunyan's idea of pilgrimage, the essay must now be seen as inevitably, inexorably placed along the way towards the confusions that beset the current combinings of technological and monetary rationalization. "Under the general name of commodity," Emerson writes, "I rank all those advantages which our senses owe to nature." Thus, under the head of "Commodity," he can refer to "Nature, in its ministry to man." While reading that section we should, perhaps, not merely be sure to interpret "commodity" in a moralistic sense that has since dropped away, but also have in mind the poignancy of the fact that—as we can now readily discern, since history is by nature a Damoclean sword—Emerson's use of the term already held in suspension the narrower contemporary meaning.

Where, then, are we? I am trying to do at least three things at once. I am trying to build up a contrast between transformation by victimage (dramatic catharsis) and transformation by dialectical "transcendence" (modes of "crossing" whereby something here and now is interpreted in terms of something beyond). I am trying to discuss precisely how these operations are performed in one particular essay, by Emerson, on Nature. (In brief, he so sets up "Nature" that it is to be interpreted in terms of Supernature.) And I further hope to indicate that the design here being discussed is employed in all sorts of terministic schemes. For the same principle is involved (there are tiny "transcendences") every time an author, no matter how empirical his claims, mounts to a "higher" level of generalization and, in effect, asks that "lower" levels of generalization be interpreted in its terms.

The third thesis should especially concern anyone who, while spontaneously shifting back and forth between different levels of generalization, might incline not to see that all such procedures are operating within the same rules, but in a fragmentary way.

So, if one feels that Emerson's essay is not tough-minded enough (and I'd be the last to assert that it is, for all my love of it), I'd contend that such a judgment is not enough to dismiss it.

If only like loving a pleasant dream, love him for his idealistic upsurge. For *it reads well*. It is medicine. Even in those days, I feel sure, both he and Whitman suspected that they might be whistling in the dark. But they loved the gesture (if whistling is a gesture)—and it is an appealing gesture. Albeit a gesture much more plausible then than now. Emerson's scheme for transcendence (like Whitman's variant) was propounded before his fellow-townsmen had lost their sense of a happy, predestinated future. There was not yet any crying need to turn, rather, and begin hoarding relics of the ancestral past, like an unregenerate Southerner, with the trunkload of Confederate money in his attic.

I V

Here is what I take to be the underlying form of the essay: it treats of Society in terms of Nature—and it treats of Nature in terms of the Supernatural. Thereby, even the discussion of Society in its most realistic aspects becomes transcendentally tinged (somewhat as though you had made a quite literal line-drawing with pen and ink and had covered it with a diaphanous wash of cerulean blue).

In keeping with such an approach to the everyday

materials of living, note how even the realm of the sensory can be interpreted as a kind of *revelation*. For whatever the world is, in its sheer brute nature as physical vibrations or motions it *reveals itself* to us *in terms of* sights, sounds, tastes, scents, touch, summed up as pleasure or pain. Thus, you already have the terministic conditions whereby even the most material of sensations can be called "apocalyptic" (since the word but means "revealing")—and Emerson does apply precisely that word. In this respect, even the crudest of sensory perceptions can be treated as the revealing of nature's mysteries, though the revelations are confined to the restrictions imposed upon us by the physical senses that reveal them. Also, the resources of dialectic readily permit us to make a further step, insofar as particulars can be treated in terms that transcend their particularity. Within the Emersonian style, this convenience indigenous to terminology would be more resonantly stated: "when the fact is seen in the light of an idea."

If Nature is to be treated in terms of Supernature, another possibility presents itself. There could be stylistic procedures designed to serve as *bridges* (or intermediaries) between the two sets of terms. The simplest instance of such a bridging device is to be seen in the dialectic of Christian theology. If you make a distinction between "God" and "Man," you set up the terministic conditions for an intermediate term (for bridging the gap between the two orders); namely, "God-Man." Similarly, in the dialectic of psychoanalysis, one might be advised to inquire whether the term "preconscious" can serve (at least on some occasions) as a bridge between the terms "conscious" and "unconscious." Fittingly, the major bridge of this sort in Emerson's essay comes in the chapter halfway through, containing the homily on "Discipline."

We'll discuss later how the chapter on Discipline operates as a bridge, a "pontificator." Meanwhile, we should note another kind of bridge: the *imagistic*. There is such a profusion of images in the essay that at first I was puzzled as to how I might discuss the imagery in the summarizing way needed for a presentation of this sort. For to deal with the images in their particularity, one would need the kind of line-by-line analysis that is possible only to a succession of sessions in the classroom.

So I propose a makeshift. Near the start of the essay, Emerson writes, "if a man would be alone, let him look at the stars." Then he continues:

> The rays that come from those heavenly worlds will separate between him and what he touches. One might think the atmosphere was made transparent with this design, to give man, in the heavenly bodies, the perpetual presence of the sublime. Seen in the streets of cities, how great they are! [I fear that that line has become a victim of technological progress.] If the stars should appear one night in a thousand years, how would men believe and adore; and preserve for many generations the remembrance of the city of God which had been shown! [This passage presumably refers to a spot in the Introduction: "The foregoing generations beheld God and nature face to face; we, through their eyes." And at that point, of course, one might turn aside to mention the favored role of eye-imagery in Emerson's transcendental vision.] But every night come out these envoys of beauty, and light the universe with their admonishing smile.

Perhaps we should add the opening sentence of the next paragraph: "The stars awaken a certain reverence, because though always present, they are inaccessible; but all natural objects make a kindred impression, when the mind is open to their influence."

On the basis of these sentences, I would propose for purposes of essayistic efficiency to suggest that Emerson's imagery in general is "starry-eyed." Recall that all three canticles of *The Divine Comedy end* on references to the stars, and put that thought together with the fact that Emerson's essay thus *begins*. Note also that, in keeping with the quality of Emersonian individualism, he equates the stars with a desire to be *alone*. And when he refers to the atmosphere as being "made transparent with this design," we are advised to note the several other incidences of the term, thus:

> I become a transparent eye-ball.

> . . . the universe becomes transparent, and the light of higher laws than its own shines through it.

> If the Reason be stimulated to more earnest vision, outlines and surfaces become transparent, and are no longer seen; causes and spirits are seen through them.

> The ruin or the blank that we see when we look at nature, is in our own eye. The axis of vision is not coincident with the axis of things, and so they appear not transparent but opaque.

And in his essay "The Poet," with reference to reading a poem which he confides in "as an inspiration," he says: "And now my chains are to be broken; I shall mount above these clouds and opaque airs in which I live,—opaque, though they seem transparent,—and from the heaven of truth I shall see and comprehend my relations."

Here is what I am aiming at: first, the essay involves a definite *crossing*, via the middle section on "Discipline," so far as the development of the *ideas* is concerned. But in the starry-eyed visionary imagery (as epitomized in the notion of the "transparent") the transcendence is *implicitly* or ambiguously there from the start, and permeates the style throughout the entire essay. To pick some instances almost at random:

> . . . like an eagle or a swallow . . . the pomp of emperors . . . the live repose of the valley behind the mill . . . spires of flame in the sunset . . . the graces of the winter scenery . . . this pomp of purple and gold . . . the dewy morning, the rainbow, mountains, orchards in blossom, stars, moonlight, shadows in still water . . . the spells

of persuasion, the keys of power ... like travel-
lers using the cinders of a volcano to roast their
eggs ... the azure sky, over whose unspotted
deeps the winds forevermore drive flocks of
stormy clouds ... a leaf, a drop, a crystal, a moment of time ... not built like a ship to be tossed,
but like a house to stand ... This transfiguration
which all material objects undergo through the
passion of the poet ... the recesses of consciousness ... faint copies of an invisible archetype
... [Nor should we omit mention of this reson-
ant set in his Introduction: "language, sleep,
madness, dreams, beasts, sex." And, characteristically, at one point he gives us the equation: "the
eye,—the mind."]

And here would be the place to cite from the transitional chapter on "Discipline," and at almost the mathematical center of the essay, his central bit of Uplift. In
these tough times, I'd not even have the courage to repeat
the passage, if I could not immediately hasten to propose a non-Emersonian translation:

> Sensible objects conform to the premonitions of
> Reason and reflect the conscience. All things are
> moral; and in their boundless changes have an
> unceasing reference to spiritual nature. There-
> fore is nature glorious with form, color, and mo-
> tion; that every globe in the remotest heaven,
> every chemical change from the rudest crystal up
> to the laws of life, every change of vegetation
> from the first principle of growth in the eye of a
> leaf, to the tropical forest and antediluvian coal-
> mine, every animal function from the sponge up
> to Hercules, shall hint or thunder to man the
> laws of right and wrong, and echo the Ten Com-
> mandments. Therefore is Nature ever the ally of
> Religion.

Going beyond the specifically theological level here,
one might note the sheerly "logological" fact that a strategic feature of the Decalogue is its urgent sprinkling of
Negatives. Elsewhere I have dealt with the all-importance

of the Negative in the development of language, in connection with the complex property-structures that depend upon the codifications of secular law (and its species of "thou-shalt-nots"), and with the modes of thinking that arise from the resources of Negativity (Alienation, or "Negativism," for instance).

But for present purposes I might offer a shortcut of this sort: you know of the great stress upon Negativity in much contemporary Existentialist philosophy. And you know of the ingenious talk about "Nothingness" (the Heideggerian concern with *nichten* and the Sartrean concern with *le Néant*). Well, in the last analysis, when Emerson grows edified at the thought that all things, for man, are permeated with the spirit of the "thou shalt not," is he not talking about the same situation, except that his particular dialectic allows him to discuss it in the accents of elation, thereby (if we may apply one of his own words) endowing his statements with the quality of the "medicinal"?

Indeed, once the pattern gets established, you will find Emerson doing with his transcendentalism much the same thing as Whitman does with his infectious cult of the glad hand. Accordingly, since Nature is viewed as disciplinary, and since (as we have already noted) the Social Structure is viewed in terms of Nature, it follows that even the discords of "Property and its filial systems of debt and credit," can be welcomed transcendentally as a primary mode of moral discipline, thus:

> Debt, grinding debt, whose iron face the widow,
> the orphan, and the sons of genius fear and hate;
> —debt, which consumes so much time, which so
> cripples and disheartens a great spirit with cares
> that seem so base, is a preceptor whose lessons
> cannot be foregone, and is needed most by those
> who suffer from it most.

v

But I have not yet made wholly clear how the chapter on "Discipline" serves as a bridge between the *Hic et*

Nunc and the "Beyond." To appreciate the dialectical maneuvers here, we should lay great stress upon the strategic sentence in the Introduction: "Let us inquire, to what end is nature?" This question sets the conditions for the pattern of development. Of all the issues that keep recurring in the maneuvers of dialectic, surely none is more frequent than the theme of the One and the Many. As I have said, I feel that it is grounded in the logological fact that terms for particulars can be classified under some titular head. And thus, when we say "the Universe," we feel that we really are talking about the Universe, about "everything," though the term certainly includes an awful lot that we don't know anything about.

Be that as it may, given the typical resources of terminology, the question, "To what end is nature?" allows for a one-many alignment of this sort: the world of our Empirical existence can be viewed not just as a great variety of *things*, but as a great variety of *means*, all related to some ultimate *end*. In this regard we can see how Emerson's dialectic pattern (of *manifold means* in the world of everyday experience emblematically or hieroglyphically announcing some *unitary end* in a realm beyond everyday experience) set up the conditions for transcendentalizing maneuvers that would be progressively transformed into William James's pragmatism and John Dewey's instrumentalism. Though work, in its *utilitarian* aspects, amasses *material* powers, in its *ethical* aspects work can be felt to *transcend* utility. Hence "Discipline" serves as the means of crossing from sheer expediency to edification.

Before the bridge, Emerson's stress is upon *uses* (a subject dear to his countrymen, who were to build, by their technology, the highest Babylonian Tower of useful things the world has ever known, though many of the uses were to prove worse than useless). In his case, of course, the many resources of utility are moralized in terms of a transcendental purpose, itself in the realm *beyond* the bridge. On this side the bridge, there are "Commodities," "Beauty," and "Language." "Beauty" endangers the design, inasmuch as it is an end in itself. But Emerson preserves the design by his concluding decision that "beauty in nature is not ultimate. It is the herald of inward and eternal beauty."

Nothing could more quickly reveal the terministic resources of the Emersonian dialectic (or, if you will, the Emersonian unction) than a contrasting of his views on language with Jeremy Bentham's "theory of fictions." Bentham laid major stress upon the fact that all our terms for spiritual or psychological states are initially terms for sheerly physical things and processes. And by "fictions" he had in mind the thought that all moral or psychological nomenclatures are essentially metaphors carried over from the physical realm and applied analogically. But Emerson's transcendental dialectic allows him to apply a tender-minded mode of interpretation, thus:

> Words are signs of natural facts. The use of natural history is to give us aid in supernatural history; the use of the outer creation, to give us language for the beings and changes of the inward creation. Every word which is used to express a moral or intellectual fact, if traced to its root, is found to be borrowed from some material appearance. *Right* means *straight; wrong* means *twisted. Spirit* primarily means *wind; transgression,* the crossing of a *line; supercilious,* the *raising of the eyebrow.* We say the *heart* to express emotion, the *head* to denote thought; and *thought* and *emotion* are words borrowed from sensible things, and now appropriated to spiritual nature.

And so on. In any case, once you thus turn things around, you see why, if the things of nature are to serve us by providing us with terms which we can apply analogically for the development of a moral terminology, then the whole subject would come to a focus in a chapter on nature itself as a source of moral "discipline." Fittingly, the chapter begins by reference to the *"use of the world"* as a discipline. And at the beginning of the next chapter, "Idealism," we read: "To this one *end* of Discipline, all parts of nature conspire." (Italics in both cases ours.) Thus, when the chapter on "Discipline" is over, we have gone from the realm of *means* to the realm of *ends,* or more specifically, one unitary end (or, if you will, the sheer *principle* of purpose).

Now that we have crossed the bridge, into the realm of "Reason" and "Spirit," Nature appropriately suffers what Emerson himself calls a "degrading." For whereas Nature rated high when thought of as leading towards the Supernatural, in comparison with the Supernatural it comes into question, even as regards its material existence. (Incidentally, this change of rating in Emerson's dialectic corresponds, in the Marxian dialectic, to a step such as the transformation of the bourgeoisie from the class that is the bearer of the future to the class that is to be buried by the future. In a ladder of developments, rung five is "progressive" with regard to rung three, but "reactionary" with regard to rung seven.) However, in this later "degrading" of Nature, he pauses to admonish: "I do not wish to fling stones at my beautiful mother, nor soil my gentle nest." He wishes, in effect, but to complete the tracking down of the positions implicit in his dialectic.

One final development should be mentioned, since it throws a quite relevant light upon the essay's methods. In his final chapter, "Prospects," while zestfully reciting the many steps that man has taken through the course of history towards the affirming of what Emerson takes to be the ultimate supernatural Oneness, the essay has so built up the promissory that we scarcely notice how airily the problem of evil is dismissed:

> Build therefore your own world. As fast as you conform your life to the pure idea in your mind, that will unfold its great proportions. A correspondent revolution in things will attend the influx of the spirit. So fast will disagreeable appearances, swine, spiders, snakes, pests, madhouses, prisons, enemies vanish; they are tempo-

rary and shall be no more seen. [This comes close to the line in "Lycidas": "Shall now no more be seen."] The sordor and filths of nature, the sun shall dry up and the wind exhale. As when the summer comes from the south the snowbanks melt and the face of the earth becomes green before it, so shall the advancing spirit create its ornaments along its path, and carry with it the beauty it visits and the song which enchants it.

He envisions in sum: "The kingdom of man over nature."

One can't do anything with that, other than to note that it disposes of many troublesome things in a great hurry. But the Marxist dialectic is not without an analogous solution, in looking upon the socialist future as "inevitable."

Two asides: as regards "the thinking of the body," there are strong hints of a fecal motive near the end of the section on "Language":

"Material objects," said a French philosopher, "are necessarily kinds of *scoriae* of the substantial thoughts of the Creator, which must always preserve an exact relation to their first origin; in other words, visible nature must have a spiritual and moral side."

I have found that readers seldom look up the word *scoriae*. It comes from the same root as "scatological." Here it conceives the realm of matter as nothing other than God's *offal*. Such images are likely to turn up somewhere in the dialectics of transformation, especially where there is talk of "discipline." And, thanks to an ambiguous use of the verb "betrays," I'd incline to see traces of it in Emerson's statement that the principle of Unity "lies under the undermost garment of Nature, and betrays its source in Universal Spirit." In his later and shorter essay on "Nature," where we are told that the universe "has but one stuff," the same tricky usage appears thus: "Compound it how she will, star, sand, fire, water, tree, man, it is still one stuff, and betrays the same properties." Surely "stuff" here is synonymous with matter in the reference to Nature as God's *scoriae*. And thinking along the same lines, we find it noteworthy that, though Unity is the best of words when applied to the realm of the Supernatural, in the chapter "Prospects" it is called "tyrannizing" when applied to the earthly animal kingdom.[1]

V I

At the end of the chapter on "Discipline," just before we cross to the realm of the Beyond, we find traces of victimage, in his solemnizing references to separation from a friend:

> When much intercourse with a friend has supplied us with a standard of excellence, and has increased our respect for the resources of God who thus sends a real person to outgo our ideal; when he has, moreover, become an object of thought, and, whilst his character retains all its unconscious effect, is converted in the mind into solid and sweet wisdom,—it is a sign to us that his office is closing, and he is commonly withdrawn from our sight in a short time.

Is not this passage a euphemism for the death, or near-death, of a close friend? And thus, does not the bridge that carries us across to the Beyond end on strong traces of tragic dignification of victimage?

Similarly, I have tried elsewhere to show that James Joyce's story, "The Dead," should be analyzed primarily in terms of transcendence.[2] But the very title indicates that the purgative force of victimage also figures here.

Without considering the story in detail, we might note this much about it: the "transcending," or "beyonding," concerns the final transformation whereby the situation of the living is viewed in terms of the dead. For if the world of conditions is the world of the living, then the transcending of conditions will, by the logic of such terms, equal the world of the dead. (And the Kantian transcendental dialectic could get in the idea of God by this route: if God transcends nature, and nature is the world of conditions, then God is the realm of the unconditioned.)

The final twist, what Joyce would call an "epiphany," is contrived by the transforming of "snow" from a *sensory* image to a *mythic* image. That is, in the first part of the story, the references to snow are wholly realistic ("lexical" snow, snow as defined in a dictionary). But at the end, snow has become a *mythic* image, manifesting itself in the world of conditions, but standing for transcendence above the conditioned. It is a snow that bridges two realms—but, as befits the behavior of snow, this Upward Way is figured in terms of a Downward Way, as the last paragraph features the present participle, "falling."

There is an interesting variant in Chaucer's *Troilus and Criseyde*. The poem tells a pagan story in a pagan setting. But in the telling, Chaucer infuses the story with the medieval terminology of Courtly Love. Now, it so happens that this terminology is a *secular* analogue of the language applied to *religious* devotion. Accordingly, the story as so told sets up the conditions for the use of this language in ways that transcend its application to a pagan love affair. The book closes on the picture of slain Troilus looking down upon "This litel spot of erthe" in the traditional Christian attitude of the *contemptus mundi,* in contrast with "the pleyn felicite / That is in hevene above"—thence finally to an outright Christian prayer involving the Mary and the Trinity.

In the early part of his trip to the Underworld, Virgil encountered those of the dead who could not cross Cocytus and the Stygian swamps. Charon would not ferry them to their final abode because they had not been buried. Then comes the famous line:

Tendebantque manus ripae ulterioris amore

(And they stretched forth their hands, through love of the farther shore).

That is the pattern. Whether there is or is not an ultimate shore towards which we, the unburied, would cross, transcendence involves dialectical processes whereby something HERE is interpreted *in terms of* something THERE, something *beyond* itself.

These examples involve modes of "beyonding" that overlap upon connotations of victimage where symbolic fulfillment is attained in the ambiguities of death and immortality (with technical twists whereby, if "death" means "not-life," "immortality" compounds the negative, giving us "not not-life"). Obviously, Emerson's dialectic of a transcendent End involves similar operations. But I would here stress the fact that the principle of transcendence which is central to his essay is not confined to its use in such thorough-going examples.

The machinery of language is so made that, either rightly or wrongly, either grandly or in fragments, we stretch forth our hands through love of the farther shore. The machinery of language is so made that things are necessarily placed in terms of a range broader than the terms for those things themselves. And thereby, in even the toughest or tiniest of terminologies—terminologies that, on their face, are far from the starry-eyed transcendentalism of Emerson's essay—we stretch forth our hands through love of a farther shore; we consider things in terms of a broader scope than the terms for those particular things themselves. And I submit that, wherever there are traces of that process, there are the makings of Transcendence.

NOTES

1. The grounds for my speculations here are made clearer in my essay on "Thinking of the Body" (*The Psychoanalytic Review*, Autumn 1963), particularly the section on the symbolism of "matter" in Flaubert's *La Tentation de Saint-Antoine*. Similar connotations flit about the edges of an expression such as "purge the eyes."

2. See the section from "Three Definitions" reprinted in my *Perspectives by Incongruity*, edited by Stanley Edgar Hyman (Bloomington, Ind., 1964).

Conservative and Mediatory Emphases in Emerson's Thought

By Harry Hayden Clark

IN FLOYD STOVALL'S JUDICIOUS review of scholarship devoted to Emerson in *Eight American Authors* (amplified edition; New York, 1963, pp. 62 ff.), he concludes that, in the face of adverse appraisals based on pessimistic criteria during the last decades, "the inspirational value of Emerson cannot be saved in an age of skepticism without first restoring confidence in his common sense." Among the conventional current charges against Emerson which Stovall cites are transcendental impracticability in worldly matters, a blindness to sin and evil, hostility to the reform of social and political evils, "a belief in perfectibility in this world," a worship of self-reliant spontaneity at the expense of the authority of tradition, and a beneficent and sentimental religion which equates individualistic or extremist impulse with the voice of an untraditional God. One might as well begin by admitting that in essays such as "Politics" and "The Conservative" that espouse a mediatory position between liberalism and conservatism—which he associates with a cosmic balance between centrifugal and centripetal forces—Emerson does make ample allowance for the values of an innovating liberalism. Naturally, he could not avoid taking on some of the romantic coloring of his Romantic Era. And in following his rhetorical method of thrust and counterthrust he provided his opponents with a multitude of apothegms which can be quoted out of context to distort his total meaning. However, the time seems ripe for trying to elucidate the role of conservative and mediatory emphases in his thought. Both *The Times Literary Supplement* (for May 6, 1965) and the MLA-sponsored *American Literary Scholarship* for 1963 (edited by James Woodress, 1965) have noted that in recent years there has arisen a new respect for Emerson, representing what Jonathan Bishop calls "our one indispensable tradition" and that the upsurge of interest in him is likely to be increased by the publication of his *Early Lectures,* correspondence, *Lectures,* and the amplified *Journals.*[1] Especially noteworthy is S. E. Whicher's *Freedom and Fate* (1953), not only for tracing the changing emphasis in Emerson's genetic development but also for establishing a fruitful *method* of interpreting his thought. In accord with Emerson's increasing concern for the complexities of outward experience, which led him to entertain the possibility of skepticism, Mr. Whicher illustrates the advantages of regarding his work as a kind of "dialogue" between Emerson's inner consciousness of spiritual potentialities and a sense of personal and outward limitations. In other words, a given statement can seldom be taken alone[2] but must be viewed in relation to a counterbalancing statement, with emphasis upon his total and complex thought on a given topic, and his fidelity to a large philosophical perspective. He enjoyed the pungency of exploring ideas viewed from opposite poles, counting on the reader to recognize his eventual mediation between extremes.

Finally, while one must beware of the biographical fallacy, I think that interpretations of Emerson are more likely to be accurate which accord with his total personality and character as we find them recorded not only in his own writings and private journals but as witnessed by a great multitude of contemporaries, such as Lowell, who listened to him under varying conditions. Even those who violently disagreed with his supposed opinions testified to his ethical elevation, decorous conduct, and faithful responsibility to every obligation to his family and his community. As a means of suggesting the ways in which Emerson's thought as a whole embodied attitudes which may be called conservative or mediatory, this essay will consider the following topics: Understanding, Prudence, and the Need for Obedience to Mundane Laws; Sin and Evil; Reformism; Tradition; Self-Reliant Individualism; and the Mediation between Extremes guided by a sense of Beauty. The essay might be organized in many other ways, but the one suggested will perhaps serve to "box the compass" according to a fairly logical progression and the hierarchy of Emersonian values. This organization also has the advantage of confronting, seriatim, the charges against Emerson listed above.

I. *Understanding, Prudence, and the Need for Disciplined Obedience to Mundane Laws*

The first essential in comprehending Emerson is to note that to him "the existing world is not a dream, and cannot with impunity be treated as a dream" (*W,* I, 303); he recognized that "The restraining grace of common sense is the mark of all the valid minds," and he emphasized a common sense that "believes in the existence of matter ..." (*W,* VIII, 3; also *J,* IV, 12). As a Yankee farmer, Emerson was keenly aware of the earthy facts of life, and many of his ideas were developed through analogy with a farmer's[3] experience, for example, orchard-grafting as a counterpart of meliorism (*W,* VI, 73). Lowell and Holmes, respectively, regarded the man they knew so well as a "Plotinus-Montaigne," a "winged Franklin." Perhaps the frequent charge that he was so mystical that he did not believe in the existence of matter is partly based on a failure to see his distinction between different levels of reality according to the principle of durability. For example, he did not question, any more than did his favorite, Newton, that the apple which fell on his head existed and was a real apple; but the law of gravity that its fall represented was much more real and enduring than that one apple which would soon decay. "Time is nothing to laws" (*JMN*, V, 169).

Because Emerson believed in Reason which provides insight into a spiritual well-being, one should not assume that he did not recognize the claims of the Understanding in its own worldly realm. The "lieutenant" (*J*, IV, 74) of the Reason, "Understanding is the executive faculty.... It mediates between the soul & inert matter.... [It] incarnates the Ideas of Reason.... [and] takes middle ground..." (*JMN*, V, 272–73). According to Emerson's pervasive doctrine of the correspondence of mind and matter, "The axioms of [Newtonian] physics translate the laws of ethics," and "The laws of moral nature answer to those of matter as face to face in a glass" (*W*, I, 32–33). He also derives this doctrine from tradition, mentioning that "Socrates says 'The laws below are sisters of the laws above.' So really are the material elements of close affinity to the moral elements. But they are not their cousins, they are themselves. They are the *same laws* acting on superior and inferior planes."[4]

With such a view of the essential reality of the "law for thing" it was inevitable that Emerson should defend a "true prudence or law of shows [which] recognizes the co-presence of other laws and [which] knows that its own office is subaltern." Prudence is "not to be a several [separate] faculty, but a name for wisdom and virtue conversing with the body and its wants." Prudence "keeps these laws that it may enjoy their proper good. It respects space and time, climate, want, sleep, the law of polarity, growth and death.... Here lies stubborn matter, and will not swerve from its chemical routine." "Nature punishes any neglect of prudence.... The beautiful laws of time and space, once dislocated by our inaptitude, are holes and dens." "Let him [man] see that as much wisdom may be expended on a private economy as on an empire, and as much wisdom may be drawn from it" (*W*, II, 222, 223, 225, 228, 234). Emerson contrasts sharply with such nonconservative romantics as Rousseau and Byron. If

Emerson emphasized spiritual laws, that was because he thought that the preceding Age of Franklin and Paine had gone to extremes in emphasizing the Argument from Design in the outward cosmos at the expense of psychological Inwardness; he transcended the emphasis of the preceding Age of Reason by including it in a larger synthesis involving the outward *and* the inward in a true "sphericity." Emerson's key passage on the organic relation between worldly prudence and spirituality shows how far he was from Hawthorne's caricature of him as a "mystic, stretching his hand out of cloudland, in vain search for something real":

> The prudence which secures an outward well-being is not to be studied by one set of men, whilst heroism and holiness are studied by another, but *they are reconcilable* [my italics]. Prudence concerns the present time, persons, property and existing forms [and "governs the world" (J, V, 314–15)]. But as every fact hath its roots in the soul, and if the soul were changed would cease to be . . . the proper administration of outward things will always rest on a just apprehension of their cause and origin . . ." (*W*, II, 236; see also *W*, IV, 152 ["Montaigne"]).

While Emerson was always basically an idealist who warned against letting a craving for things "ride mankind," he did not go to the extreme of Thoreau on the subject of wealth. For Emerson, reasonable wealth, used wisely and with moderation, could do much to enable a man to fulfill his humane potentialities through such necessary instrumentalities as costly education, libraries, cultural travel, entertainment, and hospitality. Emerson's essay on "Wealth" (*W*, VI, 83–127) is surprisingly mediatory for one who mainly wishes to transcend worldly wealth:

> Property is an intellectual production. The game requires coolness, right reasoning, promptness and patience in the players.
>
> . . . .
>
> Wealth brings with it its own checks and bal-

ances. The basis of political economy is non-
interference. The only safe rule is found in the
self-adjusting meter of demand and supply. . . .
Meddle, and you snap the sinews with your
sumptuary laws. . . . Open the doors of opportunity to talent and virtue and they will do themselves justice, and property will not be in bad
hands.

If such a laissez-faire passage sounds odd in our era
of the Welfare State, involving what some call 'regi-
mentation," we should recall that, like the transcendental
reformer Theodore Parker, Emerson would safeguard
society against the predatory spirit by relying on the
merchants and other seekers of decent wealth to regiment
or control *themselves* by inward self-discipline. Emerson's
chapter on "Wealth" in *English Traits* includes much
on the way English society has been able to use wealth to
advance the social and cultural amenities as a necessary
basis for the good life. His basic emphasis is on balance
and proportion. In Emerson's essay "The Young American" the influences of the land and of the development
of commerce through such things as the railroad are
balanced by the power of "new moral causes" (*W*, I,
364 ff.). He once defined himself as essentially "a poet in
the sense of a perceiver and dear lover of the harmonies
that are in the soul and in matter, and specially of the
correspondences between these and those."[5] After all,
Emerson's idea of worldly prudence as a good if prelimin-
ary discipline in schooling a man to obey parallel spiritual
laws was not so different from the general view of his
forebears, Cotton Mather for one. Mather's *Essays to Do
Good* had influenced the prudential Franklin—if not our
"winged Franklin"—and Mather had held that man's being
responsible to "two callings" (worldly and spiritual) is
analogous to one's needing two oars to row a boat.

Since Emerson has been charged so often with merely
following lawless impulse as a spiritual guide, it is important to emphasize his doctrine of immutable laws and
of the need for disciplining one's self to obey them. In

section five of "Nature" Emerson elaborated his thesis that while "Nature is thoroughly mediate" and "made to serve," "Nature is a discipline. . . . Labor, climate, food, locomotion, the animals, the mechanical forces, give us sincerest lessons. . . . They educate . . . the Understanding" first. "Every property of matter is a school for the understanding,—its solidity or resistance, its inertia, its extension, its figure, its divisibility. The understanding adds, divides, combines, measures. . . ." If eventually "Reason transfers all these lessons into its own world of thought, by perceiving the analogy that marries Matter and Mind," we learn best by an "ascent from particular to general," from learning that at first all things as revealed to the senses are "sundered and individual." "What is a farm," Emerson asks, "but a mute gospel" teaching the discipline of the Understanding which parallels and mirrors the laws of the Reason? In "New England Reformers" Emerson describes the great man as one who will "rely on the Law alive and beautiful which works over our heads and under our feet. Pitiless, it avails itself of our success when we obey it, and of our ruin when we contravene it" (W, III, 283). In his essay "Spiritual Laws," Emerson concludes that "By contenting ourselves with obedience we become divine. . . . Place yourself in the middle of the stream of power and wisdom which animates all whom it floats . . ." (W, II, 138–39). Such "placing" obviously involves an act of free will; but, once in accord with life's "beneficent tendency," one is conscious that "the last lesson of life . . . is a voluntary obedience, a necessitated freedom" (W, VI, 240). "There is one direction in which all space is open to him. . . . He is like a ship in a river" (W, II, 140). Those who try to make out that Emerson's is an uncritical optimism, that he makes life seem too easy, would seem to minimize the fact that he says we inevitably invite "our ruin when we contravene" or disobey the "Law alive," that the free-willed individual brings much evil upon himself by violating immutable laws, whether mundane or spiritual. "You must take their divine direction, not they yours" (W, X, 84). "Who has more obedience than I masters me, though he should not raise his finger" (*W*, II, 70; on this topic of obedience see also *W*, I, 199; *W*, II, 138; *W*, VIII, 320; *W*, IX, 360; *W*, X, 84, 208; *W*, XII, 77, 205; *J*, II, 393; *J*, VI, 212).

II. *Sin and Evil*

The claim that Emerson was blind to sin and evil as charged by contemporaries such as Melville, Hawthorne, and C. E. Norton has been a major obstacle to the later acceptance of him as a wise man, but we should remember that these very influential contemporaries wrote before the *Journals, Early Lectures,* and correspondence provided the full evidence. (Emerson himself praised Hawthorne's acid attack on Giant Transcendentalism for overlooking sin in "The Celestial Railroad.") Indeed, he had written his wife in 1842 that his opponents "fasten me in their thoughts to 'Transcendentalism,' whereof you know I am wholly guiltless."[6] Considering his sardonic tone in essays such as "The Chardon Street Convention" (of disorderly eccentrics and freaks), it is quite possible that Emerson dissociated himself from the extremist reformers popularly supposed to be marching under his banner.

If one approaches Emerson's writing chronologically, it seems clear that (as his brother Charles said after reading the manuscripts of Emerson's earliest *Journals*) the predominant note was at first one of melancholy and impotence often associated with a semi-Calvinist sense of human frailty. Stephen Whicher's *Freedom and Fate: An Inner Life of Ralph Waldo Emerson* (1953) is devoted to the thesis that Emerson steadily shifted his emphasis from the celebration of the heartening potentialities of freedom (especially in the "three challenges" of 1836–38) to a somewhat disillusioned concern with the binding ties of Fate associated with the evils of reality. Thus, Emerson gradually substituted for the image of the scholar-hero the image of the scholarly observer concerned chiefly with personal reform in the light of skepticism or an "agnostic optimism." In other words, Emerson's recognition of sin and evil during his youth and in the period after 1852 balance the optimism of his middle period. But even in "Experience" (1844–45) which includes much imagery associated with a nightmarish world of horror and fright,[7] Emerson emphasizes point of view, and he says that a wrong "act looks very differently on the inside and on the outside; in its quality and in its consequences. . . . Especially the crimes that spring from love seem right and fair from the actor's point of view, but when acted are found destructive of society" (*SW*, p. 270). Emerson's essay on "Fate" (1852) has an emphasis quite inimical to the idea in "Woodnotes" that "Nature ever faithful is / To such as trust her faithfulness"; "Fate" reflects Emerson's darker awareness of the predatory qualities of nature and man.

> The way of Providence is a little rude. The habit of snake and spider, the snap of the tiger and other leapers and bloody jumpers, the crackle of the bones of his prey in the coil of the anaconda,—these are in the system, and our habits [as men] are like theirs. . . . The planet is liable to shocks from comets, perturbations from planets, rendings from earthquake and volcano. . . .
>
> (*SW*, p. 332)

And in "The Sovereignty of Ethics," reflecting the era of Darwin's *Origin*, Emerson elaborated his compensatory view that "ferocity has uses. . . . Melioration is the law. The cruelest foe is a masked benefactor" (*W*, X, 188). The essay on "Fate"—in which "the best use of Fate [is] to teach a fatal courage" and to "generate the energy of will" (*SW*, pp. 340, 343)—was, of course, balanced in the Emersonian dialogue by the essay on "Power," just as "The Transcendentalist" was balanced by "The Conservative." It is interesting to speculate on the possibility that the change of emphasis in Emerson's later period may reflect something of the attitude of Hegel and Darwin (and the latter's forerunners).[8]

Earlier influences are apparent in Emerson's pivotal essay, "Montaigne; or, the Skeptic" (1844–45), which concludes (*W*, IV, 173–86) with one of the transcendentalist's best-sustained discussions of five "doubts and negations" relevant to the problem of evil. These involve "the levity of intellect" as in Byron, Goethe, etc.; Fate or a fear that "the laws of the world . . . often hurt and crush us"; the often unfulfilled hope of man's "free agency"; the doubt of the practical efficacy of "Charitable souls" and institutional reformers; and the "yawning gulf between . . . the demand and supply of power, which makes the tragedy of all souls." Emerson ends his discussion by urging us to try to view evil particulars in a temporal perspective, "to believe what the years and the centuries say, against the hours," to believe that through "the centuries, through evil agents . . . a great and beneficent tendency streams." Such negations must be confronted, he held, and "Every superior mind will pass through this domain of equilibration . . . [and] will know how to avail himself of the checks and balances in nature, as a natural weapon against the exaggeration and formalism of bigots and blockheads," who either preach despair or an idealism which evades negations and evil. "Equilibration" and a deeper traditionalism should help us find "the permanent in the mutable and the fleeting."

Two recent studies[9] have illuminated this topic. S. E. Whicher in "Emerson's Tragic Sense" (1953), approaching Emerson in the light of polarity, illustrates the fact that especially in his earlier period he did carry on a considerable dialogue between "a sense of impotence" engendered by experience (or what he called " 'the ghastly reality of things' ") and his faith. "For all his loss of millennial hope, Emerson in fact came to allow much to the will of man. . . . Nor do I mean to suggest that he did not find the secret of a serene and affirmative life. The evidence is overwhelming that he did." Newton Arvin in "The House of Pain" (1959), is in accord with Whicher in finding that Emerson's great middle period was one of optimism framed by an earlier and a later period in which one finds a "minor strain . . . of sadness, apprehension, and doubtfulness of the goods of existence." Arvin's main contribution involves the argument that, if Emerson's optimism is not "quite so unmodulated" as generally supposed, it is by no means unique in his personality or in the America of his time, but has "a long and august tradition behind it in Western thought and analogies with the thought not only of Europe but of the East. . . . It is the theory that identifies Evil with non-existence, with negation, with the absence of positive Being," a tradition notable in Plato, in the later period of St. Augustine associated with Neo-Platonism and Plotinus, and with "the Upanishads, or the *Bhagavad-Gita*, or the *Vishnu Purana*." In view of Emerson's kinship with such predecessors, Arvin concludes that "it is superficial to rule out the whole of him, once for all, on the ground that he lacked the Vision of Evil; to see him as nothing but a transcendental American optimist of the mid-nineteenth century, to fail to see that his view of these things was in a great philosophic and religious tradition" hundreds of years older than Emerson and his America. "Emerson is a polarized, a contradictory, writer," who balanced "Power" against "Fate" in such a way that his distinctive view of evil in relation to good provides his writing (as in "Experience") with a "moral chiaroscuro" which has its own validity and aesthetic appeal. Whatever his view of the universe as seen *ab extra* from the standpoint of the Over-Soul, on the worldly ethical level Emerson is clearly aware that "The dualism is ever present, though variously denominated" (*J*, III, 377), aware that unless one exercises free-willed self-discipline the "law for thing . . . runs wild, / And doth the man unking."

III. *Reformism*

If Emerson was clearly not a blind optimist—and his essays "Works and Days" and "The Fortune of the Republic" testify to his recognition that many evils in his era needed reform—his main interest was not in proposing how to lessen these evils but rather in suggesting methods of reform likely to be most effective *in the long run*. He often contributed to individual charitable "causes," but he was chiefly interested in the kind of reform—education, for example—which might enable the individual to depend eventually on his own resources. "What is a man born for but to be a Reformer, a Remaker of what man has made . . . ," for "the good that is here is but a little island of light amidst the unbounded ocean" (*W*, I, 248; *J*, I, 246). Alexander Kern[10] remarks that while most reformers thought of the evils to be corrected as partly determined by environment or heredity, Emerson's "assumption that the intuition of the Over-Soul was unconditioned by either environment or personality permitted him to apply his radical insights in a conservative manner." Exalting the urbanity and good taste reflected in essays such as "Manners" and "Aristocracy," Emerson was no agitator; he was temperamentally unimpressed by the shrill fanatics and exhibitionists and extremists among the reformers he described in his essay on the Chardon Street Convention on reform. Institutional reformers, he thought, suffered from at least three shortcomings. They relied on numbers and organizations at the expense of trying to improve the motivation of individuals and making them truly self-reliant. Such reformers frequently tended, he thought, toward a narrow concentration on one or two evils such as current slavery or intemperance, on the supposition that legislation against them would usher in a general Utopia. Emerson recognized, as did Hawthorne in his reformer Hollingsworth, that reformers might themselves become the victims of pride and self-righteousness. And in "New England Reformers" Emerson elaborated the thesis that "society gains nothing whilst a man, not himself renovated, attempts to renovate things around him" (*W*, III, 261).

Actually, however, Emerson took a mediatory interest in the economic problems of the day, seeking to "combine socialistic ends with capitalistic means."[11] He was active in connection with four reforms. Associated with Margaret Fuller, Emerson was interested in the crusade for Women's Rights, and he allowed his name to be used as vice-president at one of the women's conventions. He thought that if a woman really wanted the vote she should have it; but he remarked that "a woman whom all men would feel to be the best, would decline such privileges if offered," and would regard them as lessening her "legitimate" and gracious "influence" which transcended legalisms and shrill contentiousness (*LR*, IV, 230). He was interested in a mild pacifism[12] and at first suggested that the North might purchase the freedom of the slaves from the South to avoid war, a proposal he rescinded in the militant "Boston Hymn." Emerson's abolitionism developed quite gradually and with many private misgivings; but when Senator Webster and his coalition had committed the North to obeying the Fugitive Slave Law of 1850, Emerson spoke out vigorously. His abolitionism,[13] however, appears to have been based not so much on any sentimental sympathy for the slaves themselves as on his abstract theory that the enslavement of human beings was completely inconsistent with his premise of the sanctity of every individual with a heritage of equal rights and opportunities. As Ralph L. Rusk says (*The Life of Ralph Waldo Emerson*, New York, 1949, p. 247), Emerson was cool to agitators' organized reform movements as "destructive of individualism" and of his kind of self-reliance, which included encouraging the individual to improve his own motives. In the "Ode: Inscribed to W. H. Channing" (1847), explaining why he was not more active in organized Abolitionism, he gives up his earlier transient toying with disunion (ll. 46 ff.) and urges that one had better face the basic cause of slavery—the greed of individuals in both the South and the North—"Things are in the saddle, / And ride mankind." Even *after* 1850 Emerson could write privately (*J*, VIII, 316), "I have quite other slaves to free than those negroes, to wit, imprisoned spirits, imprisoned thoughts. . . ."

Emerson regarded education as "the only sure means of permanent and progressive reform," according to President C. W. Eliot.[14] Everyone knows the bare outlines of the sequence of ideas in "The American Scholar": the scholar is taught by Nature (whose laws are to be interpreted through science), by Books, and by Action; and his duties are "to cheer, to raise, and guide men" (*W*, I, 100). The chief innovation, other than urging the scholar to go beyond a rote-learning of the "courtly muses of Europe," appears to lie in his rather complex view of truly "creative reading" in the sense of individual emotional assimilation. But discussion of this topic may well be postponed until we come to the topic of Tradition.

Emerson thought that when the Primal Mind or Over-Soul reveals itself inwardly to the individual, he must be right. Thus, he played a very important role in preparing his national audience and Harvard's clientele for Charles W. Eliot's epoch-making Elective System. Eliot testified on the occasion of his ninetieth birthday celebration that the idea of the Elective System (widely imitated in other universities) originally came to him from Emerson's influence in the direction of self-reliance. When Eliot became president in 1869, Emerson had been for two years an Overseer of Harvard College, and he served on a committee which, with Eliot's encouragement, recommended the Elective System. Thus, Emerson's doctrine of self-reliance helped to prepare the minds of the public for the acceptance of the system, helped to convert Eliot himself to it, and as an Overseer Emerson himself played an immediate part in getting it framed and put into actual practice. The system is a good example of the interplay of tradition and innovation in his thinking. It should be noted, first, that no one was deprived of the right to take courses in mathematics or ancient languages; the choice was optional. (Emerson himself glorified the ancients, especially Plato and Plutarch, but he thought most students could derive their essential ideas from translations as well as from linguistic study. So far as any attack on the ancients was involved, it was not an attack on their values or ideas but on the method of studying them.) Second, Emerson tried to view the whole question in a larger perspective; he transcended it by including it in a larger circle. Mathematics, for example, was to be related to education through Nature, by classification or the discovery of a "law which is also a law of the human mind. The astronomer discovers that geometry, a pure abstraction of the human mind, is the measure of planetary motion. The chemist finds proportions and intelligible method throughout matter; and science is nothing but the finding of analogy, identity, in the most remote parts" (*W*, I, 86). By insight—not by the current rote-learning, but by imaginative *insight*—the scholar comes to "see that nature is the opposite of the soul, answering to it part for part. . . . Its beauty is the beauty of his own mind. Its laws are the laws of his own mind. . . . And, in fine, the ancient precept, 'Know thyself,' and the modern precept, 'Study nature,' become at last one maxim." And one might add that so imaginative an approach, stressing insight, made the customary education a thousandfold more meaningful.

To Emerson education was a self-realization; it depended upon a language involving a correspondence between one's individual spirit and external nature as interpreted by science. Images and laws of nature give one the essentials for exploring the soul's inmost light. Emerson's views of the proper creative reading of books, especially of the ancients, will be taken up under Tradition. One might remark here that his program did not imply a complete innovation but rather a recovery of our earlier birthright, the assumptions that prevailed before neoclassical formalism and externalism became dominant. In reading Shakespeare, he thought, we should remember that his inspiration came "direct from the soul at one end" and entered "into the play-going populace at the other" (*J*, IV, 150). The individual should appreciate the similarity between his own insights and motivations and those of Hamlet. When he reads Shakespeare with imaginative creativity, he participates in genius; and this initiation constitutes one important value of true education. In short, Emerson's educational program, while an innovation away from the strict usage of his era, was a recovery of a broader tradition.

Emerson's balance—the ability to see both sides of the reform problem—appears in his essay on "Politics" (1837–

40), where he concludes that of the current "two great parties . . . one [the Democratic] has the best cause, and the other contains the best men." He thinks that "The philosopher, the poet, or the religious man, will of course wish to cast his vote with the democrat, for free-trade, for wide suffrage, for the abolition of legal cruelties in the penal code, and for facilitating in every manner the access of the young and the poor to the sources of wealth and power." But Emerson counters such praise by saying that the sensitive man "can rarely accept the persons whom the so-called popular party propose to him as representatives of these liberalities. They have not at heart" the needed reforms. "The spirit of our American radicalism is destructive and aimless: it is not loving; it has no ulterior and divine ends, but is destructive only out of hatred and selfishness. On the other side, the conservative party, composed of the most moderate, able and cultivated part of the population, is timid, and merely defensive of property" (W, III, 209–10).

If one were to sketch Emerson's general political and social views, they would reveal a combination of liberalism and conservatism, but these views have already been studied in detail by McQuiston, Odell, and (in 1964) Maurice Gonnaud, who centers on Emerson's achievement of an equilibrium between the claims of individualism and of society. It will suffice here, perhaps, to recall that Emerson wrote an early essay glorifying Burke (*The Early Lectures of Ralph Waldo Emerson,* ed. Whicher and Spiller, pp. 183–201) and concluded that the French Revolution "taught men how surely the relaxing of the moral bands of society is followed by cruelty" (J, III, 448). Emerson had studied the records of Concord's town meetings[15] through two centuries and noted—even in his own ancestors—the endless bickerings, jealousies, rivalries, "private grudge" and "meanness and pique," and opposition to the most beneficent proposals. He was emphatically not a believer in the wholesale natural goodness of the populace (J, I, 134–35; SW, p. 357). He recognized the claims and the liabilities of both the Jacksonians and the Whigs

(*W*, XI, 237, 239-40; *J*, III, 308, 404-5; *J*, V, 76), and after meeting Lincoln he came to revere his "lawyer's habit of mind . . . not vulgar, as described, but with . . . a fidelity and conscientiousness very honorable . . ." (*J*, IX, 375).

In his essay, "The Conservative," Emerson declares the need—which he finds paralleled even in the mechanism of the cosmos—for opposed human forces, for the interrelation of the conservative and the innovator, who represent "the counteraction of the centripetal and the centrifugal forces"; and "both must continue." If innovation represents "salient energy," conservatism represents intelligent practicability; both are necessary, for they generate a creative tension, like that in "the opposition of Past and Future, of Memory and Hope, of the Understanding and the Reason" (*W*, I, 295-326). This theory invites speculation about whether Emerson had in mind something like Hegel's thesis, antithesis, and synthesis.

Emersonian political and social attitudes are Jeffersonian (*W*, X, 31-66; *J*, I, 311): they spring from belief in a natural aristocracy—the humane doctrine of equal rights that emphasizes cultivation of individual excellence, that values the production of the gentleman[16] as the authentic test of a civilization. Emerson is a striking exemplar of these attitudes in his daily life as a citizen[17] of Concord.

IV. *Tradition*

In this section consideration will be given to Emerson's view of the "creative reading" of tradition, of the "two errors" in interpreting historical Christianity, and to his views of memory.

Emerson's own range of reading[18] from the ancients up to Whitman was enormous. In the essays "Quotation and Originality" and "Books" he freely admitted the magnitude of literary tradition which made complete originality almost impossible. He likened a great writer to a great stream fed by innumerable tributaries; the greater the writer, the greater his indebtedness to others.

Among his earliest lectures was a series on "The Philosophy of History," a subject later treated in his essay "History," and he liked especially to study history in the biographies of those he later called "Representative Men." He regarded the greatness of Shakespeare as partly the result of his having drawn (cf. *Hamlet*) upon a vast popular tradition which had gradually winnowed and sifted and tested his fables to provide what was "perpetually modern" in his plays. Offhand, Emerson would appear to be the most unsuitable person to be charged with antitraditionalism.

However, at a time when the reading of college students was tested by a completely literal reciting of the texts prescribed, Emerson's "The American Scholar" and its remarks that "Books are for the scholar's idle times," and that "Meek young men grow up in libraries," scandalized college faculties. It should be noted, however, that he did include the Past as one of the three main "influences" on the scholar and he acknowledged that "Books are the best type of the influence of the past" provided that the present-day reader does not become a mere "bookworm" or antiquarian bibliomaniac immune to drawing from books a humane inspiration for his own soul, which should be respected as inviolate. When one is not able to "read God directly. . . . when the sun is hid . . . we repair to the lamps which were kindled by their ray, to guide our steps to the East again. . . ." Since true literary genius is "a larger imbibing of the common [not the idiosyncratic] heart," the "great poet makes us feel our own wealth," enables readers today by empathy to be "born into the great, the universal mind" (*W*, II, 288–89, 296). For example, Emerson would read a representative author like Milton not so much to ascertain the external peculiarities of his life or his unique sources as to find revealed in Milton the lofty potentialities of his, Emerson's, *own* spirit. Reading was to be a process of deep answering to deep, to a fresh reservoir of inward stimulation and emulation. Contrasted with literal parroting of texts in Emerson's day, such a program could, of course, be called revolutionary; but as Emerson remarked, he was merely recalling the fact that "Cicero, Locke, and Bacon were only young men in libraries when they wrote these books," and Emerson was only seeking to recover the traditional birthright of such authors. Needless to say, however, this recovery greatly enriched the experience of responding to the teachings of the Past as represented by books. Incidentally, readers of T. S. Eliot's "Tradition and the Individual Talent" will note that the advocacy in reading of "a perception, not only of the pastness of the past, but of its presence," its simultaneousness in the modern reader's mind, seems to echo Emerson, who said that Past, Present, and Future are but "Triple blossoms from one root." In 1837 he said he "read these Donnes & Cowleys & Marvells with the most modern joy,— with a pleasure ... which is in great part caused by the abstraction of all *time* from their verses. ... But for my faith in the oneness of Mind, I should find it necessary to suppose some preestablished harmony ..." (*JMN*, V, 341). By stressing the organic "act of creation" of the earlier author, instead of the static record, by stimulating the modern reader's sense of a similar psychological awareness, Emerson, paradoxically, helped to give renewed vitality to tradition.

In Emerson's mind, tradition—a socially mediated literary succession of great authors who had essentially identical general interpretations of generic man—could be likened to what Plato called Unity as opposed to Variety, an idea elaborated in the essay "History" with its thesis that throughout the literate ages "the mind [of man] is One." Identification with this Unity of tradition by the reader contributed greatly to the "enlargement and independency of the individual" and the enrichment of his inward potentialities. Much has been made of Emerson's supposed literary nationalism and disparagement of our subservience to "the courtly muses of Europe" in "The American Scholar" and of his remark (in "Considerations by the Way") that "One day we shall cast out the passion for Europe" (*W*, VI, 266), a remark which in contexture refers to the surface curiosity of antiquarian travelers. The anti-Europeanism here is incidental, and only by a willful misreading could anybody charge Emerson with antitraditionalism. His motive in these remarks is to warn against a superficial, arid antiquarianism and to celebrate implicitly an authentic, selective traditionalism—the kind that is possible when individual authors, writing out of their deepest and most original intuitions, transcend their personal eccentricities and their time and place and achieve a human centrality.

The radical feature of Emerson's religious views in his "Divinity School Address" of 1838 was his complete rejection of ecclesiasticism, his revolt against what he called "two errors" in the administration of historical Christianity. The first "is not the doctrine of the soul, but an exaggeration of the personal, the positive [or literal and miraculous incarnation of God in man], the ritual." "That which shows God out of me, makes me a wart and a wen." "The second defect of the traditionary and limited way of using the mind of Christ" is related to the fact that "Men have come to speak of the revelation as somewhat long ago given and done, as if God were dead," as opposed to emphasis on the moral "Law of laws whose [psychological] revelations introduce greatness—yea, God himself—into the open [individual] soul," without advocate or mediator (SW, pp. 105-7).

How did Emerson manage to counterbalance this apparent antitraditionalism? Is he advocating that each individual should be free to follow his private impulse as the voice of God? Considering man's susceptibility to wishful thinking, might not the impulse be the voice of the Devil, or be entirely antisocial in its mandates? Actually, tradition in the more inclusive sense of the word was one primary safeguard he invoked as a test of the genuineness of the inner voice. While he reverently admits that Jesus is "the only soul in history who has appreciated the worth of man" and who has had faith in the moral "law in us," Emerson wishes to include Jesus along with *other* traditional guides, such as the ancient

Stoics. "The sublime is excited in me by the great stoical doctrine, Obey thyself. That which shows God in me, fortifies me" (*SW*, pp. 105–6). Through the "exaggeration of the personal" in revelation ("The soul knows no persons"), Christianity has taken on the peculiarities of an "eastern monarchy ... which indolence and fear have built"; and expressions relating to Jesus' love "are now petrified into official titles" associated with a "demigod, as the Orientals or the Greeks would describe Osiris or Apollo," religious truth being "foreclosed and monopolized" and separated from the continuity of tradition as a whole (*SW*, p. 106). Such tradition being rightly viewed comprehensively, "The sentences of the oldest time, which ejaculate this piety, are still fresh and fragrant. This thought dwelled always deepest in the minds of men in the devout and contemplative East; not alone in Palestine ... but in Egypt, in Persia, in India, in China. Europe has always owed to oriental genius its divine impulses." Pure religious truth "is guarded by one stern condition; this, namely; it is an intuition. It cannot be received at second hand. Truly speaking, it is not instruction, but provocation, that I can receive from another soul." What any teacher "announces, I must find true in me, or reject," lest second-hand teachings adopted for ulterior reasons "become false and hurtful" (*SW*, p. 104). In other words, Emerson's teaching here is that our safest guide is in the *comprehensiveness* of tradition *provided* it is fully assimilated by the individual and reborn in his inner consciousness. It is true that he urges originality and self-reliance, but these relate back to universality and the belief that historically "the mind [of man] is One."

A second objection to Emerson's apparent religious individualism is that it runs counter to the majority of men's yearning for socializing, for gathering companionably with others of a kindred faith in an institution—a sectarian church—with its sacraments, frequent services, and social activities. Richness and flexibility are primary Emersonian values. Just as a man should be free to draw on all traditions, and not one exclusively, so should he be free to socialize with men of all sects, all faiths, all philosophies. Emerson stresses the *continuity* of truth, in opposition to a revelation limited to the past, "as if God were dead." Emerson's kind of brotherhood—as suggested in "Initial, Daemonic and Celestial Love"—transcends merely physical and fraternal love, and advocates drawing together all individuals (as they increase in their self-mastery) in an accord with the traditional Platonic "archetypes [that] endure," that go beyond any one time or place or sect. All society, all times, all places are the individual's patrimony. Seen in this light, the charges usually leveled against "The Divinity School Address" are not very serious. If, as Emerson said (*J*, V, 380), "In all my lectures, I have taught one doctrine, namely, the infinitude of the private man" (see also *J*, II, 224 ff.; *J*, IV, 128 ff.; and *W*, II, 268–69), his doctrine of a tradition more comprehensive than Christianity and of a society or brotherhood wider than any one revelation in the past helped to reinforce and enrich this heritage of man's private infinitude of resources in his quest for guidance toward happiness. "Far be it from me," he says (*W*, X, 203), "to underrate the men or the churches that have fixed the hearts of men and organized their devout impulses or oracles into good institutions. The Church of Rome had its saints, and inspired the conscience of Europe—St. Augustine, and Thomas à Kempis, and Fénelon; the piety of the English Church in Cranmer, and Herbert, and Taylor; the Reformed Church, Scougal; the mystics, Behmen and Swedenborg; the Quakers, Fox and James Naylor."[19]

Emerson's mature essay on "Memory" (1871) supplements his essay on "History" of twenty-seven years before by illuminating his views of tradition. Memory is "the cement, the bitumen, the matrix in which the other faculties are embedded; or it is the thread on which the beads of man are strung, making the personal identity which is necessary to moral action. Without it all life and thought were an unrelated succession" (*W*, XII, 90). This view that perception is insufficient, that memory

unites the past and the present and provides life with a
continuous "thread" reminds one somewhat of the later
Wordsworth's views, not only about the continuity of his
own life (cf. the influence of Hartleyan associationism)
but about the vitalizing conception of the past as insepara-
bly related to the present—reflected in his "Ecclesiastical
Sonnets" with their tension between "Mutability" and the
unity ascribed to continuity. (Naturally, Emerson does
not share Wordsworth's later "slant" favoring a politically
established Church as the bulwark of Toryism, but the
general stress on continuity is similar.)

Indeed, it has been said that today Emerson's shrewd
and gritty essays on the history of his native state and
his ancestors—notably the "Historic Notes of Life and
Letters in New England" and "Boston"—are more readable
than is "The Over-Soul," verging as it does on mysticism.
Reference has already been made to his careful study of
the records of New England town meetings as recorded
for nearly two centuries. His lofty concern for the timeless
was balanced by a curious fascination with time as it fled
into the past. Thus, the poem "Days," which he thought
his best, seems to vibrate with his personal fear that he
was not making the most of his own passing hours. In
this poem he pictures the "Daughters of Time" appearing
and offering him his choice of "diadems and fagots,"
"bread," or the stars and sky (symbolizing his "morning
wishes" to decipher in astronomy the immutable divine
laws). He admits that not infrequently he chooses to waste
his time on "a few herbs and apples" rather than to
concern himself with major spiritual issues, thus inviting
the "scorn" of time's "daughters" or spokesmen. This
counterbalancing of time and timelessness is treated in
much detail in Emerson's impressive essay, "Works and
Days" (*W*, VII, 155–85). His "Self-Reliance" is balanced
by "Uses of Great Men," treating the cultural heroes who
stirred his emulation as models for imitation—a doctrine
he celebrates in his stirring panegyric on his favorite
Plutarch. The essay on "Books" (*W*, VII, 187–221) suggests a breathtaking delight in Emerson as he sweeps the

centuries in his quest of a human potentiality celebrated in another essay entitled "Greatness." Sherman Paul (*Emerson's Angle of Vision*, pp. 134, 136) notes that Emerson believed that one should read history and biography as controls, as objective ways of studying the self as one studies nature (see *J*, IV, 158; *J*, III, 355, 362–63, 440-42; *W*, II, 61, 66). If he found, as he sought to find, essential identity in past biographical portraits of representative men, these examples of greatness may well have encouraged him to qualify innovation with gradualism, to mistrust innovation, sharp and complete departures from the teachings of the past. While Emerson did not have the enthusiasm of the St. Louis Hegelians (whom he visited and listened to in the Concord School of Philosophers), he may well have had some sympathy with Hegel's very broad notion that all heroes had gone through a triadic and semiuniversal pattern in their "long journey" involving alienation, flight, or initiation, and return or reconciliation; and Emerson himself exemplifies the pattern in *English Traits* (his treatment of the old home of Americans) and *Society and Solitude*.

v. *Self-Reliant Individualism*

If Emerson is most widely known as the man who said "Whoso would be a man, must be a nonconformist," who is supposed to be an iconoclast eager to "affront and reprimand the smooth mediocrity and squalid contentment of the times," it is obviously important to try to understand precisely what he means by self-reliance. It is clearly something quite different from urging the individual to do anything he pleases, quite different from licentiousness. The key to "Self-Reliance" comes near the middle (*SW*, p. 161) where Emerson says,

> . . . truly it demands something godlike in him who has cast off the common motives of humanity and has ventured to trust himself for a taskmaster. High be his heart, faithful his will, clear his sight, that he may in good earnest be doctrine,

society, law, to himself, that a simple purpose
may be to him as strong as iron necessity is to
others!

In short, Emerson's self-reliance—"a self-trust which is a
trust in God himself," God being "the Universal Mind"
(*W*, X, 65–66; *J*, IV, 61)—closely resembles Milton's idea
that anyone who wishes to cast off outward controls must
first have achieved self-control. Otherwise, says Milton in
the second sonnet "On the Detraction," "License they
mean when they cry liberty; / For who loves that, must
first be wise and good." Or as Emerson says, *before* one is
entitled to be a nonconformist in parochial matters, he
must have become almost "godlike" in his lofty mastery
of his own talent, free-willed responsibility, and insight.
Since Emerson knew that "few men since the creation of
the world live according to the dictates of Reason" (*J*,
III, 390), very few men are actually entitled to claim the
rights of self-reliance, but it is a goal toward which all
should strive.

In mentioning Self-Reliance as a subject "that needs
most" to be developed, one should note (*J*, III, 267) that
Emerson counterbalanced this "Principle" by an imperative to recognize "at the same time, how useful, how
indispensable, has been the ministry of our friends to us,
our teachers—the living & the dead! I ask advice. . . . It is
that he [my friend] may stimulate me by his thoughts to
unfold my own." And in his poem (ironically?) entitled
"Grace" (1842) he expresses gratitude to God for having
been provided with "defences" from "The depths of sin,"
defences which turn out to be the prosaic ones involved
in "Example, custom, fear, occasion slow," which safe-
guarded his self-reliant individualism. This balancing of
self-reliance by the usefulness of friends and teachers living
and dead as well as the examples of others is elaborated in
the long essay on "Uses of Great Men" prefacing *Representative Men*. Here the supposed spokesman of the Party
of Hope—as contrasted with the Party of Memory of the
great men of the past—tells us to ignore "the taunt of
Boswellism," to "stick at no humiliation" necessary to use

traditional great examples as "lenses through which we read our own minds" and thus illuminate our own potentialities. "We are emulous of all that man can do" and has done in the heroic past, and the use of traditional examples[20] is that they spring our imagination and elevate our intellect so that eventually a few of us can approach "godlike" *self*-mastery and so be entitled to claim self-reliance. Emerson's doctrine of great men, emulation, and heroism and character defined as "resistance to circumstance" should always be coupled with his far-off goal of self-reliance, which has been popularly cheapened by the slogan that one should "be a nonconformist."

His kind of self-reliant individualism should also be related to his kind of brotherhood. He concluded "The American Scholar" with the thought that in the joyful "love of man. . . . A nation of men will for the first time exist, because each [individual] believes himself inspired by the Divine Soul which also inspires all men." But his poem "Initial, Daemonic and Celestial Love" (1847) elaborates best his concept of individuals being drawn together not by a merely horizontal love of man for man, which is "the ancestor of wars / And the parent of remorse," (ll. 280–81) but by an ascent into "vision where all form / In one only form dissolves." Emerson's definition of self-reliance as a reliance on God—"the Universal Mind"—and the counterbalancing emphasis upon the need for heroic examples which stir emulation, the stern injunctions for self-discipline, and the Platonic concept of truly focused individualism culminating in brotherly unity, provide the best refutation of Vernon Parrington's[21] assertion that Emerson's gospel of individualism "was the same revolutionary conception . . . that Rousseau had come upon. . . ."

English Traits (1856, based on Emerson's observations during his sojourn in England in 1848) marks his "turn from a personal to a social perspective,"[22] to an attempt to explain men functioning *en masse,* and in the light of a long historical tradition. "The culture of the day, the thoughts and aims of men, are English thoughts and aims.

A nation considerable for a thousand years since Egbert, it has, in the last centuries, obtained the ascendent, and stamped the knowledge, activity and power of mankind with its impress. . . . The American is only the continuation of the English genius into new conditions, more or less propitious" (*W*, V, 35–36). To account for the prodigious cultural force of the English, Emerson points to the Saxon race-qualities (perhaps minimizing Norman influences), and he shows sympathetic insight into the role of aristocracy (*W*, V, 185–86) and property. Self-reliant individualism continues to be balanced by broader social concerns in Emerson's *Society and Solitude* (1870), which is one of his most gracious books. He urges that "we keep our independence, yet do not lose our sympathy. . . . A sound mind will derive its principles from insight . . . and will accept society as the natural element in which they are to be applied" (*W*, VII, 15–16).

VI. *Emerson's Central Mediation Between Extremes*

If Emerson is outstanding among Americans in having achieved a positive serenity and happiness—qualities which led Matthew Arnold to claim he had done the most important work in English prose in his whole century and was the preëminent "friend and aider of those who would live in the spirit," it behooves us to try to discover his principles of happiness. An important one is his exaltation of mediation, especially notable in his praise of Plato as a "balanced soul" who mediated between the Many and the One. "It is the little wit that is always in extremes and sees no alternative." "Measure is a virtue which society always appreciates, and it is hard to excuse the want of it. Society may well value measure, for all its law and order is nothing else. There a combat of opposite instincts and a golden mean, that is Right. What is the argument for marriage but this? What for a church, a state, or any existing institution, but just this—We must have a mean?" (*J*, VI, 22–23) And in a journal entry under the heading of "*Mediator, Mediation,*" Emerson concludes, "There is nothing else . . ." (*J*, VIII, 243). But the key passage on this central topic comes in his essay on "Experience" (*W*, III, 64–66):

> The mid-world is best. Nature, as we know her, is no saint. . . . She comes eating and drinking and sinning. . . . So many things are unsettled which it is of the first importance to settle;—and, pending their settlement, we will do as we do. . . .
>
> Human life is made up of the two elements, power and form, and the proportion must be invariably kept if we would have it sweet and sound. Each of these elements in excess makes a mischief as hurtful as its defect. Everything runs to excess; every good quality is noxious if unmixed, and, to carry the danger to the edge of ruin, nature causes each man's peculiarity to superabound. . . . A man is a golden impossibility. The line [of mediation] he must walk is a hair's breadth.

Now if one thinks over the implications of this passage, it is clear that since natural instincts invite extremism, the salvation of the individual lies not in merely following natural instincts but in imposing upon them some sort of order or mediation between extremes, an order derived from free-willed responsibility. In such an endeavor, as the passage cited indicates, the individual's aids are partly in existing institutions (marriage, a church, a state) which represent a traditional agreement, or a *consensus gentium* based on trial and error over the centuries; some help is derived from "Uses of Great Men" as heroic examples which stir the individual's capacity for emulation, using not only the ancients but Shakespeare—a "guiding torch" (*J*, III, 452)—as well as Milton; and some help is, of course, afforded by the individual's introspection or recovery of those inwardly revealed psychological impulses which Emerson differentiates from natural instincts as God-like in their universality and in their accord with the Platonic kind of love centered on the eternal "archetypes" that "endure." Closely related to

Emerson's celebration of the doctrine of the Golden Mean, which can be traced back through Horace to Aristotle and in part to Plato's idea of balancing the One and the Many, is his ideal of the "Spheral Man" or sphericity. But since Sherman Paul has anticipated me by devoting Chapter Five of his book to this very topic, I need not repeat his massive evidence. If Matthew Arnold is correct in praising Emerson's work as a whole because it shows how a modern man facing modern problems could eventually arrive at an affirmative sense of serenity and fortitude and happiness, it seems likely that the triumph was made possible through his ability to counterbalance an urge toward innovation by conservative practicality and through a willingness to mediate between extremes in accord with the durable doctrine of the Golden Mean.

What is striking about Emerson's treatment of the Golden Mean is an emphasis upon the *beauty*[23] of it. Above a merely physical and an intellectual beauty Emerson sets an ethical beauty: "Beauty is the mark God sets upon virtue" (*SW*, p. 28). In *The Journals and Miscellaneous Notebooks* beauty implies proportion (V, 409), balance of expression without too much emotion (V, 108), and it envelops "great actions" (V, 108). He quotes with approval Robert Herrick's definition of beauty as "Flashed out between the middle & extreme" (*JMN*, V, 18). The highest Beauty is beyond the "merely ornamental" but organic, and "must rest on a basis as broad as man" (*JMN*, V, 196). For Emerson the test of right conduct is whether or not it is beautiful. "The beautiful is the highest," for it escapes both extremes, the dowdiness of the good (in a negative sense) and the "heartlessness of the true" (in a merely metaphyical sense). Beauty "appeals to the Vaticinating Reason & asks whether the object be agreeable to the preexistent harmonies" (*JMN*, V, 206). His ethical teaching culminates in the praise of "the golden mean wherein grace and safety lies" (*J*, III, 195). The traditionalist Emerson traced this doctrine to his favorite, Plutarch: "Beauty is ever that divine thing the ancients esteemed it. It is, as they said, 'the flowering of

Virtue' " (*JMN*, V, 302–3). This conviction that through the practice of mediation one can approach virtue, whose crown is beauty, helps to account for the peculiar graciousness which pervades Emerson's ethical teachings.

In "The Conservative" Emerson associates innovating liberalism and conservatism with the need for cosmic balance between centrifugal and centripetal forces and seems, therefore, to allow for about 50 percent liberalism. Despite the topic of this essay, I do not wish to minimize liberal emphases of Emerson, but only to preserve his rich complexity of thought and value.

NOTES

1. References in the text will be as follows: *J* for *The Journals of Ralph Waldo Emerson*, 10 vols., ed. E. W. Emerson and W. E. Forbes (Boston, 1909–14); *JMN* for *The Journals and Miscellaneous Notebooks of Ralph Waldo Emerson*, ed. W. H. Gilman, A. R. Ferguson, M. R. Davis, M. M. Sealts, H. Hayford, and G. P. Clark (Cambridge, Mass., 1960–65); *W* for *The Complete Works of Ralph Waldo Emerson*, 12 vols., Centenary Edition, ed. E. W. Emerson (Boston, 1903–4); *SW* for *Selections from Ralph Waldo Emerson*, ed. Stephen E. Whicher (Boston, 1957); *L* for *The Early Lectures of Ralph Waldo Emerson*, ed. Stephen E. Whicher and Robert E. Spiller (Cambridge, Mass., 1959); and *LR* for *The Letters of Ralph Waldo Emerson*, 6 vols., ed. Ralph L. Rusk (New York, 1939).

2. For example, the much-quoted passage about Emerson wanting to "write on the lintels of the door-post, *Whim*," appears in his essay on "Self-Reliance," which soon veers around to the famous passage about the need to have attained "godlike" qualities of will and insight and self-mastery *before* one is entitled to abandon conformity and claim the right of self-reliance. And the passage, "I unsettle all things.... I simply experiment; an endless seeker, with no Past at my back," in its contexture in the essay "Circles," is immediately followed by the balancing statement, "Yet this incessant movement and progression [life being a perception that larger and more inclusive circles or generalizations can be drawn around smaller ones], which all things partake, could never become sensible to us, *but by contrast* [my italics] to some principle of fixture or stability in the soul. Whilst the eternal generation of circles proceeds, the eternal generator [a sense of God within us] abides. That central life is somewhat superior to creation, superior to knowledge and thought, and contains all its circles" (*W*, II, 318). In other words, seen as a dialogue, the passage as a whole

means that Emerson is contrasting the littleness of his own personal Past ("what I do") with the vastly superior "principle of fixture or stability in the soul," a view which enables him to say elsewhere that "Past, Present, and Future" are but "Triple blossoms from one root."

3. See Douglas C. Stenerson, "Emerson and the Agrarian Tradition," *Journal of the History of Ideas*, XIV (January 1953), 95–115.

4. Edward Waldo Emerson, *Essays, Addresses and Poems* (Cambridge, Mass., 1930), p. 283. Quoted in Bliss Perry, *Emerson Today* (Princeton, N.J., 1931), p. 82.

5. Quoted in J. E. Cabot, *A Memoir of Ralph Waldo Emerson* (Boston, 1887), p. 236.

6. Quoted in Cabot, p. 490.

7. John Lydenberg in "Emerson and the Dark Tradition," *Critical Quarterly*, IV (Winter 1962), 352–58, has analyzed the imagery of "Experience." He finds that while the dominant tone is essentially optimistic, isolated passages show that in 1844–45 Emerson was at times troubled by "the sense that the world of experience is mere surface, unreal; the failure of contact between souls, our helpless isolation from our fellows; the unbreakable shell which cuts off all feeling...; the masochistic tendency to court suffering as the only way to reality; the realization that there is nothing left us but the grim satisfaction of waiting for the one reality that will not slide away from us—death. All this is there, and un-typical of Emerson." Still useful is Chester Jorgenson's "Emerson's Paradise under the Shadow of Swords," *Philological Quarterly*, XI (July 1932), 274–92, although not devoted to genetic development or imagery; Jorgenson assembles many acknowledgments of sin and evil and concludes that from an overall view Emerson paid almost as much attention to these subjects as did the Puritan Milton who concluded, "All is best, though oft we doubt. ..."

8. Henry Pochman, *German Culture in America* (Madison, Wis., 1957), pp. 198 ff., has argued persuasively that Emerson's final period reflects the Hegelian-Darwinian influence.

Emphases in Emerson's Thought

In the early crucial period when Emerson was re-
signing his ministry and (after traveling in Europe)
preparing to write *Nature,* 1836, he drew special rein-
forcement from science, both Newtonian and evolutionary. As an intuitionalist he found the basic truth within
his own consciousness; he went to outward nature and
to science as its interpreter in the realm of understanding, seeking confirmation. Whether pre-Darwinian melioration—the worm in "striving to be man ... mounts
through all the spires of form"—was primarily related to
theories of emanation associated with the Neo-Platonists
and the Germans, the sources did not concern Emerson
as much as did the fact that such mounting did confirm
his optimism. In my study of "Emerson and Science,"
Philological Quarterly, X (July 1931), 225–60, I included
his reading of and concern with *both* the physical scientists and the emanationists, concluding that they "were
not mutually exclusive in their influence." (J. W. Beach,
in a study of "Emerson and Evolution," *University of
Toronto Quarterly,* III [July 1934], 474–97, minimizes
Emerson's concern with major scientists during this early
period, emphasizes the emanationists with whom he, Mr.
Beach, is temperamentally out of harmony, and thinks
Emerson did not make a "transition from the scale-of-
being phase ... to the strictly evolutionary phase" of
thought until about 1844.) Regardless of the precise
sources, what seems to me of central importance is that
amid the general scientific controversies of the time
Emerson did mediate; he recognized that a delimited and
merely empirical science could "cloud the spiritual sight,"
and he interpreted science symbolically so as to reinforce
and extend his view of correspondence, according to
which "The axioms of [Newtonian] physics translate the
laws of ethics" (*W,* I, 32–33). Briefly, as I have tried to
show in closely documented detail in my article, he used
science so as to justify his turn against ecclesiasticism and
his turn toward a faith in a relatively depersonalized
Over-Soul, perhaps best defined as a "beneficent tendency"
or as "conscious" and "animated law." (Newtonianism
would seem to have reinforced his belief in immutable
physical and ethical laws, as opposed to Calvinistic ideas
of divine caprice in "illustrious providences"; and the
pre-Darwinian evolutionists seem to have reinforced his

view of nature almost consciously tending to ascent and melioration.)

9. See the articles by S. E. Whicher, "Emerson's Tragic Sense," and Newton Arvin, "The House of Pain," conveniently reprinted in *Emerson: A Collection of Critical Essays,* ed. M. R. Konvitz and S. E. Whicher (Englewood Cliffs, N. J., 1962), pp. 39–59.

10. *Transitions in American Literary History,* ed. H. H. Clark (Durham, N. C., 1954), p. 295.

11. See John C. Gerber, "Emerson and the Political Economists," *New England Quarterly,* XXII (Sept. 1949), 336–57; and Alexander C. Kern, "Emerson and Economics," *New England Quarterly,* XIII (Dec. 1940), 678–96.

12. See W. A. Huggard, "Emerson and the Problem of War and Peace," *University of Iowa Humanistic Studies,* V (1938), 1–76.

13. See Raymer McQuiston, "The Relation of Ralph Waldo Emerson to Public Affairs," *Bulletin of the University of Kansas,* XXIV, No. 8, Humanities Studies, III, No. 1 (April 1923), pp. 1–63. A. T. Odell in *La Doctrine sociale d'Emerson* (Paris, 1931), is especially good in tracing Emerson's views of slavery and reform in strictly chronological order. He shows that after 1846, in his maturity, Emerson studied the actual life of the United States and of England (*English Traits,* 1856), in the light of his principles, lecturing on many political or social topics. Maurice Gonnaud's *Individu et société dans L'oeuvre de Ralph Waldo Emerson* (1964) is a Sorbonne dissertation running over five hundred pages, and very meticulously documented, especially from evidence only recently made available. M. Gonnaud, finding it "regrettable" that F. I. Carpenter's *Emerson Handbook* separated the treatment of the American dream from the political ideas, tries to integrate these, with emphasis on Emerson's general approach to equilibrium. Mr. Adapha Ramakrishna Rao's dissertation (unpublished), "Emerson's Attitude toward Humanitarian Reform," at the University of Wisconsin (1965) is well documented and has an up-to-date bibliography. It is interesting as having been written by a devout Hindu sympathetic toward Emerson's distinctive point of view. Other earlier studies

on related topics will be found listed by Stovall in his *Eight American Authors*, pp. 87 ff.

14. *Atlantic Monthly*, XCI (1903), 846.

15. See Emerson's essay of 1870 in the collection of *New England Society Orations*, ed. C. and E. Brainerd (New York, 1901), II, 386.

16. Edwin H. Cady in *The Gentleman in America* has an excellent chapter on Emerson, but his unpublished dissertation (1943, available at the University of Wisconsin Library) has a much more detailed analysis, pp. 368–429. No doubt Emerson's observations of the West during his lecture-trips partly reinforced some of his basic ideas of self-reliance, individualism, and optimism; however, the Westerners frequently asked him to lecture on "Beauty," "Art," and especially "Manners." See Ernest Marchand, "Emerson and the Frontier," *American Literature*, III (May 1931), 149–74, for a full discussion. Other studies of his lecture trips have been made by H. H. Hoeltje, Louise Hastings, R. B. Nye, Eleanor B. Scott, and C. E. Shorer.

17. E. W. Emerson, *Emerson in Concord* (Boston, 1888) and various articles by H. H. Hoeltje, listed in Lewis Leary's *Articles on American Literature* (Durham, N. C., 1954), give vivid personal details.

In Emerson's social and family relations, including his role in his home town, he was a strict conformist in spite of his dictum that "Whoso would be a man must be a nonconformist." Emerson is well known for his strict observance of the social forms and good taste of the gentleman, always deferential toward others; and his home town was proud to have him serve on its school board, its library board, proud to have him dedicate its cemetery and take a leading part in all civic activities. As an Overseer of Harvard he once cast the decisive vote in continuing to make attendance at college chapel compulsory, despite what one might have expected from the author of the early "Divinity School Address." Even after he resigned from the Unitarian pulpit, he spent most of his Sundays through 1838 preaching in various churches, and he was willing to have his wife and children attend church regularly and contribute to the church. He was meticulous in all his obligations as a husband and father. His son testified that he usually avoided physical disciplining of his children, securing obedience by his kindly but stern admonitions and his affection; his son remarks that if one of the children, for example, became belligerent at dinner, Emerson's method was to distract attention by asking the child to do something, to go and shut the front gate. When Charles Dickens, who worried about his mistress back in England, remarked that he would think his own son were sick unless he were promiscuous, Emerson said that among his own social class in America young men went to their marriages as chaste as their brides. The recent publication of Emerson's love letters to Ellen correct the opinion based on the heavily expurgated first edition of the *Journals* and show that his own feelings were at least as impetuous as those of the other men; but he believed that feelings should be channeled and controlled within the contexture of the family, which to him was sacred. Innovations in conventions of family morality were unthinkable.

If in this portrait of Emerson I have at times emphasized the way he lived in the 1850's rather than in the 1830's, there was little difference in basic character and motivation, although the young man may have shown more enthusiasm and concern for originality.

18. For information about Emerson's reading, the summary lists of books referred to after each period in the old edition of the *Journals* are illuminating. Walter Harding has announced the forthcoming study entitled *Emerson's Library*. Floyd Stovall, *Eight American Authors* (1963), refers to many studies of Emerson's reading and indebtedness, among them J. S. Harrison's *The Teachers of Emerson* (New York, 1910), with its acute analysis of his debt to the dualistic Platonism, Neo-Platonism, and Coleridge. Among those who have treated influences are W. L. Ustick and C. L. Young (Montaigne), R. P. Falk (Shakespeare), P. C. Pettigrew (Milton), N. A. Brittin (the Metaphysical Poets), Vivian Hopkins (Bacon), F. T. Thompson (Carlyle, Coleridge, and Wordsworth), René Wellek, F. B. Wahr, and H. A. Pochmann (the Germans), F. I. Carpenter and A. E. Christy (Orientalism), H. H. Clark and J. W. Beach (scientists), J. T. Flanagan (nov-

elists including Scott), Clarence Hotson (Swedenborg),
Richard Greenleaf and J. B. Moore (Wordsworth), and
Nathalia Wright (Horatio Greenough).

Emerson read mainly for "lustres" or inspirations and
was not concerned with consecutive summaries of individual books. Useful is K. W. Cameron, *Ralph Waldo
Emerson's Reading: A Corrected Edition* (Hartford, Conn.,
1962), as well as Haynes McMullen, "Ralph Waldo Emerson and Libraries," *Library Quarterly*, XXV (April
1955), 152–62. Edmund G. Berry's *Emerson's Plutarch*
(Cambridge, Mass., 1961), has an illuminating treatment
of Emerson's respect for the ancient classics and the doctrine of emulation. Emerson's respect for classical scholars
like Richard Bentley in connection with "learned travel-
lers" is illustrated in *JMN*, V, 250.

19. In this connection see Emerson's comments on "ancient
piety" in his essay "Boston" (*W*, XII, 193), based on his
journals of 1836 and *Lectures* of 1837–38.

20. Norman Foerster and G. E. DeMille have emphasized the
classical traits of Emerson. If his central drives are quite
distinct from those of the kind of romanticism represented
by Byron, Shelley, or Swinburne, however, he does have
much in common with the later Coleridge (beginning
with *The Friend*, 1809–10, and *Aids to Reflection*, 1825)
and with the later Wordsworth (beginning with the
"obstinate questionings / Of sense and outward things" in
the "Ode on Intimations of Immortality," 1803, and
"Laodamia," 1814)—in other words, long after these two
poets had recoiled from their earlier French revolutionary kind of romanticism and had turned to conservatism
and the Anglican Church. But since some interpreters
quibble about romanticism, perhaps it is as well if I com-
press into a footnote references to traits in Emerson's
literary theory which seem to lean toward conservatism.
These are his semi-Platonic three levels of Beauty sketched
in *Nature* (*W*, I, 16–24; see also *W*, I, 355); his anti-
mechanistic organicism (*W*, III, 24), and his view that
"The classic unfolds: the romantic adds" (*J*, IX, 25); his
criterion which emphasizes general "tone" and the elevation of "the mood of mind" which a poem can inspire
in the reader (*W*, XII, 305); his insistence that a writer

to be great should combine particulars and universality via symbolism (*W*, III, 15 ff.); his emphasis on Imagination (over Fancy) as insight into spiritual laws and the highest types of human personality (*W*, VIII, 28–29 and *W*, XII, 307–36); and his insistence that a poet may well use the particulars of the familiar American scene so long as through symbols he springs the imagination to envisage the great unseen realm of timeless universals (as in the third part of "The Poet"). These objectives seem to me to lean toward mediation, or at least the more conservative side of romanticism, but I will not press this argument. Some interpreters emphasize Emerson's presaging prosodic freedom and irregularity; mediation in prosody is suggested in Arthur H. Quinn's conclusion (*The Literature of the American People*, New York, 1951, p. 286) that while Emerson scouted mechanical "rules" "he never violated the fundamental laws of English versification . . . but with sure if unconscious instinct he followed the impulses which every great English poet has pursued."

21. Vernon L. Parrington, *Main Currents in American Thought* (New York, 1927–30), II, 390.

22. Robert Spiller, in his essay on Emerson in his edition of *Literary History of the United States* (New York, 1948). Spiller sees Emerson as "formulating the dichotomy between the vision of a Jonathan Edwards and the common sense of a Benjamin Franklin, a conflict and a balance which has always provided the creative tension in American life" (p. 358). For excellent analysis see P. L. Nicoloff's *Emerson on Race and History: An Examination of English Traits* (New York, 1961).

23. In his survey of scholarship in *Eight American Authors*, Floyd Stovall in his section on Aesthetics (pp. 88–94) refers to studies by H. D. Gray, E. G. Sutcliffe, Norman Foerster, Régis Michaud, Vivian Hopkins, Charles Feidelson, C. R. Metzger, J. R. Reaver, Walter Blair and Clarence Faust, G. E. DeMille, and others. Some of these provide interesting sidelights on Emerson's idea that "Beauty is the mark God sets upon virtue," but no one appears to have centered on the topic.

Victor Cousin and Emerson

By *Emerson R. Marks*

I

RALPH WALDO EMERSON'S EARLY ADMIRATION for Victor
Cousin, "whose lectures," he told Wordsworth in 1833,
"we had all been reading in Boston," is a matter of familiar record. Though the impact of the once celebrated
French eclectic on Transcendental thought in general has
been variously assessed, there can be no doubt that Americans took great interest in his work. Orestes Brownson
and George Ripley placed him at the head of modern
philosophers, and Henning Gotfried Linberg's translation
in 1832 of the *Introduction to the History of Philosophy*
was popular reading in New England cultural circles.
Cousin in fact enjoyed a vogue in American intellectual
life that went beyond his immediate polemical use to
members of the Transcendental Club.[1] The main channel
of his influence was apparently the *Elements of Psychology* as translated in 1834 by Caleb Sprague Henry, Anglican professor of philosophy at New York University; but
for Emerson and his friends the more important work was
the *Introduction à l'histoire de la philosophie* (1829),
which Emerson himself read in the original as well as in
Linberg's version. Brownson's review of both translations
for *The Christian Examiner* in 1836 is little more than
an approving summary, often a close paraphrase, of Cousin's arguments. "We must be eclectics," Brownson wrote,
and he closed his review with a ringing appeal for American endorsement of what he regarded as Cousin's triumphant reconciliation of philosophy and theology.[2]

In contrast to Brownson's wholesale advocacy, Emerson's own relation to Cousin is complex but in no sig-

nificant sense one of intellectual indebtedness. Their broad similarities of doctrine, indicative of some kind of influence, give no reason to suppose that, without Cousin, Emerson's thought would have been appreciably different from what it was. What most usefully emerges from a comparative reading is rather a fresh appreciation of his achievement. Because Cousin's teachings so largely reflect the attitudinal norms of the early nineteenth century, studying his published lectures helps to avoid praising or blaming Emerson for what was not of his personal contriving. It reveals some of his shortcomings for what they so clearly are, maladies of the intellectual atmosphere to which he was by temperament peculiarly susceptible. By the same token it throws into sharp relief what is owing to Emerson's own genius: what on the speculative level made him the critic, and not merely the recorder, of his age; and what on the literary level (the two levels coalesce, of course) continues to attract readers while his French mentor mainly gathers dust on the library shelves.

Reading Victor Cousin today it is easy to understand why his philosophical books have been long out of print. Their lively appeal to Emerson and his circle seems at first perplexing. One's impression even of *Du Vrai, du beau et du bien,* considered his best book, prompts the gnawing question as to what intellectual poverty of their own could have made the Ripleys and the Brownsons hail the French writer so enthusiastically. Certainly, Cousin's great contemporary *éclat* has yielded over the years to general neglect. In 1849 Sainte-Beuve still felt him worth a *Causerie* (shared with Villemain), in which he declared that some of Cousin's remarks on the beautiful belonged among the finest pages in the French language. By 1940, however, a student of Sainte-Beuve had to report that Cousin and the whole eclectic school "are in our times largely forgotten, scorned, and even scoffed at."[3]

This may seem harsh, but surely those lectures on philosophy which Cousin delivered in Paris between 1815 and 1830 must be the epitome of "unprophetic" writing. The ugly forces at work beneath or alongside the liberalism and material advance of the nineteenth century, sensed by even the most sanguine romantics, never trouble Cousin's bland assurance. The severe indictments of the century by Coleridge, Thoreau's truculent dissent from its most vaunted claims, Arnold's castigation of its vulgarity, and even Emerson's revulsion (for all his lack of a vision of evil) at the immorality of its politics and trade—all that for us today accredits a writer as a competent witness to the century that preceded and engendered the age of Dachau and Hiroshima—have no counterpart in Victor Cousin. The new political liberty, he assures his rapt hearers, will nourish an ever nobler life. "Think of it, gentlemen, nothing regresses, everything moves ahead!"—this while the young Sainte-Beuve sadly pondered the new century's *enérgie dissolvante*, so destructive, he wrote, of all conviction and faith.[4]

Cousin's myopic sensibility detracted nothing, however, from his usefulness as a purveyor of German transcendental philosophy, in lucid and simplifying French, to Americans put off by the language or by the dialectical intricacies of the original texts. In this respect he shared the general reputation of his countrymen as popularizers and interpreters of abstruse ideas. "What Mme. de Staël did by her *Germany*—what Cousin did for Hegel—that France does for western Europe and America still, all through her clear and popular mind," Emerson told a Concord audience in 1848.[5] Among the "ancestry of Transcendentalism" Professor Wellek names de Staël, Benjamin Constant, Théodore Jouffroy, and Cousin.[6] Emerson's knowledge of German philosophy came largely through Coleridge and Carlyle, but it was Cousin who taught him his Hegel and much of his Fichte.

Read in Boston, Cousin was also valued for some of the same reasons that had won him applause in Paris. In the years immediately preceding his appearance, Chateaubriand and de Staël had inculcated, in reaction against eighteenth-century scepticism and materialism, a thirst for belief; and this thirst Cousin shrewdly sensed and gratified. As Émile Faguet wrote after the century's end, his greatest appeal was to those who were Christian but, their faith shaken by the *philosophes,* were seeking a Christianity devoid of supernaturalism.[7] With obvious cultural differences, the situation with the young men and women of the Transcendental Club was roughly analogous. The Unitarianism in which they had been nurtured had its intellectual base in Lockean psychology; and though it had stopped along the sensationalist road well short of the ultimate materialism of a Helvetius, it had so far made its peace with philosophical rationalism that the first influxes of European romantic literature served mainly to arouse in these descendants of the Puritans a nagging sense of spiritual impoverishment. In the generation before them in Europe, Werther and René had stirred a like response. The American form of it was only more exacting: divines and sons of divines, the Transcendentalists demanded a system inherently theistic; liberally cultured, they required intellectual respectability, which meant a theology reconcilable with the latest and boldest speculation, if not indeed directly buttressed by it. To fit this need Victor Cousin's *spiritualisme* (the name he came to prefer to *eclectisme*) struck them as almost tailor-made.

For many, above all for Emerson, the acclaim as a lecturer that Cousin had achieved by an eloquence apparent even in print had an additional attractiveness. Such American spellbinders as Daniel Webster and Edward Everett had an ardent admirer in the young Emerson, who valued his own forensic gifts and was later to write some still provocative pages on the art of eloquence, that "best speech of the best soul." Thinkers whose truth was stamped by the accents of living speech, lending an air of fervent personal commitment, had always a special appeal to his imagination. Among such, as his contemporaries amply attest, Cousin was notable in his time.

11

Brilliant pupil of humble parentage, assigned in 1815 at the age of twenty-two to lecture on philosophy at the École Normale, Victor Cousin succeeded Royer-Collard in that function. During the ensuing five years he began to read Kant, visited Hegel at Heidelberg, and spent a month with Schelling at Munich. Dismissed from his post in 1820 for political liberalism, he set to work on editions of Descartes and Proclus, and on the translation of Plato which Emerson often used in place of the original. In 1824 he spent the six months of a political imprisonment reading Kant, Fichte, and Jacobi, thus preparing himself for a triumphant restitution in 1828, when he obtained the history of philosophy chair at the Sorbonne.

In a lengthy review of Cousin's works written in 1853, Gustave Planche revived the scene and the moment:

> After several years of silence, the professor once more appeared in his chair. Two thousand hearers thronged the hall of the Sorbonne. M. Cousin had put to good use the long period of leisure which the Villele ministry had imposed upon him, and the expectations of his audience were not disappointed. He undertook to recount all that man had thought about God, about nature, and about himself, and he was able to enliven this account and to lend it an almost dramatic interest.

Of the book that resulted from this new series of lectures, the *Introduction à l'histoire de la philosophie*, Planche wrote that every page of it was "vibrant and colorful, the brilliance of the images detracting nothing from the precision of the thought: a talent rare and outstanding."[8] Since this is the volume which mainly impressed Emerson and which especially after Linberg's translation accelerated the spread of Cousin's fame in New England, Planche's praise of it is worth notice.

By 1841, when a second edition of it was issued at Paris, its publisher Didier could point proudly to

[67]

Cousin's international reputation. In his "Avant-Propos" he quotes a passage from Linberg's preface in which the Boston translator lauds the deep veneration for the Creator that animates Cousin's lectures and the central position in his philosophy held by an infinitely wise and good personal God.[9] Linberg's praise reveals a great deal about the spiritual climate of Emerson's time, because if there is one thing no modern reader, surely no Christian reader, can detect in Cousin it is a deep veneration for the Creator. It is equally hard to find a God of any kind occupying a *central place* in Cousin's system. Insofar as he has anything fundamentally original to offer, it is his doctrine of the impersonality of the reason. His God is only a neo-Platonic one, the Infinite, or what he calls the final term of his concept of Ideal Beauty.[10] Yet Linberg's estimate was one widely shared by New Englanders, including clergymen. That they could regard Cousin in this light is a measure of the theological distance separating them from their seventeenth-century forebears. They could welcome Cousin as a religious ally only because the intervening eighteenth century had done its work. By post-Napoleonic times many cultivated people could accept only a Christianity without the Incarnation and preferably without the sacraments. They felt most comfortable in a religion that ignored miracles and mystery and made only polite references to revelation. What they wanted was a theology that meshed smoothly with their liberal faith in the human mind and with no uncouth emphasis on St. Paul's assertion that this world's wisdom is God's foolishness. These attitudes define the theological climate of Emerson's sermon of 1832 on the Lord's Supper and of Theodore Parker's later *Discourse on the Transient and the Permanent in Christianity*. In such a climate Cousin's philosophy, combining as it did a skillful defense of intellectual freedom with expressions of respect for religion, was understandably welcome.

I say "respect for religion" because it is that rather than "veneration" that describes Cousin's attitude. Quite apart from the intellectual tendencies of the age, Cousin was little given to piety in his own nature. Faguet makes the discrimination necessary to defining his temperament when he ascribes to Cousin *l'esprit religieux* but not *le sentiment religieux*. By the first term Faguet meant a mind ardent of certitude, impatient of doubt, avid of finding and transmitting to others a satisfactory explanation of everything.[11] The more one reads Cousin the more apt Faguet's characterization seems. In the *Introduction à l'histoire de la philosophie,* Emerson read, for example, that Cousin would always accord religion the profoundest respect, and was reminded a few pages later that his author had "done homage to Providence." How far short such respect and homage were from any *sentiment religieux* Emerson might already have surmised from the earlier statement that "Christianity is the philosophy of the people."[12] Whether Emerson felt this as patronizing we cannot know, though of course it could not have had for him the shock of irony it has for modern readers, unable quite to suppress its accidental paraphrase of a more brutal aphorism about religion and the people.

Fundamentally, Cousin's treatment of Christianity is a function of his belief in the idea of progress. If it is recalled that Emerson's time and country in varying degrees (and with noteworthy exceptions) shared this belief, it is understandable why pious souls may have been largely insensitive to the obvious condescension of passages like the following, and so unoffended by them:

> Philosophy is patient; she knows how things transpired in earlier generations, and she is full of confidence in the future. Happy to see the masses, the people, that is to say practically all humanity, in the embrace of Christianity, she is glad to stretch out her hand gently to them and help them lift themselves higher still.[13]

"Higher still?" An interpolation at this point in the printed text reads "marked attention in the audience." There is no reason to ascribe this hush to offended piety. It is more likely that Cousin's hearers, like the Transcendentalists themselves, were receptive to something "higher" than traditional Christianity. Yet a significant difference between Cousin's Sorbonne audience and his New England readers needs stressing. The intellectuals of Restoration France had been exposed to an Enlightenment mainly irreligious when not flatly atheistic. American rationalism, on the other hand, typified by Benjamin Franklin, had effected no break with theism, and Transcendentalism itself was deeply religious in motive and inspiration. For this reason the degree of Cousin's popularity among its exponents seems in one sense anomalous. His all-embracing progressism relegates theology to a primitive past, as a cruder form of thought from which man had advanced to philosophy. Dismissing the Persian *Zend-Avesta* as merely theological ("a theology is not yet a philosophy"), Cousin praises Confucius for having founded his doctrine on reason alone. Luther he condemns as a "declared adversary" of human reason.[14] Late in life Emerson wrote that he owed his first taste for Hindu philosophy to Cousin's resumé of the Krishna-Arjoon dialogue in the *Bhagavad-Gita*.[15] But whereas Emerson retained a life-long admiration for Indian thought, Cousin is strongly critical of its disregard for the "law of temporal succession," its wish to give all its works "the appearance of infinity and eternity."[16] In this, of course, he was attacking the feature Emerson most valued.

For the Transcendentalists the best religion was yet to come. For Cousin all religion belonged to an outgrown past. Though he wrote that religion was the basis of all civilization, his idea of intellectual advancement consists precisely in the gradual secularization of thought. In his encompassing historicism, religion represents the first of three stages of cultural progress, theology the second; growing out of theology comes philosophy, the highest stage.

If, despite all this, Transcendentalists could hail Cousin as a kindred spirit, the explanation lies in the fact that their beliefs were at bottom closer to his humanism than to real Christianity. They, too, it might be said, disliked theology. Their religious sensibility is the polar opposite to that of Pascal, Cousin's *bête noire*. Their spiritual monism is as fully opposed to Pascal's three disparate orders as their optimism is to his misanthropy. Although Emerson's taste was broad enough to allow him some relish of Pascal as an author, his praise is tolerant and mixed: "Stern & great, old-fashioned-theological, but with sublime passages."[17] It is not hard to guess that what Emerson found sublime in Pascal were the places where man is shown superior to the physical universe by his power of thought. The demonstration of man's misery without God presumably constituted the "old-fashioned" theology. In one of the most crucial of the *Pensées* Pascal locates charity in the supernatural order, which he expressly declares to be above and disjunct from the orders of bodies and minds. With tolerable simplification Transcendentalism might be summed up as one long polemic against this view. In any case, it is easy to imagine how much more congenial Emerson must have found it to turn from the implacable *Janséniste* to Cousin's brighter view of the human potential. In 1819 the Sorbonne professor assured his students that of man's dual nature the spiritual part was the essential. "Therefore let man follow his true nature, and his life will be noble and holy, because the nobility and the holiness of his nature will be reflected in it."[18] For this, the future author of "Self-Reliance" must have felt it comparatively easy to overlook anything disquieting in the French philosopher's attitude toward religion or the deity, assuming he found it disquieting at all.

Cousin's opinion of Pascal is instructive as an index of the change in outlook from Emerson's time to our own, a change which criticism must take properly into account. To an "existentialist" age no longer assured of certain certainties, Pascal's tortured journey to the Cross seems once more compelling. In Cousin's history of philosophy his place is contrastingly that of a quirk, a horrible example of the "imperious dogmatism" to which scepticism can lead. In 1842, having discovered the discrepancies between the autograph manuscript of the *Pensées* and the published editions, Cousin renewed his attack on Pascal as "a declared enemy, a contemner of the natural light of philosophy." More clearly than the edited texts, he reported to the French Academy, the manuscript lays bare Pascal's true intention, which was to employ scepticism to destroy all true philosophy in order to leave man no other refuge than religion. Vowing his opposition to this dastardly setting at loggerheads of Reason and Faith, Cousin proclaimed once again his profound respect for Christianity along with his refusal to betray the equally sacred rights of free thought.[19]

Pascal's sparring partner was Montaigne, honored among Emerson's representative men as the exponent of a "wise skepticism." In "Montaigne; or, The Skeptic," he carefully distinguishes Montaigne's resistance to philosophical assent from the wrong kind of scepticism, "universal denying . . . universal doubting . . . scoffing and profligate jeering at all that is stable and good." This discrimination of scepticisms is very like Cousin's, who wrote of "a true and a false scepticism, a scepticism legitimate and respectable, inasmuch as sincere, and a scepticism which is only a dodge, a kind of game" designed to exaggerate the weaknesses of human reflection in order to return men to the sway of Christianity.[20] Whether or not Emerson recalled these words as he contemplated Montaigne, what is most impressive is the difference of quality rather than the possibly adventitious parallel between his thought and Cousin's. Whatever anyone may think of Emerson's understanding of the *Essais* (his Montaigne is characteristically Emersonian), the distinction he makes is put to respectable use, whereas Cousin's purblind charge of insincerity against the author of the *Pensées* may strike a modern reader as little better than dishonest shuffling. Emerson's inability to accept a thoroughgoing scepticism stems partly from contemporary American hopefulness, mostly perhaps from his own cast of mind. Cousin's has too much the flavor of a bad-tempered protest against something embarrassing to his "programme."

Emerson could only have delighted in Cousin's declaration that history is God's government of an orderly world made visible, upon which he based his "high historical optimism," a phrase that might as fittingly label Emerson's own faith. What Emerson happily avoids is Cousin's frequent smugness of tone:

> I regard the idea of historical optimism . . . as the loftiest idea to which philosophy has yet attained. It alone makes possible a philosophy of history. It is the conquest of our age: it is enough to give it the quality of superiority that the latest accretion to humanity must have; it would suffice to make us thank Providence for having been born at the moment when existence is finally about to be understood and exculpated at every point of its duration, and consequently to understand and revere the more him who made it.[21]

Since this paragraph brings one of the lectures to a close, it is tempting to pass it over as so much perorational rhetoric. Unfortunately, there is good reason to take it quite literally. So unrelieved is Cousin's faith in progress that even war is among those aspects of existence that he "exculpates." War is a condition of progress because in every clash of arms new truth fights against old error, the future combats the past. Moreover, truth and the future always win and always deserve to win. Whoever wins therefore must presumably have been in the right. "Alexander conquered the Thebans, that's certain; Thebes passed from freedom into slavery; who cares?" Cousin asks. All that matters is that at Platea the future triumphed over the past. Some twenty years earlier Coleridge had told his countrymen, dismayed at the apparent invincibility of Napoleon's armies, the hard truth that a bad idea can inspire victory as well as a good one. But Cousin had to "demonstrate the morality of success," as he put it, or admit a "contradiction between morality and civilization, which is impossible. . . . Gentlemen, everything is perfectly just in this world . . . ; happiness is given only to virtue, unhappiness is imposed only on vice."[22] Little wonder he had to write a book against Pascal.

But if Emerson never descends to such fatuity of assertion, does he not preach as unqualified an optimism? Mark Van Doren is not alone in his opinion that Emerson "trusted the world not to be tragic."[23] Certainly, the theme that evil is illusory or at worst negative is too recurrent in Emerson's writings to need documenting; and to the extent that this strain has detracted from his modern reputation Cousin's doctrine may be deplored as having aggravated something regrettable in Emerson's mental make-up. This is not to take it as the "source" of Emerson's imperfect sense of evil. An entry in his *Journals* for 1832 cautions against even too hastily listing it among several such sources. "What can we see, read, acquire," it runs, "but ourselves? Cousin is a thousand books to a thousand persons."[24] Whatever he took from Cousin or anyone else was only what he wanted to take, which was mainly whatever promised to fuel the fire of his own convictions or bring them to the clearest articulation. In the lecture on "Quotation and Originality" of 1859, he declared that the books every man remembers in connection with the culminating moments of his life are those which "met his views." An interesting paragraph in "Intellect," which incidentally refers to Cousin's influence on "many young men in this country," carries the 1832 *Journal* entry further by the remark that every man passes "through a succession of teachers," with whom he is advised to "wrestle" as a condition of attaining intellectual independence.

Emerson himself consistently practiced this kind of creative assimilation. Whatever its inadequacies, his optimism is finally his own. Unlike Cousin's, it is worth respectful attention because it is neither based on the naïve and doctrinaire progressism in which the French thinker's speculation is systematically imprisoned, nor achieved by suppressing the most damaging evidence. In "Works and Days," glancing at the promise of technology to lift humanity out of its beggary to a life of godlike

ease and power, Emerson questions its political effect.
"The science of power," he notes prophetically, "is forced
to remember the power of science." Though willing to
admire technical marvels like photography and balloon
navigation ("the next war will be fought in the air"), he
is nonetheless convinced that "we must look deeper for
our salvation...." He knows that like all tools these are
"in one sense edge-tools, and dangerous." The state of
American politics, which he adjudges more corrupt and
brutal than ever before, prompts him to ask whether for all
his enlightenment man is morally improved. In Cousin he
had read of the universal betterment of all things, but
in "Self-Reliance" he reported his own observation that
society never advances. "It undergoes continual changes . . .
but this change is not amelioration." In the final lecture of
the *Introduction à l'histoire de la philosophie,* Cousin
avowed his satisfaction with the *"ordre actuel des choses,"*
alluding complacently to the *Charte,* that paragon of modern political wisdom which the lecturer himself was to
outlive by many years.[25] In contrast to this "high historical
optimism," Emerson's faith in individual moral perfectibility is based not on misapprehended history but on his
intuition of the divine spark in every human being. Beyond anything Emerson had to witness, the political
brutalities of our own time put his kind of intuitive faith
to the test, severely perhaps; Cousin's doctrine, however,
they simply discredit.

Apart from these considerations is something more
apposite to assessing the work of one who was primarily
an artist. That Emerson would now be regarded, like
Cousin, chiefly as a phenomenon of intellectual history,
were it not for his creative gift, is a fact made dramatically
plain by comparing their work. Cousin's "happiness is
given only to virtue, unhappiness is imposed only on
vice" and Emerson's "Society acquires new arts and loses
old instincts" (from "Self-Reliance") may serve as touchstones. However favorable to Emerson may be the contrast
of sense here, his superiority is as much literary as it is
doctrinal. Yet this literary superiority itself is referable

to something deeper than mere belletristic agility, a talent of which Cousin was also possessed in no small measure. The pungency of Emerson's style arises from a greater depth and breadth of vision. His antithesis of new arts and old instincts grips by its sudden revelation of his having gauged the claims of social progress against certain permanencies of human psychology. Cousin presses a thesis; Emerson looks before and after.

A related distinction separates the two men's total intellectual processes. Unable himself to give allegiance to any single philosophic system, Emerson must have felt an immediate sympathy with Cousin's eclecticism. His practice of dropping into his intellectual crucible nuggets variously culled makes the American in a sense the greater eclectic. His main objection to its French expositors was that they insisted on erecting eclecticism itself into a system. By 1838 he was complaining to Frederick Henry Hedge of Cousin's "pompous plea for eclecticism" and invoking old Montaigne against "these Frenchmen who so magnify method above the moon."[26] He might better have pointed out the logical flaw in Cousin's principle that all philosophies are true in what they affirm and false in what they deny, which so blandly overlooks the fact that any philosophic affirmation implies the denial of opposite or alternative propositions. In any case, in "Nominalist and Realist" Emerson formulates his own eclecticism in terms happily immune to logical refutation: "I am always insincere, as always knowing there are other moods." This is psychological instead of logical, and by its honesty it disarms even those readers for whom consistency is more than a hobgoblin virtue.

III

If Cousin cannot be said to have furnished Emerson any ideas, his tutelage is nonetheless discernible at crucial points of Emerson's thought. Anyone who recalls *Representative Men* is bound to be arrested by Cousin's repeated use of the term *représentant* in the *Introduction à l'his-*

toire de la philosophie. Reading this volume in the early 1830's, Emerson learned that the history of a people is the history of its great men. "A great man," Cousin taught, "is not, as such, an individual; his fortune is to represent better than any other man of his time the ideas of that time, its interests, its needs." Though everyone in a given culture shares the same ideas, these are only made articulate and conscious by *"le vrai représentant."*[27] Clearly, Emerson's representative man is more closely related to Cousin's *représentant* than to Carlyle's hero. To what others have said about this relationship[28] one significant observation may be added. Emerson's conception tends to reverse the causal order between Cousin's outstanding figures and the cultures they represent. Whereas a *représentant* derives his superior power from the cultural "idea,"[29] and is thus in some sense its creature, Emerson's representative man is apparently prior to his culture, engendering it, or some part of it. "A man Caesar is born, and for ages after we have a Roman Empire.... An institution is the lengthened shadow of one man."

This notion of human greatness is, of course, part of a total conception of history which Emerson shares with Cousin. The French historian of philosophy was eloquent in asserting a harmony of general laws linking man, nature, and history. "History thus conceived, in this universal harmony, is therefore eminently beautiful; it is an admirable poetry, the drama or epic of mankind." So rapt a vision of the human record is not really sustained in Cousin's discussion, but it may account for Emerson's enthusiastic comment to his brother William in 1831. "A master of history," he calls Cousin; "an epic he makes of man & of the world...."[30] Careful comparison of their ideas supports Professor Rusk's judgment that Emerson worked his historical theory out in his own way.[31] Certainly, it is one worthier than Cousin's of being labeled "admirable poetry." "The Gothic cathedral is a blossoming in stone subdued by the insatiable demand of harmony in man," Emerson wrote in "History." While Cousin merely affirms this consonance between man's nature and his recorded deeds, Emerson's imagery affords his readers an imaginative sharing of the conception to which Cousin's prose never rises.

Every idea common to the Transcendentalist Emerson and the French eclectic philosopher recalls Perry Miller's astute generalization about the movement to which Emerson belonged. Though "fed by deeper springs than mere aesthetics," it had to issue in "a doctrine and an attempted practice of the beautiful."[32] Quite apart from his poems, its greatest exemplar was at his best a poet in the Coleridgean sense. Between any two similar passages in Cousin and Emerson there is either the generic difference between the poet and the expositor, or a difference of degree. In the latter case it is mainly owing to Emerson's more intense verbal economy. Consider Cousin at one of his more eloquent moments:

> Every utterance is an act of faith; this is so true that in the cradle of societies every utterance is a hymn. Look into the history of tongues, of societies, and of every distant epoch, and you will find in them nothing anterior to their lyrical element, to hymns, litanies: so true is it that every primitive perception is a spontaneous apperception stamped by faith; an inspiration accompanied by enthusiasm, that is to say a religious movement.[33]

Even with the inevitable loss in translation this excerpt is a good cut above the flattest prose. Its initial clause has even something of the Emersonian pith, and every alert reader feels sure that Emerson has somewhere expressed a similar thought. It may be only after noticing that Cousin is drawing a relationship between religion and primitive utterance that a memorable sentence from "The Poet" comes to mind. "The religions of the world are the ejaculations of a few imaginative men." An important fact about the bearing of Emerson's reading on his speculation is glimpsed by noting that the ideas expressed in these two quotations merely overlap without being identical. They also belong to discrepant contexts. Cousin's string of clauses makes up a stage in his demonstration of the universal agency of the spontaneous reason. Emerson's sentence, typically without discernible connection to the brief paragraph it closes, finds its proper context only in the whole essay exalting the poet's role. This variance of contexts further reveals the distinctive quality of Emerson's writing. The noteworthy point about his sentence is that its compact suggestiveness can *bear* virtually the entire essay as "commentary." The best of Emerson's infinitely repellent particles always seem infinitely expandable. The fact that each is in turn part of the context for other memorable sentences only shows how far the artistry of his style consists in its organic unity. For all the flash of his rhetoric Cousin has nothing of this.

Probably because of their common source in neo-Platonism, Cousin and Emerson are nowhere more alike than in their aesthetic thought. Whatever the reason, almost every major point of Emerson's theory of beauty can be matched in *Du Vrai, du beau et du bien.* Like his Transcendental admirer, Cousin conceives of an ideal beauty to which any specific art work imperfectly aspires, a principle which in both men severely restricts their practical criticism by turning attention away from the concrete embodiment to the intangible ideal. Idealistic aesthetics of this kind tends, paradoxically, to a certain denigration of the arts, and it appeals mainly to persons of relatively low aesthetic sensitivity. In *Du Vrai,* Cousin's notion of form is perilously close to mere shape, outward configuration, and his chapter on French *siècle d'or* art consists mostly of tedious moralizing. Henry James might have been less surprised at Emerson's apparent indifference to the paintings in the Louvre had he recalled the statements in "Art" that "There is higher work for Art than the arts" and that all pictures and statues are "cripples and monsters." The shock of these asseverations will be diminished for anyone who discovers Emerson's warrant for them in Cousin, who declared that "in the world of forms, beauty is only shown in such a manner that, in revealing it, veils and disfigures it. What a dim, equivocal, incomplete image of the infinite idea a vast sea or a high mountain is—in other words a large volume of water and a heap of stones!"[34]

Like Emerson's, Cousin's aesthetic field is self-defeatingly broad. Besides such natural phenomena as seas and mountains—inherited from the eighteenth-century theorists of the Sublime—both writers included noble deeds in the category of the beautiful, on a par with man-made art works. Cousin instances a rich man giving alms to a beggar; Emerson, in *Nature,* the heroes at Thermopylae. If anything, Cousin's theory is the more hospitable, admitting even philosophic systems. Condillac's *Traité des sensations* is listed under the Beautiful in a grouping that assigns Kant's *Critique of Pure Reason* to the higher class of the Sublime. There are in fact, he says, three kinds of beauty: physical, intellectual, moral. Yet all three have as a common factor "moral beauty, understanding by this term, along with moral beauty properly so-called, all spiritual beauty." Never attained by any mortal artist, this supernal quality is realized only in God, in Whom it is one with truth and goodness.[35] Or, as Emerson expressed it in *Nature,* "God is the all-fair. Truth, and goodness, and beauty, are but different faces of the same All."

From these fundamentals other similarities logically follow. For both men natural or artistic objects are mere symbols of an idea; neither has any firm grasp of form as structure (though Emerson more nearly approaches it); both confound the several arts; both obscure the line between the moral and the aesthetic. These basic resemblances may suggest some qualification of Vivian Hopkins' conclusion that Emerson's "critical generalizations always bore the stamp of originality,"[36] though not to the extent of arguing indebtedness. Emerson's notions about art are what we should expect them to be; so are Cousin's. Those they hold in common merely enroll both writers among critics who believe with Sir Philip Sidney that "the skill of the artificer standeth in that idea or foreconceit of the work, and not in the work itself."

Cousin was not in any case an original aesthetic

thinker. Though he had read Kant closely and follows his crucial distinction between the agreeable and the beautiful, he neither develops it nor adds anything of his own. On the theoretical level Emerson hardly fares better. Though much has been made of his theory of the symbol, Professor Hopkins has rightly seen that his idealistic bias kept him from conceiving it as a "perfect fusion of idea with image."[37] Here Cousin could never have helped. In natural objects, he wrote,

> an immortal spirit shines through the grossest exteriors. Let us contemplate nature with the eyes of the soul as well as of the body, and everywhere a moral expression will strike us, and the form will lay hold on us as a symbol of the thought.[38]

This is the language of the purest Transcendentalism, in which the priority of the abstract spirit is always fatal to that structural conception of the symbol that has made Coleridge so fruitful to modern poetics. For him the symbol had a value of its own, unique in kind and terminal. For Cousin and for Emerson (who never learned this lesson from the *Biographia Literaria*) it was only a means to an end that might equally well be attained by other means, mystical communion for example.

Yet on this subject as on others Emerson's writings continue to avoid the general neglect that has overtaken the Frenchman's derivative speculations. His chief advantage lies in his being an artist himself, a coiner of the electric phrase, of prose expressions that have the reverberation of poetry and so allow him to convey intuitive insights that penetrate beyond the limits of a sterile theory. "We are far from having exhausted the significance of the few symbols we use. We can come to use them yet with a terrible simplicity." So wrote Emerson in "The Poet." Victor Cousin held views of the poetic symbol very like Emerson's, but he could never have spoken of the *terrible simplicity* of their use. That is the American poet's unique contribution, and for us today it is almost everything.

But there is something else. Underlying the naïve faith in human progress that diminishes Cousin's claim to modern attention is the predominant historicism of his age. In twentieth-century consciousness his conception of history has been gradually replaced by a new sense of how past and present are related that will admit neither his smug assurance of social amelioration nor his trust in the intellect. The sensibility of the age of Joyce, Proust, and Eliot is marked by a new attitude toward time itself, a suspicion that the linear notion of time is a distortion of experience. More respectful of the past, we have turned again to myth and away from history, to the timeless and away from the time-bound and the time-ridden. Though in his *Histoire générale de la philosophie* Cousin propounded a cyclical theory according to which every era begins in sensualism, rises to idealism, and declines through scepticism to mysticism, his basic preachment was of a gradual upward development. In his view Oriental mysticism and Greek rationalism are not alternative modes of thought. The Greeks are simply superior since they had attained to the notions of chronology and history, whereas in India "chronology is confounded in mythology." Toward modern mystics like Saint-Martin he is openly scornful, because "mysticism is born of a despair of speculative reason. . . ."[39] These opinions reveal an epistemological abyss separating Cousin from Emerson, whose sympathy with the mystic way to truth colors so much of his thought, just as in his consciousness of the past the mythic predominates over the "chronological." Professor Carpenter has even suggested that Emerson's preference for the symbolic and mythic modes of apprehension over the logical and discursive foreshadows the modern philosophy "in a new key" offered by Mrs. Langer.[40] By such a test Cousin's philosophy is clearly in the old key.

In the Sorbonne lectures the Transcendentalists easily found encouragement for their faith in the primacy of the intuition. "Inspiration," Cousin declared, "is characterized by enthusiasm; it is accompanied by that powerful emotion which wrests the soul from its ordinary inferior state and disengages in it the sublime, divine part of its nature." He recognized a spontaneous as well as a reflective reason. In that discussion of the *Bhagavad-Gita* which initiated Emerson's exploration of Asian thought, he gave special emphasis to "the mystical points of view."[41] Yet these tendencies, so congenial to Transcendentalism, are not really central to his own convictions. In telling contrast to Emerson's distrust of logic is Cousin's inference that the Nyaya philosophy must have been produced in a relatively advanced civilization because the syllogism appears in Gotama's writings.[42] Willing in the spirit of eclecticism to admit the claims of intuition, Cousin remained at bottom a rationalist whose avowed model was not Kant but Descartes.

Turning in later life from the dead end of eclecticism, Victor Cousin abandoned philosophy for seventeenth-century philology and public education. By then he had fulfilled the task for which he was best fitted. With erudition and eloquence he had pleaded the Idealist case to a generation glad to listen. If he ever imagined himself an original thinker, it is an estimate posterity has hesitated to endorse. At this distance of time his achievement is rather that of the great teacher, a role which best describes his relation to gifted contemporaries in France and to Emerson in America. But to number men of genius among one's pupils is perhaps no mean thing.

NOTES

1. See Georges J. Joyaux, "Victor Cousin and American Transcendentalism," *French Review*, XXIX (1955), 129, and Herbert W. Schneider, *A History of American Philosophy* (New York, 1946), p. 234.

2. Perry Miller, *The Transcendentalists* (Cambridge, Mass., 1960), p. 114.

3. Maxime Leroy, *La Pensée de Sainte-Beuve* (Paris, 1940), p. 149. All material quoted in English from French texts is of my own translation.

4. *Introduction à l'histoire de la philosophie* (Paris, 1841), p. 58. This volume, first published in 1829, contains the course of lectures Cousin gave in 1828. Hereafter cited as *Introduction*. Sainte-Beuve, *Portraits Contemporains*, 5 vols. (Paris, 1876), I, 426.

5. "France, or Urbanity," excerpted in Lestrois Parish, *Emerson's View of France and the French*. Franco-American Pamphlet Series No. 5 (New York, 1935), p. 8.

6. "The Minor Transcendentalists and German Philosophy," *The New England Quarterly*, XV (1942), 661.

7. "Victor Cousin," in *Politiques et moralistes du dix-neuvième siècle*. Deuxième série (Paris, 1903), p. 275.

8. "Victor Cousin," in *Études littéraires* (Paris, 1855), pp. 10, 11.

9. *Introduction*, p. iii.

10. *Du Vrai, du beau et du bien* (Paris, 1863), p. 169.

11. *Politiques et moralistes*, pp. 229–30.

12. *Introduction*, pp. 140, 158, 59. In the *Histoire générale de la philosophie*, an epitome of his 1829 lectures on philosophy, Cousin declares that by divorcing theology from philosophy he has guaranteed to religion "a sincere

respect" and to philosophy "a just liberty" (Paris, 1864), pp. 304–5.

13. *Introduction*, pp. 59–60.

14. *Histoire générale*, pp. 39, 271.

15. In a letter to Professor Friedrich Max Müller of August 4, 1873. *The Letters of Ralph Waldo Emerson*, ed. Ralph L. Rusk, 6 vols. (New York, 1939), VI, 246. Hereafter cited as *Letters*.

16. *Histoire générale*, p. 43.

17. *Letters*, IV, 509.

18. *Histoire de la philosophie morale au XVIIIe siècle*, Vol. III (1819) of *Cours de l'histoire de la philosophie morale*, Première série (Paris, 1846), p. 24.

19. *Histoire générale*, p. 494; *Études sur Pascal*, pp. xii, 8, 36.

20. *Histoire générale*, p. 24.

21. *Introduction*, p. 228. Compare his confident observation that Descartes' method is superior to the processes of the Greek mind "with all the superiority of our civilization over that of Greece" (*Introduction*, pp. 53–54).

22. *Introduction*, pp. 276–78, 281, 282.

23. "Introduction" to *The Portable Emerson* (New York, 1946), p. 17.

24. *The Journals and Miscellaneous Notebooks of Ralph Waldo Emerson*, ed. William H. Gilman, George P. Clark, Alfred R. Ferguson, Merrel R. Davis. 3 vols. (Cambridge, Mass., 1960, 1961, 1963), III, 327.

25. *Introduction*, pp. 433, 435.

26. *Letters*, II, 123.

27. *Introduction*, pp. 299, 300, 305.

28. J. O. McCormick credited Cousin with having "crystallised for Emerson" ideas about great figures which Emerson had developed for himself by 1827 ("Emerson's Theory of Human Greatness," *The New England Quarterly* [1954], cited in Edmund G. Berry, *Emerson's Plutarch* [Cambridge, Mass., 1961], p. 93). More recently Philip L. Nicoloff has declared the function of Cousin's great man to be "virtually identical with that which Emerson

assigned to such representative figures as Goethe and Napoleon" (*Emerson on Race and History* [New York, 1961], pp. 72–73).

29. In the *Introduction* (pp. 229–75 passim) Cousin elaborates the notion that each civilization is governed by an *idée prédominante* or *idée fondamentale* which is expressed in all its institutions. In "The Transcendentalist" Emerson speaks of the "Reigning Idea" of a period, and in "History," he sees the Greek "national mind" variously embodied in Greek civil history, letters, architecture, and sculpture. These notions have an obvious Hegelian flavor, but Emerson knew Hegel through Cousin.

30. *Introduction*, pp. 233–34; *Letters*, I, 322–23.

31. *The Life of Ralph Waldo Emerson* (New York, 1949), p. 278.

32. *The Transcendentalists*, p. 9.

33. *Introduction*, pp. 177–78.

34. *Introduction*, pp. 13–14.

35. *Du Vrai, du beau et du bien*, pp. 148, 160, 163, 169.

36. *Spires of Form: A Study of Emerson's Aesthetic Theory* (Cambridge, Mass., 1951), p. 222.

37. *Spires of Form*, p. 130.

38. *Du Vrai, du beau et du bien*, p. 167.

39. *Histoire générale*, p. 524.

40. *Emerson Handbook* (New York, 1953), p. 97.

41. *Introduction*, p. 169; *Histoire générale*, p. 80.

42. *Histoire générale*, pp. 63–64.

Personality and Style
in Concord

By Albert Gilman and Roger Brown

Is it possible to distinguish the styles of two writers living in the same time and place, educated at the same school, writing in the same genre, on the same topic, voicing the same opinion, with nothing but their personalities to keep them apart? Emerson and Thoreau provide the almost exeprimental contrast that is required. They are, to begin with, very well matched in respect of all the historical and demographic factors that can cause one man's writing to differ from that of another. Both lived in the nineteenth century, Thoreau's shorter lifetime being encompassed by that of Emerson. Both lived most of their lives in the village of Concord, Massachusetts, and both were educated at Harvard. Whatever differences there may be in the styles of the two men cannot be attributed to membership in distinct census groupings.

Because the various genres of literature set distinct problems and have distinct conventions, it is desirable to hold genre constant in looking for features of style that are determined by personality. Although Emerson and Thoreau both wrote some poetry, the present study is limited to their prose. Both men wrote personal journals, essays, and Lyceum lectures. The three forms stand in the same relation to one another for the two authors: the journals were source books from which essays and lectures were mined. The passages we will consider are drawn from these shared forms.

Style is to some extent dictated by topic. Between an

essay on the Over-Soul and an accounting of the cost of food consumed in eight months beside Walden Pond some differences of diction and grammar are to be expected. However, one need not look to personality for an explanation; the differences would be there if both passages had a single author. Since topical effects tend to obscure personality effects, we have tried to hold topic constant. That is easy to do with Emerson and Thoreau because their topical range is about the same. The great subjects of both writers include Nature, self-reliance, conscience, the state, poetry, friendship, manners, possessions, and Slavery. It is not only the topics that match but the opinions, the arguments, the general philosophies. There are even short passages that approach propositional equivalence, and we will restrict our study to these.[1] In these passages we will find some sentences, even paragraphs, that either Emerson or Thoreau might have written. We will even find passages actually written by one that would be taken for the work of the other. On most passages, however, we will discover that Emerson and Thoreau have left their stylistic fingerprints.

Of course, a man's style, unlike his fingerprint, may be as it is because he has undertaken to make it so. A difference of style, produced by intention, to correspond with an ideal, is an expression of personality but not an expression of the most interesting aspects of personality. The significance of the Emerson-Thoreau contrast is heightened by the fact that they had very similar ideals of style. Both, for example, valued compression, vitality, and straight-line direction. Emerson wrote of the good style (No. 10): "It is a shower of bullets . . . " (*J*, V, 420). Thoreau wrote: "The *art* of composition is as simple as the discharge of a bullet from a rifle" ("The Last Days of John Brown," *W*, IV, 447). The ideals are similar, but even in these phrases we notice that "a shower of bullets" has not the compression, force, and direction of "the discharge of a bullet from a rifle." And, a few sentences further on, Thoreau, suppressing his predicates, creates the rhythm of bullets thudding into a target: "This first, this second, this third; pebbles in your mouth or not" (p. 448). Emerson's next clause begins with "whilst" and has a compound subject and a compound predicate. There was something that kept the styles apart, something other than education, genre, topic, or stylistic ideal.

The Personalities

The differences in the personalities of Emerson and Thoreau, for the most part, lie in temperament and intelligence. In temperament Thoreau was more aggressive than Emerson, more *aggressive* in two senses: more *combative* and also more *vigorous*. Vigor and combativeness are distinguishable characteristics, and it may be that the two are bundled together by the English word "aggression" for accidental and arbitrary reasons. It is more likely, however, that the lexicon reflects an actual association in human and animal nature. At any rate, they were associated in Thoreau.

The difference of temperament is rather well attested by contemporaries of the two men, by incident in their lives, and by self report. John Gardner, a friend of Emerson's in Latin School days, speaks of Ralph Waldo's rather overpowering "equanimity"; Gardner thought Emerson could do with "a few harsher traits & perhaps more Masculine vigor."[2] Emerson himself wrote in early adult years of his "sore uneasiness in the company of most men and women, a frigid fear of offending."[3] Comparing himself with his brilliant brother Edward, Emerson said: "My own manner is sluggish; my speech sometimes flippant, sometimes embarrassed and ragged; my actions (if I may say so) are of a passive kind."[4]

Emerson's transcendental philosophy inspired his friends to vigorous social action, to the creation of the experimental communities, Brook Farm and Fruitlands. Emerson did not join either community. After one evening of excited talk, at his home, about Brook Farm, Emerson wrote in his diary: "Not once could I be inflamed but sat aloof and thoughtless; my voice faltered and fell."[5] In 1869 Emerson found himself temporarily a member of the Harvard faculty and scheduled to give a series of eighteen lectures which were to form a theoretical unit. He seems to have found the university lectures a serious strain and to have announced to his class a defensively modest aspiration; he would make no attempt at formulating a system but "wanted only to dot a little curve of personal observation."[6] Emerson wrote more than once of his distaste for debate with tough-minded opponents. "The men of strong understanding are a menacing rapid trenchant race—they cut me short—they drive me into a corner."[7]

Thoreau, fourteen years younger than Emerson, became a disciple when he read the essay *Nature*. The two men were well acquainted all their adult lives and in 1841–43 and 1847–49 Thoreau lived in the Emerson household. Emerson is a good authority on Thoreau's temperament: "He has muscle, and ventures on and performs feats which I am forced to decline" (*J*, IX, 522). Emerson here referred to moral and intellectual muscle, but Thoreau also had physical muscle. He was in his early life much stronger and healthier than Emerson, but he contracted tuberculosis and died at the age of forty-five, whereas Emerson lived to the age of seventy-eight. Emerson testifies to Thoreau's combativeness as well as to his vigor (No. 14): "If I knew only Thoreau, I should think cooperation of good men impossible. . . . Always some weary captious paradox to fight you with, and the time and temper wasted" (*J*, IX, 15–16).

Thoreau conducted his own experiments in living. He never married and is not known ever to have been in love. He did not smoke, would not drink wine, coffee, or tea, and was, from time to time, vegetarian. He refused to pay his poll tax and on that account spent a single night in jail. Above all, of course, he lived for two years alone in his cabin by Walden Pond. The Walden experiment was not done to show that man could live in the woods. The Walden years and all of Thoreau's life were intended to show that a man can live as he wants to live, that he can have what he truly values if he will find out what that is and single-heartedly insist upon it.

A man's temperament is often revealed in his choice of heroes. Thoreau's greatest hero was one whom comfortable folk thought a fanatic—Captain John Brown. When Brown was jailed and threatened with hanging, Thoreau called his townsmen together and delivered a plea for John Brown's life. From that plea it would appear that Thoreau took Brown for a bolder, and therefore more admirable, version of himself. "He was a man of Spartan habits. . . . A man of rare common sense and directness of speech, as of action" ("A Plea for Captain John Brown," *W*, IV, 413). And "He did not recognize unjust human laws, but resisted them as he was bid. For once we are lifted out of the trivialness and dust of politics into the region of truth and manhood" (pp. 424–25). "Read his admirable answers to Mason and others. . . . On the one side, half-brutish, half-timid questioning; on the other, truth, clear as lightning, crashing into their obscene temples" (p. 426). And (No. 20): "Think of him, —of his rare qualities!—such a man as it takes ages to make, and ages to understand; no mock hero, nor the representative of any party. A man such as the sun may not rise upon again in this benighted land. To whose making went the costliest material, the finest adamant" (p. 437).

The second difference between Emerson and Thoreau is one of intelligence. It is not a question of intellectual power, but of intellectual (or conceptual) style. Thoreau's is a more analytic mind and Emerson's a more synthetic. Thoreau gives us a world well-differentiated, the experience of concrete particulars. Emerson gives us a world processed by abstraction with similarities seen everywhere. It is the difference really between a bean patch and the Over-Soul.

In explaining his poem "The Sphinx" Emerson champions his own synthetic conceptual style. "The perception of identity unites all things and explains one by another, and the most rare and strange is equally facile as the most common. But if the mind live only in particulars, and see only differences (wanting the power to see the whole—all in each), then the world addresses to this mind a question it cannot answer, and each new fact tears it in pieces, and it is vanquished by the distracting variety."[8] To put Emerson's statement in balance one is obliged to add that synthesis without analysis is seldom compelling. If Emerson saw identity everywhere, it was partly because he had a tendency to smear.

Thoreau's analytic, conceptual style put him in some danger of contributing to natural science. Channing wrote of Thoreau: "But his habit of mind demanded complete accuracy, the utmost finish, and that nothing should be taken on hearsay he had his gauges on the river, which he consulted winter and summer; he knew the temperature of all the springs in the town; he measured the snows when remarkable."[9] Thoreau interested himself in botany and zoology and in his will he left to the Boston Society of Natural History a collection of plants and of Indian relics. Emerson's attitude toward science and disciplined study seems to have been a little different. As a sophomore at Harvard he said: "Mathematics I hate."[10] Shortly before his twenty-first birthday he wrote: "My reasoning faculty is proportionably weak" and spoke of Locke and Hume as "Reasoning Machines."[11] Later in life he confessed that "he generally felt himself repelled by physicists."[12]

The fourteen volumes of Thoreau's *Journal* are replete with descriptions and measurements that are something like scientific data. It is not imprecision that prevents them from being data but rather their scientific aimlessness. They were not recorded for the purpose of inducing or testing empirical generalizations. In the absence of scientific aim Thoreau's data would suggest a mindless compulsion to inventory Nature if we did not know that he had extra-scientific aims. As Krutch says, Thoreau always sought to experience the natural world and to transmit that experience. The generalizations he sought were metaphysical, moral, and poetic, rather than scientific.[13]

The characterization of Thoreau as analytic and aggressive does not prepare us for his apparent chastity. There is some evidence that analytic intelligence, in this society at least, tends to be a masculine characteristic,[14] and among primate species in general a high level of aggressiveness in the mature male is associated with a high level of sexual activity.[15] But, of course, a personality is not just a profile of dimensional values; it is an organized system, and the principles of organization are in part peculiarly human. We cannot now hope to discover the cause of Thoreau's chastity, but there are passages which suggest an exaggerated physical squeamishness, a squeamishness which his philosophy did not approve.[16] "We discourse freely without shame of one form of sensuality, and are silent about another. We are so degraded that we cannot speak simply of the necessary functions of human nature. In earlier ages, in some countries, every function was reverently spoken of and regulated by law. Nothing was too trivial for the Hindoo lawgiver, however offensive it may be to modern taste. He teaches how to eat, drink, cohabit, void excrement and urine, and the like, elevating what is mean, and does not falsely excuse himself by calling these things trifles" (*Walden, W*, II, 244–45).

We can feel more confident of the *consequences* of Thoreau's chastity than of its causes. He himself offers an explicit sublimation theory. "The generative energy, which, when we are loose, dissipates and makes us unclean, when we are continent invigorates and inspires us. Chastity is the flowering of man; and what are called Genius, Heroism, Holiness, and the like, are but various fruits which succeed it" (p. 243). The simple hydraulics implied by this statement and also by Freud's libido theory are probably wrong. And yet Thoreau's chastity did help to make possible his extraordinary achievements. Not for dynamic reasons, not by way of the diversion of libido, we would guess, but by keeping him free of the affectional ties that would have compromised his life of principle. To put it simply, a man without family is freer to follow his conscience than is a man with family, freer to live at Walden Pond, to spend a night in jail, to give his time to the study of Nature, to speak out strongly for John Brown. If Thoreau's absolute and uncompromising idealism has a certain adolescent quality, it is because adolescence is an age of mature intelligence and underdeveloped responsibilities, and so an age when morality is clear and absolute.

In time, the friendship between Thoreau and Emerson, which began so warmly, became strained and unsatisfying to both. We do not believe that the differences of personality alone foredoomed the friendship. A dominant, vigorous person of analytic intelligence and a less aggressive, less analytic, younger disciple compose a familiar sort of symbiotic pair. The difficulty in the case of Emerson and Thoreau was that the roles of leader and follower defined by the differences of age and reputation were fitted to the wrong personalities. The less aggressive, less analytic Emerson could not effectively play the sage with Thoreau for very long. But the dignity of Emerson's years, the extent of his fame, and the recollected pleasure of having had a disciple would not permit him to play any other role.

Both men testify to the difficulties. Thoreau wrote in 1853: "Talked, or tried to talk, with R. W. E. Lost my time—nay, almost my identity" (J, V, 188). And in 1856 he wrote of Emerson (No. 14): "He would not meet me on equal terms, but only be to some extent my patron. He would not come to see me, but was hurt if I did not visit him" (J, VIII, 199). In that same year Emerson said of Thoreau (No. 14): "Must we always talk for victory, and never once for truth, for comfort, and joy?" (J, IX, 15).

The Styles

Are there specific features in the styles of Emerson and Thoreau which express their differences of temperament and intelligence? In order to hold constant the many sources of stylistic variation other than personality we thought it desirable to work with passages matched, as nearly as possible, for content. The statistical analysis we planned to make required that the passages be matched as pairs, one from each author, and the fact that Emerson and Thoreau manifest a degree of stylistic overlap directed us to look for a substantial number of pairs. We found thirty-two of them.

There is no mechanical procedure that will select from the works of Emerson and Thoreau just those paired passages that are, in context, maximally close to identity. The trouble with nonmechanical procedures involving human judgment is the possibility that the judgments will not be sensitive to content alone but also to style. Nevertheless, judgment had to do the job. We looked for closely similar passages, attempting to disregard style, and at a time when the specific features to be counted had not yet been identified.

Passages were judged to constitute a matched pair when it seemed to us that a single proposition would convey the main point of both. Because this kind of propositional equivalence does not extend over long sequences, no passage is longer than about five hundred words. As far as possible, we made up the pairs with single continuous passages from each author. Sometimes, however, in an effort to maximize propositional equivalence, discontinuous selections from one or more works have been combined. In several instances the combination was made in order to bring into the corpus a single sentence, detached from the main body of one author's passage, which made an especially close match with something from the other author. The sources of the thirty-two passages are listed in Table I together with the abstract propositions in virtue of which each pair is equivalent.[17]

TABLE I

PAIRED PASSAGES AND THE PROPOSITIONS
THEY EXPRESS

1. Not only thought but action also is valuable.
   Em. "The American Scholar," *W*, I, 95–96. "I do. . . .
   splendid products"
   Th. *Walden, W*, II, 56. "The student . . . . to end"

2. Actual friendship involves many difficulties.
   Em. "Friendship," *W*, II, 199. "We are . . . . by solitude"
   Th. *A Week, W*, I, 294–95. "The only . . . . not under-
   stood"

3. One should not accept tradition unthinkingly.
   Em. "The American Scholar," *W*, I, 105–6. "Yes, we . . . .
   the moon"
   Th. *Walden, W,* II, 9–10. "It is . . . . nothing about"

4. One should not imitate others.
   Em. "Self-Reliance," *W*, II, 46. "There is . . . . has tried"
   "Self-Reliance," *W*, II, 83. "Insist on . . . . exhibited
   it"
   Th. *Walden, W,* II, 78–79. "One young . . . . true course"

5. One should live in the present.
   Em. "Self-Reliance," *W*, II, 67. "These roses . . . . above
   time"
   "Self-Reliance," *W*, II, 76. "He walks . . . lives al-
   ready"
   Th. *Walden, W,* II, 59. "This spending . . . . at once"
   "Walking," *W*, V, 245–46. "Above all . . . . this mo-
   ment"

6. Nature has great value for a city man.
   Em. *Nature, W,* I, 16. "To the . . . . finds himself"
   Th. *Walden, W,* II, 349–50. "Our village . . . . ground"
   Walden, W, II, 350. "We must . . . . produces fresh-
   ets"

7. I have no genius for philanthropy.

Em. "Self-Reliance," *W*, II, 51–52. "If malice .... to with-
hold"

Th. *Walden*, *W*, II, 80–81. "But all .... they will"

8. A man should set his own conscience above all conventional standards.

Em. "Self-Reliance," *W*, II, 74. "The populace .... one
day"

Th. *Walden*, *W*, II, 355. "This was .... with such"

9. Personal possessions are not important to the great soul.

Em. "Heroism," *W*, II, 252. "Yet the ... earnest nonsense"

"Heroism," *W*, II, 255. "The heroic .... its loss"

Th. *Walden*, *W*, II, 25. "Old shoes ... them do"

Walden, *W*, II, 26. "I say ... of clothes"

Walden, *W*, II, 32. "I used ... be free"

Walden, *W*, II, 72. "Thank God ... furniture ware-
house"

Walden, *W*, II, 74. "When I ... to carry"

10. The language of the street is strong and agreeable.

Em. "The Superlative," *W*, X, 169. "I am .... and agreeable"

Journals, V, 419–20. "The language .... half sentence"

Th. *A Week*, *W*, I, 109. "We are .... the pine"

A Week, *W*, I, 110. "A sentence ... the end"

Journal, I, 237. "There is ... quite cheap"

Journal, I, 237. "The scholar .... high art"

Journal, I, 237. "I like ... of nature"

11. A good style is a concentrated one.

Em. *Journals*, X, 302–3. "All writing .... a surprise"

Journals, V, 213. "There is .... of surface"

Th. *Journal*, II, 418–19. "It is .... without digesting"

12. I dislike easy familiarity, lack of reserve and of self-reliance.

Em. "Manners," *W*, III, 136–37. "I prefer .... much acquainted"

"Manners," *W*, III, 139. "The love .... to flight"

"Friendship," *W*, II, 208–9. "Let me .... unites
them"

"Behavior," *W*, VI, 186–87. "The basis .... its members"

Th. *Journal*, V, 263–65. "Here have .... beautiful reserve"

13. Temperance in food and drink is admirable.
   Em. "Heroism," *W*, II, 254–55. "The temperance ....
   before it"
   Th. *Walden*, *W*, II, 236–37. "Beside, there .... me essen-
   tially"
   Walden, *W*, II, 240. "I believe ... of tea"

14. My friendship with Thoreau (Emerson) was a difficult
   one.
   Em. *Journals*, VIII, 303. "Thoreau gives .... set aside"
   Journals, IX, 15–16. "If I .... temper wasted"
   Th. *Journal*, III, 250. "I doubt .... comprehensive char-
   acter"
   Journal, VIII, 199. "I had .... our affection"

15. Self-culture is more important than traveling.
   Em. "Self-Reliance," *W*, II, 80. "It is ... educated Ameri-
   cans"
   "Self-Reliance," *W*, II, 81–82. "Our first .... fled
   from"
   Th. *Walden*, *W*, II, 352–53. "The other .... be after"
   Walden, *W*, II, 353. "Be rather ... higher latitudes"
   Walden, *W*, II, 353. "Nay, be ... of thought"

16. An ideal friendship is a relation of love, truth, and equality.
   Em. "Friendship," *W*, II, 205–6. "I wish .... was drudgery"
   Th. *A Week*, *W*, I, 283–85. "A Friend .... for us"

17. Fine clothing is not necessary to the great spirit.
   Em. "Social Aims," *W*, VIII, 87-88. "To pass .... to
   bestow"
   Th. *Walden*, *W*, II, 23–24. "As for .... clothes on"
   Walden, *W*, II, 25–26. "A man .... of clothes"

18. The personal conscience is a higher standard than gov-
   ernment or law.
   Em. "John Brown: Speech at Boston," *W*, XI, 271–73.
   "The state .... of paper"
   Th. "A Plea for Captain John Brown," *W*, IV, 437–38.
   "Any man .... from that"

19. Slavery now impinges on my life.

Em. "The Fugitive Slave Law," *W*, XI, 228–29. "I said
.... not exist"

Th. "Slavery in Massachusetts," *W*, IV, 405–6. "I have
.... see it"

20. John Brown should not hang.

Em. "John Brown: Speech at Boston," *W*, XI, 269–70.
"It is .... poor prisoner"

Th. "A Plea for Captain John Brown," *W*, IV, 437.
"Who is .... of men"

21. Regrets and pangs of conscience are of little value.

Em. "Self-Reliance," *W*, II, 78–79. "Another sort ....
are swift"

Th. *A Week*, *W*, I, 75. "Men have .... no milk"

22. Few men understand the art of walking.

Em. "Country Life," *W*, XII, 142. "Few men .... a dog"
"Country Life," *W*, XII, 158–59. "Dr Johnson ....
call professors"

Th. "Walking," *W*, V, 205–6. "I have .... a walk"

23. My vicinity offers many good walks.

Em. "Country Life," *W*, XII, 143-44. "For walking ....
a park"

Th. "Walking," *W*, V, 211–12. "My vicinity .... to you"

24. Through books there is community of mind.

Em. "The American Scholar," *W*, I, 91–92. "Undoubtedly there .... never see"

Th. *Walden*, *W*, II, 119–20. "It is .... the board"

25. Our houses are no credit to us.

Em. "Domestic Life," *W*, VII, 110–11. "I am .... dearly
bought"

Th. *Walden*, *W*, II, 31. "From the .... mausoleum instead"
Walden, *W*, II, 32. "I used .... as this"

26. The less government the better.

Em. "Politics," *W*, III, 215–16. "Hence the .... and
flowers"

Th. "Civil Disobedience," *W*, IV, 356. "I heartily ....
standing government"
"Civil Disobedience," *W*, IV, 356–57. "This American .... the railroads"

"Civil Disobedience," *W*, IV, 358. "But a . . . . the right"

27. There is poetry in the primitive sense of words.
    Em. "The Poet," *W*, III, 21–22. "The poets . . . . a tree"
    Th. "Walking," *W*, V, 232. "Where is . . . . surrounding Nature"

28. Thought and spirit are more important than form in true poetry.
    Em. "The Poet," *W*, III, 9–10. "Our poets . . . . its poet"
    Th. *A Week*, *W*, I, 400. "A true . . . . always divine"

29. All nature and all experience feed the true poet.
    Em. "The Poet," *W*, III, 42. "And this . . . . or ignoble"
    Th. *A Week*, *W*, I, 101–2. "At least . . . . and then"

30. America awaits her poet.
    Em. "The Poet," *W*, III, 37–38. "Banks and . . . . for metres"
    Th. "Walking," *W*, V, 232. "I do . . . . than anything"
    "Walking," *W*, V, 233. "The West . . . . American mythology"

31. It is possible to find contentment in the simple things of life.
    Em. "Experience," *W*, III, 61–62. "The fine . . . . by analysis"
    Th. *Walden*, *W*, II, 361. "However mean . . . . a palace"
    Walden, *W*, II, 361. "Do not . . . . about me"

32. There is nothing in history that is not also in the present.
    Em. "Works and Days," *W*, VII, 174–75. "The world . . . . is Doomsday"
    Th. *A Week*, *W*, I, 160–61. "In every . . . . the researched"

We will begin by comparing the passages qualitatively and will find that the propositional equivalence attained is never perfect, that temperament and conceptual style always intervene to make one author express something the other does not. While these qualitative comparisons are often persuasive, they are both selective and subjective, and so one cannot be confident that they establish real differences characteristic of the two authors. We will then compare the passages quantitatively, showing that there are formally defined features, interpretable as expressions of temperament and intelligence, which appear with statistically significant differential frequency in Emerson and Thoreau.

Qualitative Comparisons

The thirty-two propositions of Table I convey fairly well the philosophy, social attitudes, and cranky opinions that Emerson and Thoreau had in common. The statements of Table I are a rather banal set. Only our reverence for the two authors deterred us from phrasing No. 31 as "The best things in life are free," and No. 32 as "History repeats itself." In part the banality of the statements in Table I is explained by the fact that they are encapsulations of the lower original passages. In part the paraphrases seem banal, whereas the sources do not because, for both writers, it is the way the thing is said that chiefly matters. Emerson and Thoreau are nearer to being poets than to being systematic philosophers or psychologists. But they are poets with distinct personalities. The same idea has never the same overtones for the two.

Consider first the difference of vigor between Emerson and Thoreau. Here is Emerson describing the benefits that Nature offers to a city man (No. 6): "To the body and mind which have been cramped by noxious work or company, nature is medicinal and restores their tone. The tradesman, the attorney comes out of the din and craft of the street and sees the sky and the woods, and is a man again. In their eternal calm, he finds himself" (*Nature, W,* I, 16). Here is Thoreau on the same subject: "Our village life would stagnate if it were not for the unexplored forests and meadows which surround it. We need the tonic of wildness. . . . We must be refreshed by the sight of inexhaustible vigor, vast and titanic features, the sea-coast with its wrecks, the wilderness with its living and its decaying trees" (*Walden, W,* II, 349–50). For both men nature is medicinal, but Emerson craves a healing balm and Thoreau "the tonic of wildness."

Emerson, thinking of the importance of living in the

present (No. 5), preaches a sermon on "These roses under my window. . . . There is no time to them. There is simply the rose; it is perfect in every moment of its existence" ("Self-Reliance," *W*, II, 67). Perfect the rose certainly is but also rather bland by comparison with "the cock crow in every barn-yard within our horizon," which is what comes to mind in a similar connection for Thoreau. "That sound commonly reminds us that we are growing rusty and antique in our employments and habits of thought. His philosophy comes down to a more recent time than ours" ("Walking," *W*, V, 246).

Emerson, comparing travel unfavorably with self-culture (No. 15), exposes a shadow of melancholy: "I pack my trunk, embrace my friends, embark on the sea and at last wake up in Naples, and there beside me is the stern fact, the sad self, unrelenting, identical, that I fled from" ("Self-Reliance," *W*, II, 81–82). Thoreau, advising us not to travel to the "other side of the globe," adds the exhortation: "Be rather the Mungo Park, the Lewis and Clark and Frobisher, of your own streams and oceans; explore your own higher latitudes. . . . Nay, be a Columbus to whole new continents and worlds within you, opening new channels, not of trade, but of thought" (*Walden, W*, II, 353).

Again and again Thoreau sounds the more vigorous note. For example, in No. 26: "I heartily accept the motto, —'That government is best which governs least' " ("Civil Disobedience," *W*, IV, 356). Emerson's near equivalent is: "Hence the less government we have the better" ("Politics," *W*, III, 215). Emerson on the subject of wine (No. 13) quotes John Eliot, the Indian Apostle: " 'It is a noble, generous liquor and we should be humbly thankful for it, but, as I remember, water was made before it' " ("Heroism," *W*, II, 254–55). Thoreau's related sentence has more athletic spring: "I believe that water is the only drink for a wise man; wine is not so noble a liquor; and think of dashing the hopes of a morning with a cup of warm coffee, or of an evening with a dish of tea!" (*Walden, W*, II, 240).

Consider next the manifestations of combativeness. Here is Emerson telling an audience that John Brown ought not to be hanged (No. 20): "Nothing can resist the sympathy which all elevated minds must feel with Brown, and through them the whole civilized world.... Indeed, it is the *reductio ad absurdum* of Slavery, when the governor of Virginia is forced to hang a man whom he declares to be a man of the most integrity, truthfulness and courage he has ever met. Is that the kind of man the gallows is built for?" ("John Brown," *W*, XI, 269–70). We have already seen some of Thoreau's lines in defense of John Brown, but here are a few others. "Who is it whose safety requires that Captain Brown be hung?... If you do not wish it, say so distinctly.... A man.... sent to be the redeemer of those in captivity; and the only use to which you can put him is to hang him at the end of a rope!" ("A Plea for Captain John Brown," *W*, IV, 437). Emerson is measured, stately, a little remote with his *reductio ad absurdum*. Thoreau is passionately and personally combative: "If you do not wish it," "the only use to which *you* can put him" (italics added). Emerson did not have the stomach for this sort of face-to-face accusation.

It is regularly the case in the thirty-two pairs of passages we have studied that Thoreau is more concerned than Emerson with destroying his opposition. Both advise us not to follow tradition unthinkingly (No. 3); Emerson in the mild words: "It is a mischievous notion that we are come late into nature; that the world was finished a long time ago" (*Nature, W*, I, 105). Thoreau is more challenging and abrupt: "What old people say you cannot do, you try and find that you can. Old deeds for old people, and new deeds for new.... I have lived some thirty years on this planet, and I have yet to hear the first syllable of valuable or even earnest advice from my seniors" (*Walden, W*, II, 9–10). With Emerson it is usually possible to feel that an attack is not leveled against anyone in particular. With Thoreau one generally feels that there is someone who will take offense.[18]

Emerson expresses his taste in manners (No. 12) as

follows: "I prefer a tendency to stateliness to an excess of fellowship. Let the incommunicable objects of nature and the metaphysical isolation of man teach us independence. Let us not be too much acquainted" ("Manners," *W*, III, 136–37). Thoreau expresses the same taste in connection with a particular acquaintance and in strongly personal terms: "I wanted that he should straighten his back, smooth out those ogling wrinkles of benignity about his eyes, and, with a healthy reserve, pronounce something in a downright manner. It was difficult to keep clear of his slimy benignity, with which he sought to cover you before he swallowed you and took you fairly into his bowels" (*J*, V, 264).[19]

When Thoreau blazes away in his most aggressive vein he reminds us of a writer with whom he is not often compared—George Bernard Shaw. The points of resemblance between Shaw and Thoreau are numerous: iconoclasm, impatience, extravagance, a taste for paradox. Both men attempted to found every action, even trivial ones, on principle. Both eschewed alcohol and tobacco, both were vegetarians, both admired fanatical men. There was a certain coolness in the private lives of both; both are under grave suspicion of chastity.

When Thoreau is least like Emerson he is most like Shaw (No. 5): "This spending of the best part of one's life earning money in order to enjoy a questionable liberty during the least valuable part of it reminds me of the Englishman who went to India to make a fortune first, in order that he might return to England and live the life of a poet. He should have gone up garret at once. 'What!' exclaim a million Irishmen starting up from all the shanties in the land, 'is not this railroad which we have built a good thing?' Yes, I answer, *comparatively* good, that is, you might have done worse; but I wish, as you are brothers of mine, that you could have spent your time better than digging in this dirt." The passage is from *Walden* (*W*, II, 59–60), but the impatience, the vigor, the extravagance, the paradox, are very Shavian. And so are they in this sentence from *Walden*: "As for the

Pyramids, there is nothing to wonder at in them so much as the fact that so many men could be found degraded enough to spend their lives constructing a tomb for some ambitious booby, whom it would have been wiser and manlier to have drowned in the Nile, and then given his body to the dogs" (*W*, II, 64).

The difference of conceptual style between Emerson and Thoreau appears, in extreme form, in their remarks on the subject of housing (No. 25). Emerson advises: "His house ought to show us his honest opinion of what makes his well-being when he rests among his kindred, and forgets all affectation, compliance, and even exertion of will. He brings home whatever commodities and ornaments have for years allured his pursuit, and his character must be seen in them" ("Domestic Life," *W*, VII, 110–11). Thoreau is rather more concrete. "I used to see a large box by the railroad, six feet long by three wide, in which the laborers locked up their tools at night; and it suggested to me that every man who was hard pushed might get such a one for a dollar, and, having bored a few auger holes in it, to admit the air at least, get into it when it rained and at night, and hook down the lid, and so have freedom in his love, and in his soul be free" (*Walden, W*, II, 32).

A contrast in level of abstraction appears in many of the paired passages including some that we have already cited to illustrate the difference of temperament. For example, Emerson lists as benefits of Nature for the city man (No. 6), the sky and the woods. Thoreau's list is more fully itemized: the bittern, the meadow-hen, the snipe, the whispering sedge, decaying trees, the thundercloud, etc. (*Nature, W*, I, 16; *Walden, W*, II, 349–50).

The association between concrete, analytic concepts and a combative tone is not entirely arbitrary. Other things equal, it is easier to disagree with a concrete statement than with an abstract generalization. On the highest level of abstraction men tend either to agree or to be unable to determine whether they do or do not agree. But when someone advises you to sleep in a box, six feet long by three wide, you know where you are.

Quantitative Comparisons

With matched passages it is possible to use a simple test for the statistical significance of obtained differences, the Sign Test.[20] Probably everyone who makes a count in connection with a study of style feels the force of the question: How large and consistent must a difference be before it is taken seriously? The question is ordinarily answered with intuitions of probability: "A difference of only 5 words in passages 1000 words long may be meaningless." Intuition does not necessarily set easier tasks than the theory of probability, but it is more partial than that theory to the investigator's hypotheses and in that respect less trustworthy.

In testing any particular hypothesis about differences in the styles of Emerson and Thoreau, we propose to treat the 32 matched samples as if they were 32 tosses of a coin. In essence we shall be asking whether the coin is an unbiased one for which the two outcomes, heads and tails, are equally probable or a biased one for which one outcome is more probable than the other. There will be in our counts two outcomes corresponding to the heads and tails of coin tossing: a difference that favors Emerson will be the one outcome and a difference that favors Thoreau the other. We shall be asking of each stylistic feature whether the outcomes are equally probable across the passages or whether we should consider that the tosses are biased and the styles therefore truly distinctive with regard to the feature in question.

With a coin that is really unbiased *any* obtained sequence of outcomes is *possible*—even, for instance, 32 successive cases of heads. However, the probability of obtaining so discrepant an outcome with an unbiased coin is astronomically small. A reasonable man who obtained such an outcome would conclude that the coin was not in fact unbiased but biased in favor of heads. What would he conclude for various less extreme outcomes, for 30 heads and 2 tails, 28 heads and 4 tails, 26 heads and 6 tails? As the outcomes approach equality they become more and more compatible with the conclusion that the coin is actually unbiased. Mathematical theory (the expansion of the binomial) assigns exact probabilities to each sequence of results on the assumption that the coin is unbiased. However, the drawing of the line where one will begin to believe that the coin is biased is a partially arbitrary decision. It is conventional in the use of tests of significance of this kind to treat results which have a probability of occurrence no greater than 5 times in 100 (p = .05) as significant results, as evidence that the outcomes are not equally likely.

As an example let us apply this statistical model to one count. The hypothesis is that Thoreau makes greater use of the first-person, singular pronouns, "I," "me," and "my," than does Emerson. Because the first selection of such a pronoun in a sentence tends to constrain subsequent selections in that sentence, we decided to count each sentence just once—as containing a first-person singular pronoun or as not containing one. The count was made for each passage and expressed as a ratio with the number of sentences containing a pronoun as the numerator and the total number of sentences in the passage as the denominator. Expression as a ratio is necessary because the paired passages are not exactly matched in length.

In No. 3 Emerson used no first-person singular pronouns in his 11 sentences ($\%_{11}$), whereas Thoreau used pronouns of this type in 4 sentences from his total of 14 ($\frac{4}{14}$). The Sign Test of significance directs us to ignore the size of a difference of this kind and simply to record its direction. The difference is given a plus sign if, as in the present instance, it is in the predicted direction and a minus sign if it goes contrary to the prediction. In short, the outcomes are dichotomized into heads and tails. With the numerical data, of course, one sometimes gets a tie; there were 7 ties in the present comparison. A tie is like the case in which a coin rolls down the register and cannot be read. The outcome does not count either way and the number of tosses is reduced by 1.

Of the 25 pairs of passages usable for the pronoun

analysis, Thoreau exceeded Emerson 19 times and Emerson exceeded Thoreau 6 times. A table of probabilities for the expansion of the binomial (Table D in Siegel)[21] tells us that an outcome as extreme as this would not happen more than 7 times in 1000 ($p = .007$) if the two writers really used the first-person singular pronoun equally often in passages of matched content. Being reasonable men we conclude that the coin is biased, the styles in this respect distinct, and the hypothesis confirmed. Of course, careful readers of Thoreau and Emerson have known all along that Thoreau made greater use of "I," but our tests will demonstrate that some other things which careful readers believe are probably not true. Since not all of our impressions will survive the test, we can feel more confident of those that do.

Aggressiveness

The difference in the tendency to use the first-person singular pronoun is one of the formal features that we consider to be expressions of differential aggressiveness. It is so because it occurs with another set of features, the negative forms "not," "none," "no," and the like.[22] Negatives were counted only once per sentence and the ratio of negative to affirmative sentences counted for each sample. There were no matches in the entire set of 32 pairs. In 24 pairs Thoreau had the greater proportion of negatives, whereas Emerson had the greater proportion in only 8 pairs. A difference as large as this would be obtained by chance less often than once in a thousand times ($p < .001$) if there were really no difference in the styles of Emerson and Thoreau. We also counted sentences marked by the conjunction of a first-person singular pronoun and a negative. There were 16 untied cases, and Thoreau led Emerson in 14 of them; a difference significant with $p = .002$.

Why should negatives in conjunction with the first-person singular pronoun be considered an index of aggressiveness? Why, for instance, is it aggressive of Thoreau to write (No. 4): "I would not have any one adopt *my* mode of living on any account" (*Walden, W, II, 78*)? The sentence is aggressive because it implies the existence of another mind that holds to the affirmative form of the proposition being negated. One does not negate propositions that no one is entertaining. We say, "It is not sunny out," only if someone thinks it is, and "It will not fly," only if someone thinks it will. Thoreau's sentence, "I would not have any one adopt *my* mode of living on any account," implies the existence of someone who believes that Thoreau *would* have him adopt *his* mode of living. And indeed Thoreau refers to "one young man of my acquaintance" (p. 78) who did think just that.

The development of an argument by means of a succession of negative propositions represents a preoccupation with the mistaken ideas that must be set aside before the truth can be established. Thoreau consistently attempted to get at the false propositions in the mind of the opposition so that he might strike them down. The use of the first-person singular pronoun made the combat a personal one, Thoreau against the conventional ideas of his time.

Our impression of a temperamental affinity between Thoreau and Shaw is strengthened by the finding for negatives. Richard M. Ohmann, in his study of Shaw, considers the "posture of opposition" to be one of the most characteristic features of Shaw's style.[23] Ohmann supported his qualitative impressions with word counts, comparing passages from Shaw with a control set of passages from Chesterton, Wilde, the Webbs, Yeats, and Bertrand Russell. Ohmann made no tests of statistical significance, but he counts many more negatives in the passage from Shaw than in the other passages.

There are formal features other than the negative that reveal Thoreau's combativeness. The logical structure of discourse in English is sometimes explicitly marked with such connectives as "because," "if"–"then," "therefore," "though," "but," and "yet."[24] Thoreau uses more of such connectives than does Emerson, and the difference is significant, though only barely so. The logical connectives in general are not clearly related to combativeness, but one subvariety, the contrasting conjunction, does seem to be.

Contrasting conjunctions like "but," "though," and "yet" encode a relation of negative implication linking two propositions or two modifiers of a single head word (which commonly transform into two propositions). One says, in English: "There was thunder and lightning *but* no rain"; "I liked her *even though* she hated me"; "She was beautiful *but* dumb, poor *but* happy." In each of these constructions an expectancy is generated and then violated. Negative implication is a kind of conflict, and the writer who develops his argument through the use of negative implication—as, for instance, does John Donne—sounds more combative than one who does not. Thoreau uses a larger number of contrastive conjunctions than does Emerson in 20 passages; Emerson uses more in 9 passages. The difference is significant with $p < .05$.

The passages from Emerson and Thoreau listed as No. 1 illustrate the contrast between argument by positive implication and argument by negative implication. Emerson begins with the general assertion that he does not see how any man can afford "to spare any action in which he can partake." This assertion implies that action is valuable, and the remaining sentences of the passage assert that it is so indeed and list the ways. It is "pearls and rubies" to his discourse; it is an instructor "in eloquence and wisdom"; it is the "raw material out of which the intellect moulds her splendid products" ("The American Scholar," *W*, I, 95–96). The entire paragraph is a harmonious unfolding of the implications of the first sentence.

Thoreau's way is different. His first sentence asserts that the student who foregoes action and experience makes a mistake. This sentence, like Emerson's first sentence, implies that action is valuable. Instead, however, of listing the various ways in which it is valuable, Thoreau throws up a challenge to the implication. " 'But,' says one, 'you do not mean that the students should go to work with their hands instead of their heads?' " And then a challenge to the challenge: "I do not mean that exactly, but I mean something which he might think a good deal like that." The conclusion which fights its way through the several challenges is: the student should not *"play life"* or *"study it merely"* but "earnestly *live* it from beginning to end" (*Walden, W,* II, 56).

Conceptual Style

As one index of the synthetic-analytic contrast of conceptual style, we have used a ratio of abstract nouns to concrete nouns. The noun form that seems to us to convey the strongest sense of abstraction is the singular common noun without any determiner.[25] Emerson uses 6 of them in the following sentence (No. 1): "Drudgery, calamity, exasperation, want, are instructors in eloquence and wisdom" ("The American Scholar," *W,* I, 95). The addition of a determiner (*a calamity* or *this calamity* or *some wisdom*) would limit the abstraction. Pluralization seems to fragment it (*calamities, wants*). There is one sort of singular noun without determiner, the mass noun referring to a physical substance (e.g., *sand, water*), that does not convey a strong sense of abstraction. These latter we counted as concrete, along with all plurals, all proper nouns, and all singular nouns with determiners. The differences between Emerson and Thoreau are large and consistent. Emerson was more abstract in 23 cases and Thoreau in 8, a difference significant at better than the .001 level. Emerson knew of this difference between himself and Thoreau: "In reading him, I find the same thought, the same spirit that is in me, but he takes a step beyond, and illustrates by excellent images that which I should have conveyed in a sleepy generality" (*J,* IX, 522).[26]

As a second index of conceptual style we have used a ratio of sensory-and-motor verbs to the total words in a passage. Sensory verbs are those that make reference to sensation in a particular modality, such verbs as "see," "hear," "smell," and "feel." Motor verbs are those that make reference to some definite picturable activity, such words as "walk," "run," "cut," "stand up," "pluck," and "bounce." It seemed to us that this count would capture the difference between Thoreau's tendency to render concrete experience and Emerson's tendency to abstract and synthesize. The quantitative difference turned out to be a very large one. In 21 cases Thoreau uses more sensory and motor verbs than does Emerson, while Emerson uses more of them in just 2 cases ($p < .001$).

The common sensory and motor verbs in English all have multiple meanings including usually several abstract meanings. One can *see* the sky or—the point of an argument; one can see a client, see that something is done, see someone home, etc. Thoreau and Emerson do not differ significantly in the raw frequencies with which they use the *words* in question; their differences are with respect to the sensory and motor meanings of the words. Thus Emerson uses "see" in No. 17 ("Social Aims," *W*, VIII, 87) and uses it again in No. 18 ("John Brown," *W*, XI, 271), but the object of the verb in the former passage is "moral benefit" and in the latter "the use of a judge." In Emerson's No. 16 ("Friendship," *W*, II, 205) we have the verb "vaults" but with "friendship" as subject; in his No. 10 (*J*, V, 420) we have "walk" and "run" but with "words" as subject. On the other hand, when Thoreau uses "see" in No. 9 (*Walden*, *W*, II, 32) it is with himself as subject and "a large box" as object. In No. 5 ("Walking," *W*, V, 246) he "hears" the "cock crow" and in No. 6 (*Walden*, *W*, II, 350) "smells" the "whispering sedge." In No. 32 his "thrust" (*A Week*, *W*, I, 160) is of a "stick"; in No. 6 it is "the mink" that "crawls" (*Walden*, *W*, II, 350) and in No. 9 "an immigrant" who is seen "tottering under a bundle" (*Walden*, *W*, II, 74). In sum, Thoreau's sensory verbs are likely to name physical sensations and his motor verbs are likely to name physical actions, whereas Emerson's sensory and motor verbs are likely to be used with extended metaphorical meanings. It is a count of meanings rather than words that distinguishes the writers.

Personality and Style in Concord

Indirection, Archaism and Other Features

Not everything we counted served to distinguish Emerson from Thoreau, and not everything that distinguished them can be interpreted in terms of conceptual style or temperament. We had thought it likely that Emerson would make a higher score for the use of "elevated" diction (such words as "firmament," "poetry," "divine"). We had expected Thoreau to use more superlatives, more negative affixes (for example "un-," "dis-"), more all-or-nothing words (for example, "all," "each," "nobody"), and more imperative constructions, to italicize more often, and to use the exclamation point more liberally. The absolute frequencies were in the anticipated direction in almost all cases, but the differences were not consistent enough to be judged significant. Some of these features would almost certainly register as significantly different if one were to compare passages selected at random. It should be remembered that the design of the present study demands more than is usual of stylistic features; they are required to demonstrate diagnostic power in passages matched with respect to everything but the personalities of the authors.

There are, finally, two features that do distinguish Emerson from Thoreau and do certainly contribute to the reader's perception of the two styles but which seem to be related to both personality dimensions rather than to either one alone. One of the features is the balance between direct constructions and indirect constructions. We mean by a direct construction a declarative sentence (identified by the author's own end punctuation) in which the main subject, verb, and predicate object (or predicate adjective or predicate nominative) occur in that order. An indirect construction is any declarative that breaks this order; for example, Emerson's (No. 14): "Centrality he has, and penetration" (*J*, IX, 15) and his (No. 21): "Welcome evermore to gods and men is the self-helping man" and "For him all doors are flung wide; him all tongues greet," both from "Self-Reliance" (*W*, II, 78). The difference between the two authors is again significant, though not quite so consistent as others we have reported. In 18 cases Emerson uses a larger proportion of indirect constructions, while Thoreau does so but 9 times (p about .05).

Many readers have noticed that Emerson often used archaisms.[27] In our passages we find quite a few of these. In No. 1 an inanimate object is assigned gender: "the intellect moulds her splendid products" ("The American Scholar," *W*, I, 95–96). In No. 7 we find the archaic negative: "Expect me not" ("Self-Reliance," *W*, II, 52). The archaic use of "be" with the intransitive verb "come" occurs in No. 3 ("The American Scholar," *W*, I, 105). Archaic subjunctives appear in many passages; for example, No. 20: "It were bold" ("John Brown," *W*, XI, 270). The archaic pronoun "thou" is used and the associated archaic verbal inflections ("shouldst," "couldst"), and "very" is used in the archaic sense of "truly." In 11 passages Emerson used a larger proportion of archaisms than Thoreau, whereas Thoreau used a larger proportion in only 2 passages.[28] The numbers are small, but the disproportion is great enough to be significant with p about .01.

The one frequent archaism in the Thoreau passages is the word "perchance" and, in the nineteenth century, this term was archaic in only some of its uses. What is interesting is the fact that Thoreau uses "perchance" in 6 different passages whereas Emerson does not use it at all. This is the sort of word that would be useful if we were studying style in order to fix the authorship of doubtful works. It is this sort of word, in conjunction with a statistical model, that has recently enabled Mosteller and Wallace to establish the authorship of the disputed *Federalist* papers.[29]

When indirection, abstraction, impersonality, and archaism come together, we have Emerson's extreme manner, the stately, "composed" style that is farthest removed from Thoreau's tart, personal, concrete manner. We have quoted examples of Thoreau's extreme; here now are some lines from Emerson (No. 3) that Thoreau could not have written. "It is a mischievous notion that we are come late into nature; that the world was finished a long time ago. As the world was plastic and fluid in the hands of God, so it is ever to so much of his attributes as we bring to it. To ignorance and sin, it is flint. They adapt themselves to it as they may; but in proportion as a man has any thing in him divine, the firmament flows before him and takes his signet and form" ("The American Scholar," *W*, I, 105).

Self-Representation

Heredity and childhood endowed Emerson and Thoreau with unlike temperaments and conceptual styles. Probably endowments like these are not alterable in adult years, but their effects are nevertheless not fully determined for the reason that a man may or may not recognize that he has them, may value them or regret them, may accept them or struggle against them. One of us (Albert Gilman) remembers hearing Austin Warren say in 1949 that there was a difference between Emerson and Thoreau on the level of self-representation and self-acceptance. It seemed to Professor Warren that Emerson had the stronger sense of personal deficiency, the greater need to wrestle with his own nature.

Very early in this paper we quoted passages to show that Emerson and Thoreau had similar ideals of style, but even in those few phrases there were signs that the ideal was more easily realized by Thoreau than by Emerson. That impression is confirmed by other closely matched sentences on the subject of style. Emerson wrote (No. 10): "I am daily struck with the forcible understatement of people who have no literary habit. The low expression is strong and agreeable" ("The Superlative," *W*, X, 169). Thoreau's very similar sentence is: "We are often struck by the force and precision of style to which hard-working men, unpracticed in writing, easily attain when required to make the effort" (*A Week*, *W*, I, 109). We notice that Emerson in praising plain, honest speech says something not strictly true; he cannot have been *daily* "struck with the forcible understatement of people who have no liter-

ary habit." In praising the style of people with "no literary habit" he employs the very literary phrase, "I am
daily struck," and he characterizes the stylists he admires
in terms they would never use, as persons "who have no
literary habit" and who are given to the "low expression."
They would be more likely to describe themselves in
Thoreau's terms as "hard-working men, unpracticed in
writing." The shared ideal of style seems to have cor-
responded more closely with Thoreau's natural inclinations than with Emerson's.

The central ideal in the philosophy shared by Emerson and Thoreau was self-reliance or independence. A
man should find his own way of life and insist upon it for
himself, whether or not it is approved by tradition and
convention. Both writers were perfectly clear that the
claims of personal conscience are superior to those of any
law or any social pressure. This sure morality, independ-
ent of the present consensus, made it possible for them to
oppose the Fugitive Slave Law and to champion the imprisoned John Brown.

Though Emerson first articulated the philosophy of
self-reliance, it was more congenial to Thoreau. Thoreau,
like the salmon whose migration upstream is guaranteed
by a seasonal need to push against pressure, felt himself
only in opposition. Thoreau makes on us the compact
impression of a man whose natural inclinations agree with
his convictions. Emerson seems more dispersed, the line
he describes less clear.

Independence and self-reliance were values that Emerson chose rather than values that directly expressed his
temperament. He was not fond of combat but was rather
inclined to compliance. However, having adopted a creed
of independence, he struggled with his own nature and,
at important points, did what his conscience required. He
resigned from Second Church in 1832 because he could
not in conscience continue to administer communion. He
knew that his Divinity School Address in 1838 would
bring obloquy upon him, but he was not deterred.

When conscience required it, Emerson could act

against his inclinations, but he knew what his inclinations were and knew that they were fundamentally unalterable. Most impressively he saw that the philosophy of self-reliance required that he choose his own nature (No. 4): "Insist on yourself; never imitate. Your own gift you can present every moment with the cumulative force of a whole life's cultivation; but of the adopted talent of another you have only an extemporaneous half possession" ("Self-Reliance," *W*, II, 83).

William James in his address at the Emerson centenary in Concord especially praised the philosopher-poet for knowing and accepting his own nature. "This duty of spiritual seeing and reporting determined the whole tenor of his life. It was to shield this duty from invasion and distraction that he dwelt in the country, that he consistently declined to entangle himself with associations or to encumber himself with functions which, however he might believe in them, he felt were duties for other men and not for him."[30] Even on the issue of slavery, which strongly engaged his conscience, Emerson concluded: "I have quite other slaves to free than those negroes."[31]

The United States in the 1960's creates an appetite for leaders of sure morality and uncompromising conscience. Morality has been so thoroughly displaced by consensus that even our liberal statesmen are willing to call extremism an evil. It has become possible to talk as if departure from the great central stream—in whatever direction—were necessarily bad. That is the way things are, but it is not the way they have always been. We all know that there is an honorable American tradition of extremism in a good cause, and we feel some yearning for the moral confidence that made that tradition honorable. In these circumstances Thoreau's clear, confident voice is extremely impressive.

But there is more than one standard by which to judge a man's thought and style and personality. If we take account of the complexity of the problem solved, the integration of Emerson's personality is the more impressive achievement. His experience was richer than Thoreau's—he lived in the American South and traveled in Europe and Africa; he had talked with Coleridge, Wordsworth, Carlyle, and other great men of the age. Thoreau had little direct acquaintance with the world outside of Concord and Boston. Emerson had a more refractory temperament, more extended sympathies, and loyalties necessarily more divided. The problem life set him was more like the problem life now sets us. "I am always insincere, as always knowing there are other moods" ("Nominalist and Realist," *W*, III, 247).

Emerson's experience was more comprehensive and so was his understanding. We have repeatedly quoted him on himself, on Thoreau, on their styles, and on their friendship. Not so often Thoreau, since he seems not to have seen so far round their lives. This present paper is no more than an expansion of such exact Emersonian observations as this one concerning Thoreau and himself: " 'T is as if I went into a gymnasium, and saw youths leap, climb, and swing with a force unapproachable,—though their feats are only continuations of my initial grapplings and jumps" (*J*, IX, 522).

Thoreau is the uncompromising idealist. Only perfect friendship is worthwhile; alcohol, meat, and even a dish of tea must be eschewed since they do not accord with principle; no law is too trivial to be disobeyed if it is morally wrong. Emerson is more compromising—or temperate. He thinks it (No. 13) not worth his while to denounce "flesh-eating or wine-drinking" ("Heroism," *W*, II, 254). He sees (No. 16) that "friendship should have feet, as well as eyes and eloquence" ("Friendship," *W*, II, 205), that there is some value in "the municipal virtues of justice, punctuality, fidelity and pity" (p. 205). If we ask which man is the rarer type today, the more striking and invigorating, the answer is Thoreau. If we ask which man we would prefer to trust with power, today and over ourselves, the answer is Emerson.

NOTES

1. All references to these passages will be indicated by the number assigned to them in Table I and by the appropriate volume and page reference to the standard edition in the parentheses following the quotation. For Emerson: *The Complete Works of Ralph Waldo Emerson,* 12 vols. (Boston, 1903–4) and *The Journals of Ralph Waldo Emerson,* 10 vols. (Boston, 1909–14). For Thoreau: *The Writings of Henry David Thoreau,* 6 vols. (Boston, 1906), and *The Writings of Henry David Thoreau [Journal],* 14 vols. (Boston, 1906). A passage from Emerson or Thoreau quoted but not given a number is a passage that was not used by us in the stylistic analysis and for which Table I does not give a reference.

2. Quoted in Ralph L. Rusk, *The Life of Ralph Waldo Emerson* (New York, 1949), p. 67.

3. Quoted in Rusk, p. 104.

4. Quoted in Rusk, p. 128.

5. Quoted in Rusk, p. 289.

6. Quoted in Rusk, p. 443.

7. Quoted in Rusk, p. 235.

8. Quoted in Rusk, p. 313.

9. Quoted in Joseph Wood Krutch, *Henry David Thoreau* (New York, 1948), p. 141.

10. Quoted in Rusk, p. 75.

11. Quoted in Rusk, pp. 103–4.

12. Rusk, p. 457.

13. Pp. 144–48.

14. See, for instance, Jerome Kagan, Howard A. Moss, and Irving Sigel, "Psychological Significance of Styles of Conceptualization," *Basic Cognitive Processes in Children,*

ed. John C. Wright and Jerome Kagan (Ohio, 1963), pp. 73–112. Monographs of the Society for Research in Child Development, Vol. XXVIII, No. 2. The conceptualization of the analytic style by Kagan, Moss, and Sigel does not exactly coincide with the distinction we made between Emerson and Thoreau, but there is some similarity.

15. There is even some evidence that among mature males differences of aggressiveness are related to differences in the production of the male sex hormone. Males of many species have an organized dominance order such that the higher ranking animals have rights of precedence to space, food, and females. Several studies have shown that when a male animal who is low in dominance order is given injections of male hormone he will fight his way up to a higher position. See, for instance, John Paul Scott, *Aggression* (Chicago, 1958), pp. 68–88, and G. Clark and H. G. Birch, "Hormonal Modification of Social Behavior," *Psychosomatic Medicine,* VII (1945), 321–29 and VIII (1946), 320–31.

16. Raymond Gozzi in his doctoral dissertation, "Tropes and Figures: A Psychological Study of David Henry Thoreau [*sic*]" (New York University, 1957), has attempted a psychoanalytic study of Thoreau's personality. It seems to us that his case is not convincing because the data are too few and their relevance too remote. For a summary of the dissertation see Carl Bode, "The Half-Hidden Thoreau," *The Massachusetts Review,* IV, (1962), 68–80.

17. To facilitate location of the passages we have given the title of the work, volume and page, and the first two and last two words of the passage.

18. O. W. Firkins has shown that Emerson's tone is on occasion brusque, rough, even coarse (*Ralph Waldo Emerson* [Boston, 1915], pp. 244–52). It is our impression, nevertheless, that combativeness and vigor are more *characteristic* of Thoreau, characteristic in two senses: the qualities are frequent and also unstudied. On the infrequent occasions when Emerson is rough he seems to be so from principle rather than temperament—perhaps in a deliberate effort to "invigorate" his style. This is, of course, only an impression, but the case does not chiefly

rest on the impressions reported in this section of the paper but rather on the quantitative comparisons of the next section.

19. The comparison may seem unfair for the reason that the Thoreau quotation is from his journal whereas the Emerson quotation is from an essay. However, as J. Lyndon Shanley in *The Making of "Walden"* (Chicago, 1957) suggests, Thoreau's writing was not necessarily sharper in the journals than in the essays. Satire sometimes became more pointed and exaggeration more extreme in the passage from the journals to *Walden* (p. 37). We make a similar inference concerning Emerson's journals and essays from the fact that Firkins, in demonstrating that Emerson could be brusque, cites about as many passages from the one as from the other (loc. cit.).

20. See Sidney Siegel, *Nonparametric Statistics for the Behavioral Sciences* (New York, 1956), pp. 68–75.

21. P. 250.

22. We were here guided by a discussion of negation in the terms of transformational grammar. See Edward S. Klima, "Negation in English," *The Structure of Language: Readings in the Philosophy of Language,* ed. Jerry A. Fodor and Jerrold J. Katz (Englewood Cliffs, N.J., 1964), pp. 246–323.

23. *Shaw: The Style and the Man* (Middletown, Conn., 1962), see ch. 3 and p. 177.

24. Jonas A. Barish has made brilliant use of such connectives in his study *Ben Jonson and the Language of Prose Comedy* (Cambridge, Mass., 1960), see especially pp. 23–40.

25. See Ralph B. Long, *The Sentence and Its Parts* (Chicago, 1961), p. 227. Long's definition is more useful for our purposes than the definition of abstract nouns in terms of transformation grammar offered by Robert B. Lees, "The Grammar of English Nominalizations," *International Journal of American Linguistics,* XXVI (1960), 14.

26. For a discussion of Emerson's use of abstractions from another point of view, see Paul Lauter, "Truth and Nature: Emerson's Use of Two Complex Words," *English Literary History,* XXVII (1960), 66–85.

27. See, for instance, Firkins, pp. 239–40 and André Celières, *The Prose Style of Emerson* (Paris, 1936), p. 14.

28. In his master's thesis, "A Formal Study of H. D. Thoreau" (University of Iowa, 1948), William Drake states that such poetic archaisms as "o'er," "e'er," "yon," "methinks," "ye," "oft" make a "negligible appearance" in *Walden*. He also points out that in working over journal material for *A Week*, Thoreau "modernized" the "archaic form" "o'er" to "over." Portions of the thesis are reprinted in *Thoreau: A Collection of Critical Essays*, ed. Sherman Paul (Englewood Cliffs, N.J., 1962), pp. 63–91, see pp. 66 and 74.

29. F. Mosteller and D. L. Wallace, *Inference and Disputed Authorship: "The Federalist"* (Cambridge, Mass., 1964).

30. Reprinted in *Emerson: A Collection of Critical Essays*, ed. Milton R. Konvitz and Stephen E. Whicher (Englewood Cliffs, N.J., 1962), pp. 18–23, see p. 19.

31. Quoted in Rusk, p. 368.

Emily Dickinson and the Crisis of Self-Reliance

By Glauco Cambon

> *Nothing is at last sacred but the*
> *integrity of your own mind.*
> —R. W. EMERSON, "Self-Reliance"

ONE WAY TO APPROACH poetry might be (and traditionally was) to come to it from the outside and explore its relationship to what came before as well as to what surrounded it in the immediate cultural topography of its time. Another way (perhaps The Way, by now) is to concentrate on the poetry from the start and proceed on the assumption that it constitutes a self-sufficient world. But if we place ourselves within that world, it need not be a prison; the very act of installing ourselves in it will make it the contingent center of a cognitive horizon, and if so, we shall have to find there some references to the other worlds of language, experience, and thought with which it shares at least part of its substance and space. To do this is to postulate a third way of penetration, neither externally genetic nor atomistically formalist. Our approach, that is, would be internal, and yet cognizant that the special universe of one poetry might enclose or reflect related universes. No poem is a closed monad.

It no longer matters so terribly, then, if we start from the historical antecedents of Emily Dickinson's poetry to narrow down the focus on its individual physiognomy, or if conversely we take our place within its magic circle to inspect the enclosure inch by inch and then look out on what lies beyond, once its relationship to that "beyond" is properly understood. Between two cultural realities

[*123*]

there can be such a thing as dialectical implication. The child (to change the metaphor) is and is not its parents; its individuality contains and consumes theirs. The poetry of Emily Dickinson is and is not whatever nurtured it. Just as the child cannot be predicted from the parents, Emily Dickinson cannot be resolved into her cultural ancestors, whether Metaphysical, Puritan, or (in this case) Transcendentalist. Like any true artist, she is irreducibly herself; yet she has a recognizable ancestry, and to recognize some of the salient family traits need not mean to violate the integrity of her poems and of the inherent poetics.

With this cautionary premise to a probing of the Transcendentalist vein of Emily Dickinson, I can leave the historical task of defining American Transcendentalism to a number of available authorities, from Frothingham to Matthiessen. More specifically, however, I must refer to Ralph Waldo Emerson himself, in whose essays on "Self-Reliance," "Circles," and "Experience" it is not hard to find a cluster of Dickinsonian sources.[1] Indeed, her Transcendentalist lineage has been seen as a case of qualified Emersonianism, whether by George Whicher[2] (who hastens to add that in her poetry the Emersonian component blends with altogether different ones), by Austin Warren[3] (who emphasizes her affinity for Emerson's verse rather than for his philosophy), or by Charles Anderson[4] (who remarks that her propensity for Emerson's organic-effusive conception of Nature is sharply offset by her unromantically craftsmanlike poetics). Roy Harvey Pearce[5] should also be remembered, in this connection, as a scholar who posits a much closer link between our two writers. And more recently, Clark Griffith[6] in a brilliant monograph notes that Miss Dickinson, in her time and place, could hardly avoid absorbing the Transcendentalist ideas and the Emersonian spirit in particular—with the result that she became a "post-Emersonian, or, still more accurately perhaps, a sort of Emersonian-in-reverse."[7] For Emily Dickinson had Emerson's "knife in the brain" and she used it to dissect what the master had left intact in his sweeping buoyancy.

Emily Dickinson

Generally speaking, the self-reliance of Emerson and Thoreau is a posture of expansive certainty, and it assumes the possibility of achieving an immediate communion with society and the world at large; Miss Dickinson's mental self-reliance repeatedly involves doubt, terror, despair. If one reads Emerson's "Experience" backwards, one will be following her inner itinerary, for the opening question of his essay ("Where do we find ourselves?") is her conclusion. She confronts the final instability of experience—that prime source of knowledge and action which in the end had come to seem so reliable to him:

> I stepped from Plank to Plank
> A slow and cautious way
> The Stars about my Head I felt
> About my Feet the Sea.
>
> I knew not but the next
> Would be my final inch—
> This gave me that precarious Gait
> Some call Experience.

This autobiographical epigram (Poem No. 875 in Thomas H. Johnson's numbering[8]) defines one important bias of hers toward existence and knowledge (notice the tentativeness, the slowness, the sense of danger and the uncertainty about a final goal: she is stepping on a half-submerged pier, but to what boat, if any?). Elsewhere in the universe of her poetry, to be sure, the precariousness is counterpointed by sudden flashes from another sphere, "Experiences" perpendicular to "experience." Here, she is charging with irony the glib and smug use of the word "experience," which the poem refocuses as denoting a tentative process ("precarious Gait") in flat refutation of the popular idea that experience is an accumulated store of vested wisdom. In so doing, Miss Dickinson unwittingly revives the very origin of the word: *ex-perior,* "to go through," with the closely related *periculum,* "peril," and this determines the semantic structure of the whole poem. A significant poem by Emily Dickinson often takes shape as an act of radical inquiry. Essays of the self-critical imagination, I should like to call them, or, to stay with my chosen etymological cue, *experiments* beset by perils and sometimes rewarded by accruing experiences. That points to a structural analogy with the inner form of an essay by Emerson or Thoreau, where we witness the heuristic, not syllogistic, use of intelligence. Which is to say that Emily Dickinson shares with them both an attitude of critical openness to experience without which her whole poetical adventure, and the very shape of each poem, would be inconceivable. Unlike them, however, she lets crucial questions and denials outweigh the affirmations. They resolve everything in an exhilarating cosmic identity (since Nature is Thought precipitated, and the world therefore a metaphor of the self), while she now and then crashes into a barrier of inaccessible or chaotic otherness (since for her certain residues of Calvin's inscrutable God have proved refractory to the Transcendentalist solvent).

Frothingham remarked that "The first article in Mr. Emerson's faith is the primacy of Mind. That Mind is supreme, eternal, absolute, one, manifold, subtle, living, immanent in all things, permanent, flowing, self-manifesting; . . . the universe is the result of mind. . . ."[9] Now, in her poetry Emily Dickinson insistently probes beyond the phenomenal into a world of mind which can only be called noumenal—a sky and an abyss, a light and an engulfing darkness, where she cannot dwell in peace but only waver between visitations of bliss and the anguish of being utterly lost. Emerson's ubiquitous Over-Soul, the protean deity conceived as the safe locus of the individual searching mind, gives way with her to an inviolable "Circumference," a merely glimpsed completeness. His spiritual Everywhere becomes in her experience a menacing Nowhere. The ancestral God has not vanished; he has become unreliable. If for Emerson the Other was Self, an irresistible benevolence, for Miss Dickinson it was the self that could become a demonic Other.

As for Thoreau, he does not have to leave the world of tangible phenomena to experience the world of mind;

his ecstasy is a contemplative recognition of their inter-
penetrative unity, and thus the climactic raptures of
Walden can take place without deranging the contempla-
tor, who is merely expanding his consciousness, not dis-
placing it. And if the etherealized baroque of a Thoreauvian poem like "Haze," with its chain-reaction of
metaphors, comes very close to the gaudy style of so many
nature poems by Emily Dickinson (the Oriole poem, for
instance, numbered 1466 by Johnson, or the sunset poems,
or the ecstatically Walden-like No. 321 with its perceptive synaesthesia, or even the Hummingbird poem, No.
1463, on the verge of a sharper abstraction), there is
nothing in his quietude to compare with her poetical
ventures into "otherness." She can lose herself in the
Nowhere that impinges on the limits of her mind; he is
at home in the acclimatized self and in the spiritualized
nature his mind never lost touch with. He is never world-
less; she knows the terror of cosmic alienation. Thoreau's
nature is philosophically like Schelling's, while Dickinson's
view of reality approaches Kierkegaard's.

The threshold experience of being lost (which is
something other than physical death, for it has to do with
the crisis of identity) lurks all around the "precarious
Gait" of the poem I took for my initial text, but it takes
over, shatteringly, at the unending conclusion of the related poem, No. 280:

> And then a Plank in Reason, broke,
> And I dropped down, and down—
> And hit a World, at every plunge,
> And Finished knowing—then—

It is easy to see why the early editors lopped off this fifth
stanza from the body of the poem. It was too much for
them; they could not accept this downward transcendence,
especially since it supervenes as a sudden rupture of the
trance-like quiet on which Stanza 4 had come to rest:

> And I, and Silence, some strange Race
> Wrecked, solitary, here—

That suddenness, however, is intrinsic to the dynamics of the poem, which heightens a weird experience of inner tension to breaking point. This is what can happen when one keeps stepping "from Plank to Plank" in the course of rational experience, but without shrinking from the ultimate *periculum* of a nonrational Experience. The former procedure is imaged as gradual, tentative, and horizontal; the latter, as abrupt, peremptory, and vertical. In this crisis, the mind loses any support to plunge into the noumenal Nowhere.

Since the poem moves in the noumenal sphere, it does without any visual reference. It starts from the self-imprisoned mind ("Brain") with a Chinese-box effect (the coffin in the brain) to break through into a tolling "Space" which is both inner and outer, encompassing the self that generated it (Stanza 4). Then, paralyzed inertia reverses itself into dizzy motion, and we reach the point where the self "unselves" itself; the mind can no longer know what or where it is. Tactile, auditory, and kinetic images have embodied this process: Line 1 says "I *felt* a Funeral, in my Brain," not "I saw" or "I envisaged" (just as Line 3, Stanza 1, of the other poem speaks of *"felt"*— not "seen"—stars); then the "Mourners" *tread,* and drums are both felt and heard (like a projection of the pulse at the temples), then the boots *creak,* space *tolls,* a plank *breaks*, and she *hits* worlds in her fall. The self can no longer be a safe shelter, as it had been for Thoreau and Emerson; it hides a Pascalian abyss ("This Chasm" of Poem No. 858), a negative infinity. Otherwise, it can be a prison, as at the beginning of the poem just discussed. Having no Over-Soul to rely on, Emily feels her separateness. Her moments of communion with Being are rare and problematic.

Such is her existential predicament, but she can muster a desperate kind of self-reliance to face it:

> No Rack can torture me—
> My Soul—at Liberty—
> Behind this mortal Bone
> There knits a bolder One—

You Cannot prick with saw—
Nor pierce with Cimitar [*sic*]—

For in the last resort, freedom and captivity are functions of consciousness:

Except Thyself may be
Thine Enemy—
Captivity is Consciousness—
So's Liberty.
(Poem No. 384)

If so, there would seem to reappear an Emersonian "primacy of mind," which indeed Emily Dickinson momentarily affirms in the arrogance of a Transcendentalist poem like No. 632:

The Brain—is wider than the Sky—

.   .   .   .
The Brain is deeper than the sea—

.   .   .   .
The Brain is just the weight of God—

But the mind has no safeguards against itself. What was a solution for the self-assured Emerson is a problem for the restless experimenter of introversion, diving in the "polar privacy" of her "soul admitted to itself," the "Finite Infinity" of Poem No. 1695. Any assurance, any bliss or promise of bliss, can only be provisional; the questioning rises anew, and no certainty endures, since, as one of her last poems (No. 1770) has it,

Experiment escorts us last—
His pungent company
Will not allow an Axiom
An Opportunity

—an aphorism William James and John Dewey would have subscribed to. There had been from the very start a pragmatic temper in the Transcendentalist dreamers who managed such experiments as Brook Farm, Walden, and the Masonic Temple school of Boston, and this was part of their bequest to the solitary writer of Amherst.

For Emily Dickinson, poetry as such is experiment

and knowledge, action being out of the question for her as it had not been for a Margaret Fuller. The results are never predictable; at the limit, we can posit an equation of experiment-peril-experience:

> Experience is the Angled Road
> Preferred against the Mind
> By—Paradox—the Mind itself—
> Presuming it to lead
>
> Quite Opposite—How Complicate
> The Discipline of Man—
> Compelling Him to Choose Himself
> His Preappointed Pain—
> (Poem No. 910)

The inflexible urge to know thus brings her to question everything—life and death, God and world and self ("Scarlet Experiment! Sceptic Thomas!" No. 861)—and she can say of herself (in one version of Poem No. 561),

> I measure every Grief I meet
> With analytic eyes—

until the instruments of analytic knowledge renege, and then she knows only by "unknowing" (Poem No. 510):

> It was not Death, for I stood up,
>
> .   .   .   .
>
> It was not Night, for all the Bells
> Put out their Tongues, for Noon.
>
> It was not Frost, for on my Flesh
> I felt Siroccos—crawl—
>
> .   .   .   .
>
> But, most, like Chaos—Stopless—cool—
> Without a Chance, or Spar—

Once again, we are plunged into the noumenal, where the standard categories of knowledge no longer apply, where they are discarded for a disconcerting Experience beyond definition: the experience of naked consciousness, swaying in utter exposure between terror and ecstasy, freedom and paralysis or "Bandaged moments" and "moments of Escape" (Poem No. 512). Then language strains itself to the limits of violence:

> The soul has moments of Escape—
> When bursting all the doors—
> She dances like a Bomb, abroad,
>
> . . . .
>
> Touch Liberty—then know no more,
> But Noon, and Paradise—
>
> The Soul's retaken moments—
> When, Felon led along,
> With shackles on the plumed feet,
> And staples, in the Song,
>
> The Horror welcomes her, again. . . .

At its unique climax, the experience becomes a coincidence of opposites, a "perfect—paralyzing Bliss— / Contented as Despair" (Poem No. 756) or "so appalling—it exhilirates [*sic*]— / So over Horror, it half Captivates," and because "Terror's free" the soul "stares after it, secure" and has a "Gay, Ghastly, Holiday!" (Poem No. 281).

This really sounds like a final crisis, a last threshold. Yet she rises from the zero point of experience, again and again, with the posthumous voice of somebody who has returned from hell, known madness and chaos. Unknowing has become deeper knowledge, *docta ignorantia,* and we find the word "ignorance" in positive key, as in Poem No. 552, in Poem No. 568 (which talks of an "Ignorance . . . Diviner than the Childhood's"), and in Poem No. 477 (where "ignorance" becomes "the Angel" that guides man through the storm of despair). One cannot help remembering Kierkegaard's equation of innocence and ignorance in *The Concept of Dread.*

Emily Dickinson's very private kind of paradise regained is accessible (if intermittently) to the "Costumeless Consciousness" of Poem No. 1454, the mind that has died to itself, discarded its superstructures, and faced its naked terrors. From dark abysses wonder is reborn, reality is bracketed in a phenomenological suspension which unveils essence. Emily Dickinson can go on writing to the very last, meeting reality every time in endless availability, yet all the time posthumously. The posthumous tone was already implicit in our first text, where a great distance is implied between the crisis undergone and the present recounting of it. How convincingly this poet can say "I died"; how well the Goethean *"Stirb und Werde"* could be predicated of her resolution to confront extremes and wrest a continuity of consciousness from its very discontinuity. New England, as Perry Miller once remarked, is a state of mind, and if both Puritan rigor and Transcendentalist exuberance were its major historical phases, then Emily Dickinson's radical experiment in sharpening consciousness to the vanishing point can be broadly defined as a third phase, consummating the earlier two in a kind of critical Transcendentalism. For, like Emerson, but in her unique way, she made approaches to "the Maker" beyond "the Made"; and along with the Maker, the Making and the Unmade.

NOTES

1. "Circles" in particular must have fostered in Emily Dickinson her predilection for the germane writings of Sir Thomas Browne and her addiction to that protean key word, *Circumference*. Another emphasis of Emerson's that could hardly leave her indifferent was the conception of nature as a coded language for the poet and inspired thinker to decipher, the cosmic and literary symbolism, that is, as expounded chiefly in "Nature."

2. George Whicher, *This Was a Poet* (Ann Arbor, 1957); see also "A Centennial Appraisal," originally published in *Emily Dickinson: A Bibliography* (Amherst, Mass., 1930), now reprinted in *The Recognition of Emily Dickinson,* ed. Caesar R. Blake and Carlton F. Wells (Ann Arbor, 1964).

3. Austin Warren, "Emily Dickinson," originally published in *The Sewanee Review*, LXV (Autumn 1957), 565–86, as an essay-review of Thomas H. Johnson's critical edition of Emily Dickinson's complete poetry, and now reprinted in *The Recognition of Emily Dickinson*, pp. 268–86.

4. Charles Anderson, *Emily Dickinson's Poetry: Stairway of Surprise* (New York, 1960); see especially the chapter called "Center," now reprinted in *The Recognition of Emily Dickinson,* pp. 287–300.

5. Roy Harvey Pearce, *The Continuity of American Poetry* (Princeton, 1961).

6. Clark Griffith, *The Long Shadow: Emily Dickinson's Tragic Poetry* (Princeton, 1964).

7. *The Long Shadow,* pp. 10–11.

8. All my quotations of Emily Dickinson's poetry are from *The Poems of Emily Dickinson*, 3 vols., ed. Thomas H. Johnson (Cambridge, Mass., 1955).

9. Octavius Brooks Frothingham, *Transcendentalism in New England* (New York, 1959), p. 238.

PART TWO

The Current

The Identities of
John Jay Chapman

By Sherman Paul

I

IN 1928 JOHN JAY CHAPMAN PUBLISHED a translation of *Philoctetes*. Like his other translations from the *Iliad* and *The Divine Comedy* and of *Antigone* and *Medea,* its freshness and fidelity won the reluctant approval of scholars; for like all of his invasions into literature, whether into Plato, Shakespeare, Balzac, Goethe, or Emerson, it was issued under the banner of an "amateur" who used every occasion to assault "the camp-followers and sumpter mules of learning." He only claimed that the translation was the pastime of an elderly gentleman with time on his hands.

But Chapman had more than time on his hands. He was not simply refurbishing his Greek, not even, as one always suspects, finding another way, however polite or remote, of relieving himself in attack. Nor was his profound concern for revitalizing the humanities at the bottom of this work. He had no literary preoccupations. "Belles Lettres is the devil after all," he had once remarked of Lowell. "It spoils a man." He might reverse his political views, but not his literary ones. He was not a gentleman of letters like Lowell, a "literary fop." Everything he wrote was struck from the rock of his life. With him the essay became again what it had been for Emerson and Thoreau and would become for Randolph Bourne, the robust and challenging expression of Man Thinking. Even his lesser work, his traditional poems and plays, especially his plays for children, reveal the man for whom time had created insupportable burdens.

By 1928 the aging reformer and "agitator" had earned the right to let Philoctetes speak for him. Nearly three decades before, he had broken under the strain of unsuccessful political reform activity and the sudden death of his first wife, Minna Timmins. When he began to write again several years later, the fairy tale trappings of his plays for children disguised his self-analysis. "To tell thy guilt dissolves it," one character says; he wrote to confess and to assuage himself, to ask forgiveness. *The Hermits*, for example, reenacts the jealous rage that led to his assault on Percival Lowell and the expiatory act of self-mutilation. He now asks pardon and accepts solitude as repentance. In *King Ithuriel, Christmas in Leipsic*, and *A Maid's Forgiveness* he recalls the loss of his son who drowned in 1903, a "sacrifice" which restored the disabled father much in the same way as did the loss of another son in the war. *The Lost Prince* treats of "mother love" and the restoration of right. He is haunted by remorse for the "betrayal" of his first wife in *A Maid's Forgiveness*—its setting is the kingdom of "Minneberg." The kings in *King Ithuriel* and *A Maid's Forgiveness* are old, brainsick, put upon, unkinged; one is willing to renounce a crown that isn't rightly his, the other to be delivered from the need to be a king. Old age, ebb of life, loss, solitude are the themes of *Christmas in Leipsic;* here the aging husband will be a child to his wife, as the invalid Chapman undoubtedly was to Elizabeth Chanler, his second wife.

Obviously, these plays were not meant for children. But the children's play was congenial to Chapman's imagination. Pitting good against evil, it permitted him to express his sense of evil and his conspiratorial mentality. His evil characters work by means of *Realpolitik*, his good characters by means of love. His moralism is strong because his view of morality is weak. His world is composed of simples, of "two hierarchies of power." He sees it as a child sees it.

The sense of conspiracy still oppresses Chapman in *Philoctetes*. He identifies himself with Philoctetes because he, too, believed that he had been abandoned by others because of his illness; he, too, had a "nameless, blasting wound" and had become (especially in the 1920's) "a maniac in hate." He can understand the pain that makes Philoctetes desire to cut off his foot, for in his youth he had himself been driven to destroy an offending hand. But he feels his kinship most when Philoctetes tells Neoptolemus, who in Chapman's case might represent the younger generation,

> O infamy of outrage! Not content
> With casting me out, they kill my fame
> By keeping silence: not a word of me
> Lives in the land of Hellas! O my son,
> Hast thou perchance heard tell of Philoctetes. . . .

Fortunately, recognition came. In 1929 Edmund Wilson broke the silence with a long review in the literary supplement of *The New Republic*. He assessed Chapman's career in order to show that he had "much to say to the younger generation," that here was a genuine humanist who loved literature and wrote poetry, not a schoolmaster like Babbitt or More. He praised Chapman's early companion volumes, *Causes and Consequences* and *Practical Agitation,* connecting them to his generation by noting their influence on Croly's *The Promise of American Life*. Acknowledging Chapman's crankiness, he emphasized the sage and prophet rather than the agitator, and placed him in the intellectual tradition of Emerson. The intensity of his spirit, the brilliance of his literary gift, the continuity of thought embodied in Chapman's work—these, he concluded, made him "an American Classic."

When *The Times Literary Supplement* devoted its lead article to the "American Moralist" in 1930, Chapman felt that at last he was "afloat." More than this, however, was needed to keep alive a reputation that had never been secure. Thirty years earlier he had won the praise of Henry James, had been acclaimed as *the* American critic, and he knew that people now had the right to ask, "But where are the works of this man?" His answer—"The works of this man perished in the Eruption of Vesuvius" —was true enough. The fires that kindled him had also destroyed him. He had created in his fiery engagement with his times the lava of his own oblivion. His most substantial claim to fame was in his letters, published posthumously in 1937. They showed how brilliant and destructive the fires had been, and how much his reputation, in his time and ours, depended on sympathy for and fascination with his temperament and predicament.

Based on Chapman's letters, Edmund Wilson's later essay in *The Triple Thinkers* was the most important critical study of Chapman and is probably the source of whatever general enthusiasm for him there has been ever since. Now his reputation rests with the graduate students, whose scholarship Chapman would have deplored ("the earthworms of scholarship are destined to go on forever fertilizing the soil by going up and down in it"), but who nonetheless have treated him carefully and well. They have uncovered almost all that can be found in the ruins of his Pompeii. His thought has been explored and systematized in the theses of David M. Stocking and Melvin H. Bernstein. The study of his life, which his friend M. A. DeWolfe Howe did not sufficiently make in *John Jay Chapman and His Letters,* Richard B. Hovey undertook in a thesis covering the early years. Mr. Hovey published the first book on Chapman, *John J. Chapman: An American Mind,* in 1959; Mr. Bernstein's *John Jay Chapman* appeared in 1964.

One soon learns in reading about Chapman that nothing tells as much as his own words. Chapman's words are bolts of character. What he said of Emerson can be said of him: "Open his works at hazard. You hear a man talking." His voice is still one of the most engaging in American letters. Essayists are out of fashion and memorialists are rare; Chapman's literary achievement is in the essay and memoir. This must be acknowledged. But this is not so much in question as his stature.

John Jay Chapman

Ferris Greenslet once told Chapman that the history of his "education (*à la* Henry Adams) would be a record of the American people during the epoch and one of the greatest books ever written." Whether Chapman refused to make good this suggestion because, as he claimed, the past bored him, or because he had mixed feelings about Adams' *Education,* or because to rethink the past and explicitly note where he had failed would have unsettled his precarious serenity, one will never know. The book was never written, only the briefest of "recollections." But critics who glean the passing references, such as F. O. Matthiessen's coupling of Adams and Chapman as "two of our most symptomatic minds," are often led to make untenable claims. For the fame Chapman gains by association, he loses by comparison; and none of Chapman's critics has taken the risk of comparing him. Is he, as one gathers from the testimony of Jacques Barzun and from Mr. Hovey's subtitle, an American mind, a critic whose reputation can no longer be deferred because we stand in need of his qualities? Does he belong in another order, that suggested by Austin Warren when he said that Chapman was "a saint writing about saints, himself not the least of them"? Or is he after all, as Mr. Bernstein believes, only a minor representative figure? And one wonders most just what it is (since it is not his skill as an essayist) that we have overlooked, and what arouses the sympathy of his recent champions.

II

Whenever one attempts to measure Chapman's achievement he should remember that his contemporaries included such notables as Thorstein Veblen, Louis Sullivan, Paul Elmer More, Irving Babbitt, George Santayana, Owen Wister, Theodore Roosevelt, and Alfred Stieglitz. He belonged to the generation that was born about the time of the Civil War, whose entry into manhood might be marked by the enactment of the Sherman Anti-Trust Act in 1890, and whose energies and intellects were absorbed by a revolution in economic, political, and social life. For Chapman, molded by the legacies of Jay steward-ship and Chapman abolitionism and trained at St. Paul's, Harvard College, and Harvard Law School to carry on the traditions of his class, most disturbing was the fact that the changes he witnessed constituted a "status-revolution." Edmund Wilson speaks of that "difficult" time in a mem-oir of his father, who belonged to Chapman's generation. The young men, he explains, had been educated to serve as their fathers had, and they had become casualties because of their "fundamental lack of adjustment to the American life of the period." Wilson tells us that "of his father's close friends at college, but a single one was left by the time he was in his thirties: all the rest were dead—some had committed suicide." And Chapman, explaining his brother Henry's death in 1913, attributes it to the fact that "it's a pretty killing age . . . the society of it was at its worst just in our time." Other casualties, like those of Chapman and Wilson's father, were of a subtler neurotic sort, so that just "to have got through with honor that period from 1880 to 1920!" was, Wilson feels, a kind of victory.

By birthright and nurture Chapman had a special burden to carry into the new America—an urgent con-science. In everything else a cosmopolitan New Yorker, in his conscience he was a New Englander. He had the "excess of the individual spirit manifested in the exalta-tion of conscience" that William C. Brownell ascribed to Puritanism. Religious training at St. Paul's School had only exacerbated it, and the boy was shattered. "Early holiness in boys," he later remarked, "goes with pneu-monia." Nevertheless, this training fixed the religious dis-position that provided the hidden link of a life broken over the problem of how to make conscience a direct agent in human affairs. It strengthened the Hebraic, the ethical passion with which Chapman struck in word and deed. At the end of his life he could identify himself with Lucian because he had "a non-Hellenic, ethical passion, which has the heat of religion, yet does not appeal to authority or use the symbols of religion." Like Lucian's, his theme was conduct, his appeal to courage; he employed his talent to a similar end, "to break down every screen of theory that lies between the private mind and practical life." It was easy for Chapman to welcome Lucian in his attack on the "disease" of the Greek mind because earlier he had embraced Emerson and Garrison, the "purgers" of what Chapman believed to be the chronic American disease of moral cowardice, a disease bred alike in the slavery of Emerson's time and the "commercialism" of his own.

Emerson and Garrison were Chapman's heroes of conscience. During much of his life he pitted them against each other as he wavered between the efficacy of saying and the efficacy of doing. Courageous men both, they needed each other; they were the "head" and the "heart" Chapman hoped but failed to unite in himself. Emerson was the seer, an artist of ideas, for whom utterance was enough; he wanted to reform society without visible means. Garrison, however, knew what Chapman had learned as an agitator, that "reform consists in taking a bone from a dog. Philosophy will not do it." Where Emerson, with the "better element" in New England, responded to slavery only when Webster defected, Garrison, twenty-five years before, had made the "agonized protest" and had brought the heat and passion and action needed to stir a cold and conciliatory age. He was not a moralist who read lectures; he enacted lessons; and he broke the conspiracy of silence that followed the Missouri Compromise. Garrison had the prophet's emotion in the face of innocent suffering; he laid hands on visible, particular evil. Had he been a "no-organization" man capable of standing alone, the Chapman who wrote his own farewell to reform movements in *William Lloyd Garrison* would have found him the perfect practical agitator.

Chapman's criticism of Emerson was severe not simply because the seer lost power by not acting, but because Emerson had become profoundly a part of himself. No one ever gave himself over so entirely to Emerson as

Chapman did. Speaking of his "rag-dolls" (Emerson and Goethe), Chapman recalls that he found his Emerson "in an old family trunk" and that long ago he began "to show signs of wear and tear." He was always grateful to Emerson for standing him on his feet; the college boy had been "intoxicated with Emerson." "He let loose something within me which made me in my own eyes as good as anyone else. . . ." On completing "Social Results of Commercialism" he told Elizabeth Chanler: "It's all Emerson. I should have had neither the ideas reduced so clearly nor the public to understand them if it hadn't been for Emerson. I can't imagine what I should have been if it hadn't been for Emerson." Though he later repudiated the "Emerson madness"—the fanaticism and self-will Emerson had released—he never repudiated the individual moral heroism that had made it acceptable.

No, Emerson failed Chapman where he was most vulnerable—in the heart. When he wrote his brilliant essay on Emerson in 1897, Chapman qualified the praise with reservations he had earned: "Regarded as a sole guide to life for a young person of strong conscience and undeveloped affections, his works might conceivably be even harmful because of their unexampled power of purely intellectual stimulation." Not only had Emerson made a dogma of the moral law, but he had "lied" about human nature when he preached the self-sufficiency and invincibility of individual spiritual power. He had the "anaemic incompleteness" of the Puritan; he needed "incaloration." He never understood life "in its throb and passion," and his asceticism was simply the old cross on which New England had always crucified the natural instincts. After his own devastating experience of conscience inflamed by love and hate, Chapman was ready to learn from Browning that "it was right to love, hate, and be angry" and that "we had some inheritance in the joys and passions of mankind."

But Chapman personally tested Emerson in another way: he animated him with the Garrisonian passion. He became a full-blooded "American Scholar." Garrison, he felt, best fulfilled "Emerson's ideal picture of the influential individual"; he was "self-reliant, self-assertive, self-sufficient." And Chapman began his career as a Garrisonian. When he entered the political reform movement in New York City in 1888, he believed that he was making good just where Emerson had failed. Chapman's activity—cart-tailing, organizing the Goo-Goos, writing the *Political Nursery*—turned out to be the "excursions into pragmatic romance" that Veblen said typified "the contingent of well-to-do irregulars." He had achieved nothing; the bosses remained. But Chapman learned the lesson of compromise, though he put his own interpretation on it: "In all the politics I have ever known compromise means change of faith. . . ." He was unwilling to sacrifice conscience to the pragmatism of politics, as he believed that Theodore Roosevelt had—and for which Roosevelt had called him a traitor. He preferred to work alone and to limit the reformer's activity to the educative function of raising moral issues. By this time, the action he had undertaken to restore his psychic health had partly broken his spirit; "I feel like Atlas, lifting the entire universe." Family disaster completed the breakdown in 1901. And by the time he wrote the *Garrison,* it was too late to apply the lesson his life had taught him, that if the end of agitation is education, then by writing he might have truly influenced his generation—might have provided, as William James said, "a gospel for our rising generation."

Now Chapman could turn again to Emerson and accord him the lasting victory. Acts, Chapman believed, are more expressive than words, but the "great artist is the most educative influence upon the globe." Garrison had been luckier than Chapman: when he blew the "brazen trumpet" the walls of Jericho fell. But Garrison's power died with him. "The small, inner, silver trumpet of Emerson," Chapman now realized, "caught and sounded the same note, and it continues to sound the note, shaking down the walls of inner Jerichoes of men of later and even later generations." The victory of the artist had been one of passivity; he had dissolved his will in God and had become a channel for the spirit, the ultimate "influence." Thus, having abdicated the self-will of his early Emerson, Chapman accepted the mysticism of the Emerson who had always drawn his power and solace from the Over-Soul. Outbursts, such as those occasioned by his fears of Germany, of the Jew, and of the Catholic, marred Chapman's later life. But whatever serenity he had was the result of a lifetime's struggle with the will. "At first we desire to help vigorously," he explained, "and we do all in our power to assist mankind. As time goes on, we perceive more and more clearly that the advancement of the world does not depend on us, but that we, rather, are bound up in it, and can command no foothold of our own. At last we see that our very ambitions, desires and hopes in the matter are a part of the Supernal Machinery moving through all things, and that our souls can be satisfied and our power exerted only in so far as we are taken up into that original motion, and merged in that primal power." Chapman not only wished to return to the "Mansion of Religion" which enclosed the "Houses" of philanthropy, art, social caste, and grief in which he had lived, he wished to yield up to God that American conscience which no one had been strong enough to bear.

III

None of Chapman's critics sympathizes with his escape into a personal transcendental religion. They prefer the early Chapman of the Emersonian will. One gathers from the moral touchstones they cite that they are attracted to the Chapman who went alone to Coatesville to do penance for a lynching that had occurred there. His strenuousness, his courage and nonconformity, his willingness to be the conscience of his age and to serve only the authority of the moral sense, attract them. His individualism and moral intransigence make him a type we do not like to see become obsolescent; we would like to believe that a man of his qualities could still be a power in American life. From Emerson's day to ours, the intellectual has hungered for individual influence and has felt guilty because of his ineffectualness in liberating the "beneficent energy" and making the "good" turn the wheels of society. Nostalgia for the time when the individual could earnestly accept the calling of the American Scholar with the duty to bring about "the conversion of the world," perhaps self-pity because of the difficulty of becoming an intellectual force in our time—these may account for the respectful attention Chapman has received. What the cowboy is to the lowbrow, the hero of conscience emboldened by the "nerve of failure" may be to the highbrow.

Chapman's attractiveness, as Edmund Wilson's special relationship to him makes it easier to see, is due not only to the fact that Chapman is a fascinating case of what he called "the nemesis of temperament," but to the fact that he was patrician. He is an example of the democrat with an aristocratic sensibility. A cultivated amateur, a critic in the world of affairs rather than in the academy, he was more genuinely humane in his concern for the classics and the humanities than were the scholars themselves, and he reproved them for opening the universities to the commercial interests of the time. His humanism was acceptable because it united an awareness of the social values of continuity, standards, and tradition with the need for romantic impulse. Unlike Babbitt, he knew that art was the language of the emotions, that it ministered to emotional health, and that America needed not so much the will to refrain as nourishment at its emotional roots. In his youth he had discovered that Europe was his "natural habitat" and that America was a "desert," and yet this man of culture wrote one of the first and best indictments of expatriation. Though he enjoyed the social arts and was at home in club and country house, he was seriously interested in the problem of art and society. The study of how commercialism corrupts society and frustrates art in *Causes and Consequences* and *Practical Agitation* is still worth reading and places Chapman in the line of critics who, like Wilson and Trilling, devote themselves primarily to matters of cultural health.

In these books, in *Emerson and Other Essays,* and the *Political Nursery,* Chapman had much to say to a younger generation as deeply concerned with the politics of culture as he was. His attacks on the genteel tradition, on the reputations of Stevenson and Kipling, and on the "iron grey commercial civilization" which fostered in "half-educated people" a taste for "second-rate things," should have become their starting point. His views on art were romantic; he stressed its unconscious sources and expressive ends. And the polar terms of his cultural analysis —"selfishness" and "unselfishness"—were simply the moral equivalents of "acquisitiveness" and "creativity" which were later used by Van Wyck Brooks. If only Brooks had found the Emerson of his *America's Coming-of-Age* in Chapman instead of in Vernon Lee! If only the few years between the generations had not opened such an unbridgeable gap!

But Chapman was already out of things when the younger generation came of age. In 1910, in *The Treason and Death of Benedict Arnold,* a play which was Chapman's most poignant statement of his position in American life, Arnold puts on his old American uniform, exhibits the sword-knots Washington had given him, and says, "I must go back / To where I lost the way." In 1915, Chapman wrote that "we are becoming the oldest generation." By 1918, he confessed that the new age presented "strange symbols that I could not understand." *Memories and Milestones,* published in 1915, seemed to be a valedictory volume; and the critic who never got beyond Shaw and Ibsen, and who had said of Whitman, the saint of the younger generation, that he had the "soul of the tramp," was easily put aside with the Babbitts and Mores. Followers of John Dewey, the younger generation disliked the moral rhetoric of the elders; they were suspicious of a "belated abolitionist" who, as Wister said of Chapman, was a "soldier of God against Mammon." They did not see the World War religiously, as an occasion for self-sacrifice. Believers in a "trans-national America," they resented the hysteria of an Anglo-Saxon crusader, hardened in caste, who occupied himself with the affairs of private schools and Harvard College and who fulminated against immigration and found support for his prejudices in an alliance with the Ku Klux Klan.

An abolitionist who writes poetry for the Klan! This is but one paradox in Chapman's career. But this and the other paradoxes that one finds in Chapman are the detritus of social change. They are common enough in "stranded" intellectuals who after a lifetime's devotion to American culture may feel, as Edmund Wilson does now, that "I don't want any more to be bothered with the kind of contemporary conflicts that I used to go out to explore.... When, for example, I look through *Life* magazine, I feel that I do not belong to the country depicted there, that I do not even live in that country." The choruses in *Benedict Arnold* chant: "For an old [man], only death remains. He hath no strength for new things." And when Arnold dies, they chant Chapman's epitaph: "Surely the past must be allowed to all men.... What good there was in us cannot be lost. God forgets not the virtue of those who have failed; and why should men seek to judge them? Verily all courage is immortal...."

Santayana as a Critic of Transcendentalism

By Joe Lee Davis

(The lengthened shadow of a man
　Is history, said Emerson
Who had not seen the silhouette
　Of Sweeney straddled in the sun.)
　　　　T. S. ELIOT, "Sweeney Erect"

Drink up, drink up, until we meet in Hell
With Cabell, Santayana, and Marcel!
　　　　—MLA toast, 1963

I

ALL THE TERMS OF MY TITLE should be understood broadly.
The Santayana of my concern is neither the earlier nor
the later thinker exclusively, but *both*, conceived as a
spirit steadily harmonizing its many-sidedness. The critic
I am seeking to define is not the literary critic only or
primarily, but the critic of philosophy and culture as
well. Transcendentalism includes the European and the
American varieties and refers to a persistent subjectivist
tendency in Western thought and literature, especially
since the Reformation.

　Before describing—certainly before assessing—a critic's
criticism of anything, it is only fair to make allowances
for his presuppositions about the nature of criticism itself.
In Santayana's case these presuppositions can be derived
from a thorough study of his aesthetics, ethics, ontology,
and impressive array of essays in literary criticism and
theory, but in this paper I shall have to content myself

with the shortcut of relying on a few brief but explicit statements in more personal sources—his letters, his "Apologia Pro Mente Sua" or reply to his own critics in *The Philosophy of George Santayana,* edited by Paul Arthur Schilpp, and *The Last Puritan.*[1]

In a letter from Rome December 13, 1928, thanking Thomas Munro for a presentation copy of his *Scientific Method in Aesthetics,* Santayana contrasts the looser, freer, more humane temper of art criticism in the 1890's with its more rigorous, less humane orientation in the dying 1920's:

> You must remember that we were not very much later than Ruskin, Pater, Swinburne, and Matthew Arnold: our atmosphere was that of poets and persons touched with religious enthusiasm or religious sadness. Beauty (which mustn't be mentioned now) was then a living presence, or an aching absence, day and night: history was always singing in our ears: and not even psychology or the analysis of works of art could take away from art its human implications. It was the great memorial to us, the great revelation, of what the soul had lived on, and had lived with, in her better days. But now analysis and psychology seem to stand alone: there is no spiritual interest, no spiritual need. The mind, in this direction, has been *desiccated:* art has become an abstract object in itself, to be studied scientifically as a *caput mortuum:* and the living side of the subject—the tabulation of people's feelings and comments—is no less dead.[2]

In a letter from Rome March 29, 1922, to George Lawton, a doctoral candidate in philosophy at Columbia, Santayana assigns criticism—especially of literature—a role in culture considerably less central than some literary theorists, both of the nineteenth century and of our own time, have claimed for it. Young Lawton, more impressed by Santayana's essays in literary criticism than in metaphysics, had written to advise him that he should devote all his energies to the former. Since Santayana at that time was composing *Scepticism and Animal Faith,* the prolegomenon to the ontology of *Realms of Being,* it is understandable that he should have courteously but perhaps overemphatically rejected Lawton's well-meant but ill-timed advice and graded criticism gratuitously down in order to grade philosophy unnecessarily up. But even though we suspect the exaggeration of pique in his response, we must take his reasons seriously, for they arise out of his distinction between essence and existence and reflect his skeptical strategy of bracketing existence while refusing to hypostasize essence or universalize spirit:

> Criticism is something purely incidental—talk about talk—and to my mind has no serious value except perhaps as an expression of *philosophy* in the critic. When I have been led to write criticism it has never been for any other reason; and you don't know me at all if you suppose me capable of *reading up* Meredith or Thomas Hardy or any one else who hasn't come in my way, in order to describe them to other people. If you like that sort of vicarious literary nourishment, read Croce, or any other competent person who sets out to express the impression which literature has made upon him. But I should advise you to read the originals instead, and be satisfied with the impression they make upon you. You know Plato's contempt for the image of an image; but as a man's view of things is an image in the first place, and his work is an image of that, and the critic's feelings are an image of that work, and his writings an image of his feelings, and your idea of what the critic means only an image of his writings,—please know that you are steeping your poor original tea-leaves in their fifth wash of hot water, and are drinking slops. May not the remarkable sloppiness and feebleness of the cultivated American mind be due to this habit of drinking life in its fifth dilution only? What you need is not more criticism of current

authors, but more *philosophy:* more courage and sincerity in facing nature directly, and in criticising books or institutions only with a view to choosing among them whatever is most harmonious with the life you want to lead.[3]

In "Apologia Pro Mente Sua" Santayana defends *Egotism in German Philosophy*—his World War I monographic venture into criticism of philosophy and culture—against the aspersions of Professor Edward L. Schaub, among which was the charge of irresponsibility. The defense distinguishes between criticism and exposition. Schaub, he remarks, "seems not to regard my sketch as criticism at all, but thinks it was meant to be, or ought to have been, exposition." Exposition, in Santayana's view, operates within a framework of terms, dogmas, and criteria derived from the thing exposited. Criticism transports the thing criticized out of such an expository framework into a framework of discovery whose terms, dogmas, and criteria are derived from two sources: (1) knowledge of that common ground of life and the world, that existential backdrop, so to speak, to which both the critic and the thing criticized owe what they are; (2) the critic's own total philosophy or world-view: "Knowledge of this common world, and of the human passions that govern it, is presupposed in all criticism. . . . When I said that I endeavoured to understand German philosophy, I by no means intended to lay aside, even for a moment, my own dogmas, which I had already examined and reduced to the minimum compatible with honest living, that is, to materialism."[4] Criticism, as thus conceived, is responsible, but its responsibility is different from that of exposition. Its ultimate obligation is not to texts or monuments or history but to the free spirit's pursuit of what it takes to be happiness and truth.

In *The Last Puritan,* when Oliver Alden and Mario Van de Weyer are discussing Harvard professors, Oliver mentions Santayana by name, and Mario attributes to Santayana the view that "in any system of philosophy you can find something important—to avoid."[5]

From these bits of evidence it becomes clear that Santayana's presuppositions about criticism took shape in the late nineteenth-century climate of opinion, in which transcendentalism was still an important factor, and represent an eclectic combination of generalist, relativistic, dogmatic, and iconoclastic attitudes.

I hasten to add that I am using none of these adjectives with such overtones of derogation as are unmistakably intended in certain of the epithets that Santayana devises to enliven his critical characterizations but that sometimes succeed in irritating rather than persuading his readers, as, for example, when he dubs the American transcendental tradition "genteel" and the German "egotistic" or discusses Browning and Whitman as practitioners of "the poetry of barbarism."[6] He himself identified the temper of his own criticism as eclectic when he chose the *nom de plume* "Victor Cousin" for his first piece on transcendentalism—his unsuccessful Bowdoin Prize essay of 1886 on "The Optimism of Ralph Waldo Emerson."[7] To be eclectic is not necessarily to lack originality or a center, but to rove heedfully the past in seeking to arrive at a synthesis distinctively personal. To be a generalist rather than a specialist need not involve superficiality: it may lead to the kind of breadth that plumbs the depths of more than a single discipline. The generalist at his best is an eclectic who has extra lasting power because he has not stuck to his last. Relativism, rather than being the avoidance of convictions or the inability to achieve them, may be defined as a form of openness that is essential to insure the autonomy and integrity of the generalist-eclectic by guarding him against the absolutisms lurking in tradition-direction and other-direction. To be dogmatic may mean to insist on a doctrine, or be unyielding about a criterion, after having established them by all the positive means that eclecticism and generalism have made available and by all the precautionary postures and measures that relativism represents. Inevitably, as the critic employs such a doctrine or criterion in the examination of perspectives alien to his own, or those kindred to his but by no means identical with it, he becomes more or less iconoclastic; and this iconoclasm may without inconsistency boomerang or ricochet upon occasion to do its reductive or destructive work against aspects even of his own professed allegiances. But we do not have to think of such iconoclasm as either negativistic or nihilistic.

These semantic preliminaries will not be complete unless I raise the question whether the adjective "phenomenological" is also applicable to Santayana's critical approach as I have so far described it. The term has become so faddish that Norman Mailer, in the third paragraph of his *An American Dream*, has his narrator-protagonist of the Absurd—"Raw-Jock" Rojack—talking about being "phenomenologically precise."[8] The fact remains, however, that Santayana in the role of critic is like a Castilian chef serving up a *tour de force* of an *olla podrida*. He has put almost everything into it, including highly seasoned dicings of subject-object relationships. We must also remember that in *Realms of Being* he places Husserl on the witness stand as one of the corroborators of his own doctrine of essences.[9] H. B. Van Wesep, in his *Seven Sages: The Story of American Philosophy* (1960), has no doubt that the ontology of *Realms of Being* is the product of the phenomenological method:

> This new method of approaching philosophy is not exactly skepticism, nor is it common sense, nor is it deduction or induction; it is a special artifice by which everything is put afresh into a single hopper, and out of this at the end will come some new classifications. In Santayana we get the American version of this special technique, and we get it couched in books that are infinitely more readable than the German volumes (even in translation) of Husserl. Whether Santayana owes anything to Husserl is doubtful. The two methods have some striking similarities, but Santayana's way of tackling the question of Being was in all likelihood an independent in-

vention. The times called for a new approach, and Santayana himself calls his own phenomenology a species of skepticism.[10]

Thomas N. Munson, S.J., in his *The Essential Wisdom of George Santayana* (1962), is more cautious:

> The reader who is abreast of current developments in Europe will be led to compare and to contrast Santayana's animal faith and Husserl's idea of intentionality, or Husserl's *Abschattung* and Santayana's essence. . . . Santayana may even appear at times to try to shake off the traditional subject-object dualism when, for example, he elaborates his concept of the psyche and of substance. But he was too deeply immersed in traditional thought-patterns to make the break, and one runs the risk of distorting him by trying to make him into a contemporary.[11]

Herbert W. Schneider in the present volume suggests that Santayana's "intellectual escape to phenomenology" helped prepare the way for, and progressively accompanied, his "physical escape to Europe." At this point I shall simply adopt a good Husserlian or phenomenological tactic, suspend judgment on these divergent views, and bracket my questions until I have dealt further with Santayana as a critic of transcendentalism.

II

Gabriel Marcel—whose thought, it has been aptly said,[12] "defies classification" by "presenting elements of phenomenology, existentialism, idealism, and empiricism all consorting together in symbiotic bliss"—has stressed how important for his Coleridgean-Kierkegaardian "secondary reflection" or "spiritual research" are expressions like *"being at home"* or *"being at another's home"* and feelings like "the distress felt by a child during a trip or change of residence."[13] He has also helped give currency to one of the key-phrases of modern speculation by remarking: "I believe that a contemporary philosopher who wanted to rewrite Hume's *Treatise* would have to entitle it *A Treatise of Man's Condition* rather than a *Treatise of Human Nature*."[14] Readers of Santayana's autobiography, *Persons and Places*—wherein by a Proustianly cavalier handling of chronology he manages to be "phenomenologically precise" if not always factually accurate about the *Mitwelt* and *Umwelt* of his recaptured past's *Dasein,* to borrow Heidegger's terms—will note that his sense of the human condition was shaped by his "being at home" in Castilian Ávila, and then having—some months before his ninth birthday—to cross the Atlantic via Liverpool and find a new home in the Boston-Cambridge world of the 1870's, where Emerson (whom he never saw) and Longfellow (with whom the young man shook hands at a garden party) lived on until the spring of 1882 as secular deities revered almost like Ávila's Saint Teresa.[15]

Ávila prefigured for Santayana's awakening sensibility and nostalgic memory humanity's age-old relation to the natural and the supernatural. The little walled city of the foothills owed its survival to the agriculture of its environing valleys, and yet in its numerous Gothic religious structures—dominated by the Cathedral—it aspired to heaven. The market day and the sacred rite or festival provided weekly spectacles, equally colorful. Materialism and piety blandly coexisted in the folk's inner lives, each credo tempering the other and both disciplining the self to accept its animal place and spiritual destiny in the economy and order of the universe.

The Atlantic crossing, although made miserable by bouts of seasickness and by inability to talk English or to follow it when spoken, was not an entirely distressful experience, since there was some novelty in sights and ship's acquaintance, no untoward accidents occurred, the boy's father—even if afflicted with deafness and indigestion—was on hand, and the boy could look forward to reunion with his mother, his half-sisters, and half-brother after more than three years' separation. But the tug to Britain and the Cunard steamer out from Liverpool—"an old tub" appearing "rusty and almost derelict"[16]—were precarious modern substitutes for the ancient city, as must have been likewise the restive, leveling democratic sea-scapes for the stable, coigned, aristocratic Castilian land-scape. Even the eternal heavens were probably somehow different—the too-big sky of the long way west. I think of another poet-to-be, Edward Taylor in his middle twenties, making that same crossing two centuries before and noting in his diary such potentially symbolic details as the "rough, hoarse noise" of a whale "blothering in the water" and the "blue pigeon" shot down by the boatswain from its perch on "the main-topsail yard" and falling in such a way that it "was struck overboard" and forever lost, un-less, as God's messenger, it came later in the form of the "white peckled dove pigeon" that flew out of the stormy Cambridge night against the window casement "and there sat," he and his companion letting it into their chamber, trying fruitlessly to catch it as it "cooed and bristled at us," and letting it out unhurt in the morning.[17] For the much younger and perhaps less sober-spirited Santayana, it was also a crossing not without some impressions that were at the same time insights into the mysterious dichot-omies of existence. The dualism of the natural and the supernatural was taken for granted, but the dualism of the self and the world now assumed a new and poignant import. Santayana was to be haunted all his life by the image of a cockleshell tossed on its course "in the midst of overwhelming forces and everlasting realities." The sanity of Ávila, however, persisted as a cardinal tenet of his thinking: ". . . but those forces are calculable and those realities helpful, if we can manage to understand and obey them."[18]

Santayana's superb American and European education —as student, as teacher, as incredibly productive "senior citizen" of the world—was to enrich and subtilize immeas-urably, but never to change fundamentally, his early sense of this pair of basic dualisms and of the equally dualistic prescription for facing up to them implicit in the folk-ways of Ávila. A good statement of his mature disinclina-tion to resolve the dualistic habits of his earliest thought and feeling occurs in his sympathetic discussion of Freud in "A Long Way Round to Nirvana":

> I am glad that Freud has resisted the tendency to represent this principle of Love as the only principle in nature. Unity somehow exercises an evil spell over metaphysicians. It is admitted that in real life it is not well for One to be alone, and I think pure unity is no less barren and graceless in metaphysics. You must have plurality to start with, or trinity, or at least duality, if you wish to get anywhere, even if you wish to get effectively into the bosom of the One, abandoning your separate existence.[19]

On skeptical grounds he sets limits to human knowledge of nature, since this knowledge is of essences—the images and ideas funded by the senses and the faculties, some admissible to the realm of truth, some not; but on the basis of animal faith, as opposed to skepticism, he asserts nature's very real existence as the realm of matter out of which all arises that becomes knowable by assuming essence and in which a great deal still unknown must exist, including possibly something resembling the traditional supernatural. The self exists in this realm of matter as the animal psyche, but this psyche develops a dimension of awareness that is spirit and that is capable of infinitely refined intuitions of essences, both simple and complex. The self as psyche is subject to matter's dominations, but can—as both psyche and spirit—turn these dominations into powers for the enlargement of its own freedom and the achievement of that combined internal and external harmony that constitutes the life of reason and must be the ground of all genuine enhancement of the spiritual life. In short, as we go through *Scepticism and Animal Faith, Realms of Being, Dominations and Powers,* and the late revised version of *The Life of Reason,* the original dualisms are all there, no matter how treacherous the terminology and even though the celestial "presences" of Ávila's Roman Catholic faith are scarcely the same after a categorical shuffling that has changed them into essences not yet true and into powers no longer able to function as dominations.

Once we have recovered the profoundly personal origins of Santayana's dualistic thinking and are aware that its primal scenes involve somewhat different versions of the self's predicament and yet point toward the self's coming to terms with the human condition rather than wilfully or overrighteously rejecting any such compromise or mediation, we are better prepared to understand the peculiar ambivalence that runs through most of what he has to tell us about transcendentalism. We are even justified in being a bit ambivalent ourselves and in speaking of him as a semitranscendental critic of transcendentalism before we consider any other label.

Highly conscious of his debt to transcendentalism and at the same time of his mixed reactions to specific transcendentalists, Santayana rationalized this ambivalence in his famous address on "The Genteel Tradition in American Philosophy," which was delivered at the University of California on August 25, 1911, and which is fully as important a document in the study of American culture as Emerson's "The American Scholar" or Frederick Jackson Turner's "The Significance of the Frontier in American History":

> Transcendentalism is systematic subjectivism. It studies the perspectives of knowledge as they radiate from the self; it is a plan of those avenues of inference by which our ideas of things must be reached, if they are to afford any systematic or distant vistas. In other words, transcendentalism is the critical logic of science. . . . Transcendental logic, the method of discovery for the mind, was to become also the method of evolution in nature and history. Transcendental method, so abused, produced transcendental myth. A conscientious critique of knowledge was turned into a sham system of nature. We must therefore distinguish sharply the transcendental grammar of the intellect, which is significant and potentially cor-

rect, from the various transcendental systems of the universe, which are chimeras.[20]

When we relate this address to some of Santayana's other writings, notably *Egotism in German Philosophy, Character and Opinion in the United States,* and *The Genteel Tradition at Bay,* what made these systems chimeras, at least from his dualistic perspective, becomes clearer. They tended to conceive the human will in such absolute terms that, on the one hand, as will-to-duty, it served as a basis for denying or ignoring the animal in man, and, on the other hand, as will-to-power, it provided a warrant for man to play God. These systems misappropriated the great tradition of idealism—the tradition of Plato and Berkeley—for the ultimately maleficent purposes of interiorizing external nature and thus, so to speak, denaturing its check on the human will or of projecting into external nature a God congenial to this will's determinations.

To convey his distaste for these developments, Santayana perhaps relies too much on the pair of derogatory epithets previously mentioned—"genteel" and "egotistic." The justification for them is that each performs the double function of conveying an essential aspect of the type of transcendentalism to which he applies it and of suggesting Santayana's criterion of interpretation and judgment. Subjected to the criterion of his naturalism or materialism, with its realm of matter—a criterion most interestingly set forth in the essay on Lucretius in *Three Philosophical Poets*—the transcendentalism that will not face up to the animal in man or tries to moralize away this inescapable natural condition of his psyche does unquestionably appear "genteel." Subjected to the criterion of what may be called Santayana's *als ob* or "as if" Catholic supernaturalism, with its realms of essence and of spirit—a criterion that can be grasped from his essay on Dante in *Three Philosophical Poets*—the transcendentalism that impels man toward playing God seems certainly "egotistic."

Other features of this brilliant, if oversimplified, de-mythologizing of American and German transcendentalism deserve brief comment, since they show how Santayana manipulates the philosophical-anthropological techniques of defining indifferences and differences, connections and disconnections, affinities and oppositions, in cultural history.[21] As an instance of these techniques working together, consider his relating of the Protestant tradition, European romanticism, transcendentalism, and the Greek tradition. The Protestant tradition, identified with Calvinism, contributes, through the American Puritans, to the shaping of the American "genteel tradition." The Protestant tradition, again, is seen behind Kant and other German moral—or "moralistic"—"egotists" (Santayana is a cunning epithetician!), until it disappears in the "egotism" of the antimoral or amoral, action-oriented, and hence "barbarian" or "barbarous" Nietzsche. Romanticism, as exemplified by Goethe—the climactic culture-hero of *Three Philosophical Poets,* as he is for Fräulein Irma Schlote, the unforgettable epistolarian of *The Last Puritan*—is diffused in Germany, England, and France to swell the "egotistic" stream. This composite foreign stream, carrying subjectivism both valid and chimerical in its current, flows into the American: the confluence helps produce Emerson and the New England Renaissance, with its Indian summer radiance of "moralism." The entire background accounts for much in the intellectual climate of Santayana's Harvard, as depicted in *Character and Opinion in the United States, The Last Puritan,* and *Persons and Places*—a climate dominated by the trans-"egotistic" "moralism" of Royce's philosophy of loyalty and the post-"genteel" "barbarism" of William James' philosophy of action. The Greek tradition—explored so lovingly in much of Santayana's writing, but especially in *The Life of Reason, Three Philosophical Poets, Plato and the Spiritual Life,* and *Dialogues in Limbo*—supplies a cultural countertendency, whatever its prerational limitations or rational exclusions, to all transcendental folly, not only through the legacy of materialism and realism in metaphysics, but also through the ethical legacy of introspection, measure, and humility summed up in the maxims "Know thyself," "Nothing too much," and "Think as a mortal." These maxims are central, respectively, to the wisdoms of the Platonic Socrates, of Aristotle and Epicurus, and of the best Greek tragedies. The essence of romantic, transcendental myth-making is to overdo or pervert introspection and to disregard or flout measure and humility as ways and means to the good life and the good society.

Some of my phrases and allusions, chosen in the interest of brevity, may unintentionally blur Santayana's picture, but they will have to stand. As for those I use to convey his view of the Greek tradition, I have hit on them deliberately to bring to mind the American Neo-Humanists, especially Paul Elmer More and Irving Babbitt.[22] Although their classical, anti-romantic, and aristocratic biases may suggest some of Santayana's attitudes, these Neo-Humanists were anathema to him because of their "moralistic" assault on the old-fashioned naturalism or materialism that is one of the bases of his dualistic thinking. For it is naturalism in all its forms, Baconian and Rousseauistic, that is their villain of the modern world. Their villain, it is important to note, differs from Santayana's in that theirs was spawned by the *virtu* of the Renaissance rather than by the virtue of the Reformation. Hence Santayana, in *The Genteel Tradition at Bay*, concludes his assessment of the Neo-Humanists and their disciples with such statements as: ". . . I can find little in their recommendations except a cautious allegiance to the genteel tradition" and ". . . absolutism smells of fustiness as well as of faggots." This little volume of 1931 would be a first-rate example of his craft of defining indifferences or connections in cultural history, did it not contain the following "howler": "Even in politics the masters who are most determined and intelligent, like those diverse Greek lawgivers, or like the Fascists of our day, do not dream of imposing their chosen polity on all nations. They are proud, with a local and schoolboy pride, of their special customs." This is not the craft of the cultural historian, even a Fascist one, but the innocence of the chronological primitivist, musing on the halcyon essences of a long-fled Hellas—or perhaps of an eternal Ávila.[23]

More than with the dualism of Paul Elmer More and Irving Babbitt, Santayana's brand has affinities with that of their arch enemy, James Branch Cabell, Virginia's and Florida's Episcopalian hellion, whose ghost, I hope, will be long honored in Richmond and St. Augustine.[24] Cabell portrays one of his most provocative embodiments of *homo sapiens,* the roguish Jurgen, as subjecting all essences to his own particular stance of gallantry or skepticism and thinking of himself as "a monstrous clever fellow." But the reader alert to the Cabellian irony knows that Jurgen, whether he will admit it or not, has glimpses of ultimate truth. Two of these are appalling naturalistic revelations of the absurdity of existence made by the Brown Man with Queer Feet and by Mother Sereda.[25] But there is also the spiritual beauty of the illusory Christian God and Heaven believed in by Jurgen's grandmother. For Jurgen, as well as for the reader, the upshot of all such knowledge is a chastening that invests with an odd pathos both chastity and the chase, whether in the flesh or on the well-wrought urn. Early in *Persons and Places* Santayana remarks:

> If I were looking for ancestors there is only one known to fame to whom I might attempt to attach myself, and he is Gil Blas, whose blood I should rather like imagining I had in my veins. I feel a natural sympathy with unprejudiced minds, or if you like with rogues. . . . When the rogue tires of the game or is ruined by it, he may unfeignedly turn his free spirit towards higher things, or at least, like the good thief in Calvary, may recognize their existence.[26]

This intellectual libertinism sounds more like Montaigne or Cabell than Irving Babbitt, but how far a cry is it from the Emerson who said: ". . . if I am the Devil's child, I will live then from the Devil" and "Life is a pitching of this penny,—heads or tails"?[27] Again I shall bracket my question, until I can deal in more detail with the relation between Santayana and Emerson, as a means of bringing to a sharper focus what has already been said about Santayana's ambivalence toward transcendentalism generally.

III

A systematic canvassing of all aspects of the relation between Santayana and Emerson would call for a lengthy book. Since it was recognized early that Santayana was a kind of Emerson with a difference and since elaborating the whole paradox or merely one side of it became conventional gambits of Santayana criticism, there would have to be an introductory chapter, in our hypothetical study, on the history of this parallel-and-contrast-mongering.[28] Because Santayana couldn't get Emerson off his mind, wrote several critical pieces about him, and referred to him in occasional provocative contexts in his later writings, a chapter on what Santayana actually said about Emerson would be next in order.[29] Then, a series of chapters might place in full distinguishing comparison their achievements in autobiography and letters, in poetry, in criticism—especially of representative men and books—and in virtually all the recognized departments or divisions of philosophical concern, beginning, perhaps, with aesthetics and ethics and ending with religion and politics, as did Santayana, or maybe trying to fit Santayana into the somewhat different sequence or career of preoccupations discoverable in Emerson's development as a thinker.[30] At this point a chapter on their prose styles would be a demanding and conceivably rewarding "must." Throughout these later chapters, such problems as Emerson's possible influence on Santayana and the extent to which the total thought and the characteristic style of each were a response to the challenge of a different phase of American and world culture would have to be kept in mind and might yield a rich harvest of new insights for the book's conclusion.

At first glance a major difficulty seems to confront us in bringing off, without seriously loose ends or sagging symmetry, such a Plutarchian study or mutual interpretation.[31] What shall we do with *The Last Puritan,* since Emerson had too much good sense—or too little self-reliance or animal faith—to attempt a novel? On second thought, a simple solution suggests itself as we consider Santayana's paragraph in *Persons and Places* on his early friend Edward Bayley as one of the numerous models for the character of Oliver Alden:

> In his spiritual heritage there were doubtless certain naturalistic maxims that may have struck him in sermons or in casual reading. There was Milton with his Latinity and his Italian sonnets; and there was the young Emerson, a sort of Puritan Goethe, the Emerson of *Nature,* before he had slipped into transcendentalism and moralism and complacency in mediocrity. I may be reading ideals of my own into that very young man, in whom nothing of the sort may ever have come to light; but potentially I cannot help thinking that in him there was something more that those great men never possessed: I mean humility and renunciation. A dumb inglorious Milton who was not a prig, an Emerson with warm blood, who was not proud or oracular or cosmographical, and never thought himself the center of the universe. Young Bayley was my first, perhaps my fundamental, model for *The Last Puritan.*[32]

Since this paragraph discloses that *The Last Puritan* is really a novel about Santayana's own traditionally dualistic, semitranscendental ambivalence toward Emerson and transcendentalism, why not insert—between our chapter on what Santayana said about Emerson and our chapter on their achievement in autobiography and letters—a kind of transitional chapter or interchapter and entitle it *"The Last Puritan* and the Ghost of Emerson" or *"The Last Puritan* as an Exercise in Loving Exorcism"?

Santayana's ambivalence toward Emerson appears to have gone through four stages, each exhibiting the eclectic spirit and some or all of the generalist, relativistic, dog-

matic, and iconoclastic attitudes described in the first
section of this paper. In each of these four stages, also, the
presence of Santayana's dualistic thinking is evident.

In the first stage, well defined in "The Optimism of
Ralph Waldo Emerson"—the unsuccessful Bowdoin Prize
essay of 1886 to which reference has already been made—
the eclecticism, generalism, and iconclasm are those of
the precocious undergraduate. The essay is divided into
three parts. In the first, Santayana draws from a wide range
of reading to demonstrate that Emerson's optimism does
not rest on the usual bases of antipessimism in nineteenth-
century culture. It is not arrived at by an appeal to the
Benthamite calculus of pains and pleasures, or to the
"suspicious theology" of Leibnitz committed to "the doctrine that no better series of events than the actual is
possible," or to sentimental Protestantism's "method of
silencing pain with the promise of sugar-plums" in the
hereafter, or to "the superstition of progress"—"the promise, not of a heaven of pleasure, but of a millenium on
earth, or at least a perpetual melioration." The second
part develops the thesis that Emerson's optimism depends
on a mystical monistic conception of the universe that is
achieved by starting from a dualistic insistence on the
world as idea versus the world as experience, contempla-
tion versus sympathy, the larger view as opposed to the
partial view. The larger view sees unity in all things
because it is the view of the individual soul when it has
merged in the universal soul and thus grasped the truth
"that one power produces all things, and therefore that all
things have an equal right to be." Santayana the generalist
is at home with Emerson's poetry and quotes "Brahma."
Santayana the relativist points out that the same dualism
on which this monistic, optimistic faith is built in Emerson is the foundation of pessimism in Schopenhauer and
that the premise of God's overriding creativity in Calvin's
theology leads to conclusions that are scarcely optimistic.
In the third part Santayana the dogmatist emerges. Like
other Harvard intellectuals of the 1880's,[33] he is clearly
too much taken by Schopenhauer's refusal to surrender

the mind's detachment to the world-will and uses this dualism as a criterion to characterize Emerson as unsystematic, illogical, and temperamental. Santayana invokes more traditional criteria when he asserts: "Surely neither Plato, nor the Christian saints, nor Marcus Aurelius, nor anyone with whom Emerson's philosophy seems to associate him, walked this earth with a bland and persistent smile." Emerson is "the mystic turned dilettante," "proud to plead guilty to the charge of viewiness," "the prophet of a fair-weather religion." And yet we find in him "a quick eye for beauty, a turning aside from pain and sorrow, a mystical elevation of spirit," "many encouraging words, much perception of the beauty and excellence of things . . . we must be dull and morbid indeed, if we are not charmed by so much sweetness and serenity." It is interesting to note that in all three parts Santayana introduces incidental references to actual evils, mostly in society past and present, that for him make difficult the mystic's larger view: here is the young materialist declining to be won by idealistic rhetoric.[34]

The second stage of Santayana's ambivalence toward Emerson is that of the elegant young teacher of philosophy obliged to publish professionally but still intent on creative writing, especially poetry and poetic drama, and compromising for the time being by producing literary criticism, like an ex-bachelor torn between his new wife and his old mistress and seeking peace of mind in a third liaison. Two texts are relevant—the essay on Emerson in *Interpretations of Poetry and Religion* (1900) and an uncollected article that is exclusively concerned with Emerson's poetry and that appeared in the Emerson supplement of the *Boston Daily Advertiser* of May 23, 1903, after being delivered as an address at Harvard during Emerson Memorial Week. The *Interpretations* essay begins where the Bowdoin essay left off, by developing more maturely the thesis that "the source of his power lay not in his doctrine, but in his temperament, and the rare quality of his wisdom was due less to his reason than to his imagination." This power was not really "a revelation from above" but "an insurrection from beneath." In other words, Emerson's Over-Soul was a poetic myth that liberated the Under-Soul of his followers. "To reject tradition and think as one might have thought if no man had ever existed before was indeed the aspiration of the Transcendentalists, and although Emerson hardly regarded himself as a member of that school, he largely shared its tendency and passed for its spokesman." Remarkably akin to "the German romantic or idealistic philosophers," he had the good sense to stay clear of their system-making: hence, his distinction in "transcendental speculation" is that he "retained its true value and avoided its greatest danger." Some of his orthodox contemporaries, however, were disturbed by his turning away from the Church and by the vagueness of his lay preaching; Santayana, while implying that such orthodoxy is virtually a lost cause, feels that its concern over Emerson is still partly justifiable in other terms:—for does not poetic license wafted into mysticism do too much damage to our understanding, our common sense, "our hold on fact," and, in the last ironic upshot, even "to the imagination and all its works"? Herein, Santayana insists, lies the menace of mysticism: "The lights of life must be extinguished that the light of the absolute may shine, and the possession of everything in general must be secured by the surrender of everything in particular." On the whole, however, Emerson kept his imagination "near to experience" and his mysticism "within bounds," except perhaps when he used his Over-Soul myth to postulate "the unity of all minds" and evil's "evaporation in the universal harmony of things." At this point Santayana suggests that not only the freedom of Emerson's poetic imagination, fed from many sources, is to blame for such excess but likewise the American Puritan tradition. The pessimism that the Bowdoin essay attributed to Calvinistic theology is now seen to have its optimistic side in the doctrine of "a providential government of affairs for the ultimate and positive good of the elect." Even though this operation of the Calvinistic God held out "no very roseate picture of the destinies of mankind"

as a race of sinners, it fostered a habit of worship founded
on moral fervor, the "willingness to be, as the phrase is,
'damned for the glory of God.'" Emerson's Over-Soul
was simply a philosophical and poetic substitute of beneficent force and law for the theological providence of
Puritanism. The substitution got rid of the necessities of
both church-going and damnation, made the government
of the world more certain of eventual good for all men,
left the impulse to worship intact, and enhanced its moral
fervor. Rather than a philosopher, Emerson may be called
"The Psyche of Puritanism" which, released even from
the mild doctrinal bonds of Unitarianism, "ranged abroad
over the fields of history and Nature, gathering what ideas
it might, and singing its little snatches of inspired song."
Although he was in the world of his time to the extent of
supporting democracy, furthering antislavery, and approving scientific and material progress, he remained a detached
prophet of the eternal and fulfilled for his countrymen
something of the function of the prophets of old—"the
Hindoos and the Persians . . . the Platonists and the Stoics."
Thus, despite all that Santayana has said about Emerson's
antitraditionalism, he allows him a place in a very ancient
and great tradition, even though pointing out that he is
"not a star of the first magnitude" in that firmament and
deserves to be there largely because of "the originality and
beauty of the expression" he gave to borrowed ideas.
Writing for Emerson Memorial Week, Santayana is less
qualified in his praise, becoming so carried away by
enthusiasm for Emerson's expression in verse that he is
willing to hail his thought generally as a "fountain of
truth" in its synthesis of faith and reason, its projection of
"beauty and mind" into "all the forms of matter."[35]

The third stage of Santayana's ambivalence toward
Emerson is that of the famous visiting lecturer addressing
audiences representative of two entirely different environ-
ments, even though both were academic. The University
of California audience to which "The Genteel Tradition
in American Philosophy" was delivered in 1911 was made
up for the most part of the grown grandchildren of a west-

ward movement that had left disdainfully behind the evils
of the Old World and the effeteness of the New England
culture, that had put into energetic practice the Emersonian ethic of self-reliance and thus embodied William
James's pragmatism without having any notion that it
would ever be concocted, and that had been acclaimed by
Walt Whitman in such poems as "Pioneers, O Pioneers!"
and "Passage to India." To this audience Emerson must be
presented, not merely as a transmuter of Old World Calvinism or as New England's "representative man," but
rather as a kind of creative naturalistic thinker who looked
beyond "the genteel tradition" and preached the wisdom
breathed by the Rockies and the Great Plains. And so
Santayana presents him as the inspirational middleman
in a spiritual and intellectual revolution that Whitman
and William James carried further.[36] By contrast, *Character and Opinion in the United States* (1920) was expanded from lectures delivered in England at a time
when Santayana was still smarting from the irritations that
had played their part in causing him to abandon America
forever in 1912, namely, the conviction that his promo-
tions at Harvard had been slow and grudging and the
knowledge that underground gossip had spread widely
there about his moral character, particularly the extent of
his latent homosexuality, which the philistine mind had
inferred from his mannerisms, associations, failure to
marry, and frequent absences in Europe.[37] Under such
circumstances, his analysis of American culture confirmed
many of the stereotypes of the cultivated British view
and infused into them, from out of the depths of his own
disillusion, a subtle derogation of "moralism" in all its
forms, "genteel," "egotistic," and "barbarous." Santayana
praises the leading spokesmen of academic idealism and
pragmatism, Royce and James—to both of whom he owed
so much—but in a carefully designed context of their
faults that is sharply reductive of their stature. He reidenti-
fies Emerson with "the genteel tradition," dubs his originality as of an "incidental character," and relegates him to
the status of marking a transition between Jonathan Ed-

wards and William James. That this is no huge distinction is apparent from Santayana's characterization of Edwards as "perhaps the greatest *master* in false philosophy that America has yet produced" and his remark that both Emerson and James "lisped their logic, when the logic came."[38]

The fourth stage of Santayana's ambivalence toward Emerson is that of the aging cosmopolite laboring leisurely over his massive writing projects while the Europe to which he had come fondly home reeled from the early *coups* of Hitler and Mussolini through the partial materialization and final destruction of their monstrous fantasies of power. After the publication of *The Last Puritan* (English edition, 1935; American edition, 1936), Santayana embarked, while engaged with the long-gestating *Dominations and Powers* and the final volume of *Realms of Being,* on another ambitious project, involving Emerson, but never completed it. In a letter of May, 1937, to Mrs. C. H. Toy, he thus describes the project:

> I am deep now in nothing but Americana, being still haunted with the idea of writing something about *The Old Mind of the New World.* I want to illustrate my thesis by some observations on Jonathan Edwards and Emerson—hard or stiff minds—and Poe and Hawthorne—soft minds. . . . I have procured an immense volume of Emerson's works, over 1000 pages, in which I have already reread *"English Traits"* and *"Fate."*[39]

Another letter of that same month to Daniel Cory comments on the experience of revisiting Emerson:

> I am reading Emerson with pleasure. Apart from a few oddities, his English is good and there are flashes of intuition and eloquence. I also feel that the skeleton of his philosophy is discernible, in spite of a hopeless inconsecutiveness and literary freedom on the surface. He is still a fanatic at bottom, a radical individualist, with a sort of theism in the background, to the effect that the individual must be after God's or Emerson's

heart, or be damned. I have read his *English Traits*, and see he admires England (as my father did) for being successful materially, but has no love for what is lovely there. Emerson is not really free, but is a cruel physical Platonist.[40]

These passages, placed alongside the Bayley passage quoted earlier from *Persons and Places*, show that Santayana was trying to come to terms with Emerson almost until the very end and succeeding only in keeping his original ambivalence alive and kicking, now in this direction and now in that.

The identification of Oliver Alden with the ghost of Emerson is supported by a passage in *The Last Puritan*. After Oliver, on his pilgrimage to Harvard in September before the opening of the term, has chosen a room in Divinity Hall, he hears the janitor remark: "Ralph Waldo's name isn't there. Guess he hadn't a diamond to scratch it with." The text continues:

> On one of the window panes there were indeed some names and dates and initials scratched rather illegibly by former occupants.
> "Ralph Waldo?"
> "Yeah, Ralph Waldo Emerson. They say he lived in this room. It weren't in my day. *I* don't swear to it."
> Strange, Oliver thought, that he should have chosen Emerson's room without knowing it. Irma and his mother, except that it was wrong to be superstitious, would think it a special Providence. All protests against the meanness or discomfort of his lodging could now be silenced with a word. "What was good enough for Emerson is good enough for me."[41]

In the light of this passage, Santayana's treatment of Oliver as a tragic Hamlet-Christ figure, a spirit with infinite possibilities immolated in a basically absurd world, may be regarded as in part a reflection of what drew him to Emerson.[42] On the other hand, the subjection of Oliver to a clinically detached analysis with reference to the criteria of Freudian "fixations, transferences, inhibitions" and "the modernness of the new Italy," which "sucks in all the sap of the past,"⁴³ suggests Santayana's tendency to condemn those aspects of Emerson that did not square with his own quasi-Catholic materialistic dualism, veined by a tolerance at once so amoral and so saintly that it curiously unfitted him to be a sound critic of the neo-paganism gathering all about him to sup mankind on horrors.⁴⁴ Since criticism has yet to do justice to *The Last Puritan*, and the job is far too complicated to be even initiated here,⁴⁵ I will confine myself to observing that the contrast between Oliver and Mario, on which so much turns, need not be interpreted as Santayana's exorcism of his American past in favor of a Fascist future, but rather as an attempt to weigh the inner-directed personality of nineteenth-century transcendentalist ethics over against the autonomous personality demanded by the twentieth century's complex transvaluation of values and of the conditions of existence. Viewed from this Riesmanian perspective,⁴⁶ the novel adds a dimension to Santayana's already imposing stature as an "essentialist" critic of culture and as a connoisseur of moral and psychological polarities.

IV

The two questions bracketed earlier in this paper—(1) should Santayana's critical approach be called phenomenological? (2) did he really appreciate the Devil and the penny-pitching dualist or gamester polaritist in Emerson? —can now be brought forward for answers. They are related questions, and related in such a way that to answer the first is to dispose of the second, at least in a fashion. As I understand the matter, the theoretically aware phenomenological critic, alleging epistemological naïveté, rejects Matthew Arnold's principle of seeking "to see the object as in itself it really is," and in its stead proposes the principle of using the object to see the subject as it really is in its involvement with this object and with other objects and subjects. Phenomenological criticism is not to be confused with expressionistic impressionism, which is more a mode of exposition than criticism, to employ Santayana's distinction—exposition now of the object, now of the subject, displaying, at its best, great funambulistic charm, but eschewing carefully any real engagement, since its purpose is to effect, through the stimulus of curiosity and the contagion of gusto, a catalysis between the audience, on the one hand, and the work and its creator, on the other, rather than to conduct an analysis of the latter two that is also a judgment.[47] Good examples of phenomenological criticism are such otherwise vastly different books as Jules de Gaultier's *From Kant to Nietzsche*, Nicholas Berdyaev's *Dostoevsky*, D. H. Lawrence's *Studies in Classic American Literature*, and Edward Dahlberg's *Do These Bones Live*.

In so far as Santayana tells us more about himself in his discussions of transcendentalism and of Emerson than he does about the nature of the tendency, the movement, or the man, as a great historian of literature and ideas like Perry Miller or a great biographer like Ralph Rusk knows and presents them, then he is phenomenological. As such, it is not necessary that his criticism take into account all aspects of the object. It may ignore any aspects of the object that failed to make their impact during his encounters with it; such aspects lie outside the radius of involvement. In contrasting criticism with exposition and absolving the critic of the obligation to "read up" or go out of his way to provide others with surrogates for real encounters, Santayana showed a good understanding of the negative side of phenomenological criticism. In demanding that the critic put the thing criticized in as full a context of discovery as possible, he clinched his grasp of the positive side.

If, from the negative side, the phenomenological critic leaves out, as beyond the radius of his involvement, too many aspects of the object, his criticism will seem too much of an act of falsification. Most objects worth grappling with critically are many-relational and many-leveled. Enough of these relations and levels must be brought into the picture to score an approximation of truth, even though some are omitted. If, from the positive side, the phenomenological critic as "spiritually researching" subject brings an insufficient context of discovery to his task, his criticism will seem a too perfunctory and too arbitrary performance. Ideally, this "researching" subject has to be many-perspectived, drawing upon all the knowledge-structures he has spent his life in building; and these knowledge-structures, to be perspectives, have to possess some depth.[48]

Judged in such terms, Santayana's criticism of transcendentalism and of its leading American spokesman, Emerson, presents the spectacle of a many-perspectived subject and a many-relational, many-leveled object in sustained conjunction and confrontation. It is a spectacle at once absorbing, enlightening, and exciting, even though some relations and levels of the object never appear and not all the subject's perspectives possess the same depth. Santayana's historical perspective, for instance, suffers from his own residual transcendentalism and is more a knowledge-structure of essences or ideas affecting each other in a phenomenological ether than of existence in all its density interacting with ideas in the successive societal phases of the long flux of human time. Rather than seeing transcendentalism as the essence of the "egotistic" impinging on the essence of the "genteel" to produce the essence of the "moralistic" and rather than attempting to fix the essence of Emerson in such phrases as "a cruel physical Platonist," "hard or stiff," Santayana should have speculated more on the cultural situations, in all their complexity, that transcendentalism in its different varieties and through its many spokesmen sought to contend with, in its effort—as Gabriel Marcel might put it in one of his Mozartian perorations[49]—to assist *homo viator* along the winding path, out of and beyond the broken world, toward the divine life and the full society, where mystery and problem stand in creative and fraternal syzygy.

It is only fair to add that if Santayana could peruse

this conclusion in some "genteel" houseboat on the Styx or serene alcove of Limbo especially reserved for a "Catholic Agnostic," as Richard Butler, O. P., has called him— an alcove only a short distance from the cells allotted to Catholic existentialists or neo-Socratics—he might be inclined to mutter, like Cabell's Jurgen: "Of course you may be right; and certainly I cannot go so far as to say you are wrong: but still, at the same time—"[50]

NOTES

1. The following are the best discussions of Santayana as a critic: George Howgate, *George Santayana* (Philadelphia, 1938), pp. 142–226; Philip Blair Rice, "The Philosopher as Poet and Critic," *The Philosophy of George Santayana,* ed. Paul Arthur Schilpp (Chicago and Evanston, 1940), pp. 265–91; Irving Singer, "Introduction: Santayana as a Literary Critic," *Essays in Literary Criticism of George Santayana,* ed. Singer (New York, 1956), pp. ix-xxviii, and *Santayana's Aesthetics: A Critical Introduction* (Cambridge, Mass., 1957), pp. 195–222; William Walsh, "Santayana as a Critic," *A Review of English Literature,* V (January 1964), 69–77.

2. *The Letters of George Santayana,* ed. Daniel Cory (New York, 1955), pp. 238–39; italics his. This volume is hereafter referred to as *Letters.*

3. *Letters,* pp. 195–96; italics his.

4. Santayana in Schilpp, ed. cit., p. 550.

5. Santayana, *The Last Puritan* (New York, 1936), p. 431. In the Triton Edition of *The Works of George Santayana,* 15 vols. (New York, 1936–40), this passage occurs in XII, 162. The Triton Edition is hereafter referred to as *Works.*

6. "The Poetry of Barbarism" is ch. VII of Santayana's *Interpretations of Poetry and Religion* (1900); see *Works,* II, 118–52. For William James's reaction see *The Letters of William James,* ed. Henry James (his son), 2 vols. (Boston, 1920), II, 123. Frederic I. Carpenter, *American Literature and the Dream* (New York, 1955), pp. 51–62, and George Boas, "The Legacy of Santayana," *Revue internationale de philosophie* (Bruxelles), XVII (1963), 37–49, take Santayana to task for his use of "genteel" and "egotistic."

7. Published with a note by Maurice F. Brown, *Emerson*

Society Quarterly, No. 37, IV Quarter 1964, Part 2, pp. 60–70. This item will hereafter be cited as *B-ESQ*.

8. Norman Mailer, *An American Dream* (New York, 1965), p. 2.

9. Santayana, *Realms of Being* (New York, 1942), pp. 171–74. At the close of this postscript, Santayana points out that Husserl's approach to essences is more purely transcendental than his own, the tendency of which is "to look for the genesis and meaning of immediate experience in the material and animal world" rather than to take the "malicious" path "that isolates mind in mind." Other witnesses whom he summons are Alfred North Whitehead and René Guénon; in *Works*, XIV, 175–79, Proust is added from Santayana's *Obiter Scripta* (New York, 1936), pp. 273–79.

10. H. B. Van Wesep, *Seven Sages: The Story of American Philosophy* (New York, 1960), p. 286.

11. Thomas N. Munson, S.J., *The Essential Wisdom of George Santayana* (New York, 1962), p. 155.

12. Kenneth T. Gallagher, *The Philosophy of Gabriel Marcel* (New York, 1962), p. 1.

13. Gabriel Marcel, *Creative Fidelity* (New York, 1964), p. 90. The translator is Robert Rosthal; the original title *Du refus à l'invocation* (Paris, 1940).

14. *Creative Fidelity*, p. 28; cf. p. 91.

15. Santayana, *Persons and Places: The Background of My Life* (New York, 1944), p. 50. Most allusions to *Persons and Places* in my text are to the entire autobiography, now available in a one-volume edition (New York, 1963) under this title and containing *The Middle Span* (New York, 1945) and *My Host the World* (New York, 1953) as well as *The Background of My Life,* which was originally issued as *Persons and Places.* Since the pagination of the original three volumes is retained in the one-volume reissue, footnoting offers no difficulties when the separate subtitles are included.

16. Santayana, *Persons and Places: The Background of My Life,* p. 132.

17. "Diary of Edward Taylor," *Proceedings of the Massa-*

chusetts Historical Society, XVIII (1881), 4–8, is the ultimate source of these quotations, but their immediate source is Joe Lee Davis, John T. Frederick, and Frank Luther Mott, eds., *American Literature: An Anthology and Critical Survey,* 2 vols. (New York, 1948–49), I, 178–79, where Taylor's spelling is modernized.

18. Santayana, *Persons and Places: The Background of My Life,* p. 130. The image of the cockleshell is also used in a more general connection, ibid., p. 2. In *My Host the World,* p. 56, Santayana identifies himself with a roulette ball, a kind of variant of the cockleshell image. M. M. Kirkwood, *Santayana: Saint of the Imagination* (Toronto, 1961), p. 14, comments on Santayana's employment of water imagery to express the human condition. Norman O. Brown, *Life Against Death: The Psychoanalytical Meaning of History,* Vintage Books ed. (New York, n.d.), p. 183, quotes a curious psychoanalytical opinion to the effect that use of the man in the little boat as a symbol may have something to do with male transvestitism!

19. Santayana, *Works,* X, 220.

20. Santayana, *Works,* VII, 133–34. The address was published originally in *Winds of Doctrine* (1913), a volume that went through several later editions and appeared with *Platonism and the Spiritual Life* in the Harper Torchbooks in 1957.

21. Richard McKeon, "The Flight from Certainty and the Quest for Precision," *The Review of Metaphysics,* XVIII (December 1964), 234–53, contains some interesting reflections on indifferences and differences as a concern of twentieth-century philosophy.

22. Paul Elmer More, "Delphi and Greek Literature," and "Nemesis, or The Divine Envy," in his *Shelburne Essays,* Second Series (Boston, 1905), pp. 188–253, discusses more fully than does Santayana the role of "Know thyself," "Nothing too much," and "Think as a mortal" in Greek culture and literature.

23. Santayana, *Works,* VIII, 167, 169, and 160 respectively, for this paragraph's three quotations from *The Genteel Tradition At Bay.*

24. James Branch Cabell, *Some of Us: An Essay in Epitaphs*

(New York, 1930), especially pp. 3–12 and 121–31, ironically castigates the Neo-Humanists. That Cabell and Santayana have much in common has been noted by Paul Elmer More, *The Demon of the Absolute* (Princeton, 1928), p. 61, and Henry Steele Commager, *The American Mind: An Interpretation of American Thought and Character Since the 1880's* (New Haven, 1950), pp. 117–18, and explored in some detail by Arvin R. Wells, *Jesting Moses: A Study in Cabellian Comedy* (Gainesville, 1962), pp. 13–22, 26, 44, 45, 49, 62, 118–19, and 134.

25. James Branch Cabell, *Jurgen,* Avon Library ed. (New York, 1964), pp. 106–9 and 239–40; in the Storisende Edition of *The Works of James Branch Cabell,* 18 vols. (New York, 1927–30), these passages occur in VI, 132–36 and 319–21.

26. Santayana, *Persons and Places: The Background of My Life,* pp. 11–12. Cf. the rogue protagonists in Cabell, *There Were Two Pirates: A Comedy of Division* (New York, 1946) and *The Devil's Own Dear Son: A Comedy of the Fatted Calf* (New York, 1949).

27. These statements are taken from Emerson's "Self-Reliance" and "Montaigne"; see *Selections from Ralph Waldo Emerson,* ed. Stephen E. Whicher, Riverside Editions (Boston, 1957), pp. 150 and 284, where these essays are placed in a revealing chronological arrangement of Emerson texts.

28. This chapter would include, among others, William James, *Letters,* ed. cit., II, 234–35; Baker Brownell, "Santayana, the Man and the Philosopher," in Schilpp, ed. cit., pp. 56–61 particularly; John Crowe Ransom, *The World's Body* (New York, 1938), pp. 304–5; Albert J. Lubell, "George Santayana and the New England Mind," *The South Atlantic Quarterly,* LVII (Summer 1958), 295–310, particularly 303.

29. Paul C. Wermuth, "Santayana and Emerson," *Emerson Society Quarterly,* No. 31, II Quarter 1963, Part 2, pp. 36–40, has admirably anticipated some of the findings that would have to go into this chapter.

30. M. M. Kirkwood, op. cit., and Stephen E. Whicher, *Free-*

dom and Fate: An Inner Life of Ralph Waldo Emerson (Philadelphia, 1953), provide schema for planning this part of our hypothetical history.

31. Henry Seidel Canby, *Turn West, Turn East: Mark Twain and Henry James* (Boston, 1951), pp. ix-xii and 294–97, comments on the rationale of what I have called "a Plutarchian study"; Mark Spilka, *Dickens and Kafka: A Mutual Interpretation* (Bloomington, Ind., 1963), suggested in his subtitle my other term.

32. Santayana, *Persons and Places: The Background of My Life,* p. 184.

33. Maurice F. Brown, "Santayana's American Roots," *The New England Quarterly,* XXXIII (June 1960), 147–63, throws much light on the Harvard intellectualism of the 1890's and some of its interests that were already stirring in the 1880's during Santayana's undergraduate years. Enthusiasm for Lucretius and Spinoza antedated Santayana's passion for Schopenhauer, which was a phase of his senior and graduate years.

34. All the quotations from this paragraph are from *B-ESQ* (see note 7), those from the first part of the essay being on pp. 62–66; the second part, p. 68; the third part, pp. 69–70.

35. All the quotations from the *Interpretations* essay are from Santayana, *Works,* II, 154, 155, 157, 158, 159, 161, 162, 163, 164. Santayana does not use the term "Under-Soul," but I am indebted to Vivian C. Hopkins' use of it with a lower-case "s" in her *Spires of Form: A Study of Emerson's Aesthetic Theory* (Cambridge, Mass., 1951), p. 179. The quotations in the last sentence of this paragraph are from Santayana, "Emerson's Poems Proclaim the Divinity of Nature, with Freedom as His Profoundest Ideal," *Boston Daily Advertiser,* May 23, 1903, p. 16.

36. Santayana, *Works,* VII, 138–42.

37. This interpretation of the main motives behind Santayana's abandonment of America is based on his *The Middle Span* (Vol. II of *Persons and Places*), p. 159, and Daniel Cory, *Santayana: The Later Years* (New York, 1963), pp. 40–43.

38. Santayana, *Works*, VIII, 10–11.

39. Santayana, *Letters*, p. 317.

40. Cory, *Santayana: The Later Years*, p. 186.

41. Santayana, *The Last Puritan*, Scribner Library ed., p. 416; *Works*, XII, 146.

42. Santayana, *Letters*, p. 82, uses the phrase "Hamlet-like" with reference to Emerson; the identification of Oliver Alden with Hamlet occurs in his defense of the character in *The Last Puritan*, Scribner Library ed., pp. 234–35; *Works*, XI, 253–54; the identification of Oliver Alden with Christ is made in *The Last Puritan*, Scribner Library ed., pp. 223–24; *Works*, XI, 240–42.

43. Santayana, *The Last Puritan*, Scribner Library ed., pp. 601 and 600; *Works*, XII, 344 and 342.

44. Learned Hand's and Bernard Berenson's impressions of Santayana in 1937 and 1939 respectively, as set down in *The Selected Letters of Bernard Berenson*, ed. A. K. McComb (Boston, 1964), pp. 144 and 171–72, provide confirmation.

45. The job has been initiated—generally in the right direction—by Frederick W. Conner, "*Lucifer* and *The Last Puritan*," *American Literature*, XXXIII (March 1961), 1–19; James C. Ballowe, "The Art and Criticism of Santayana's *The Last Puritan*," unpublished University of Illinois doctoral dissertation, 1963; and William H. Marshall, "An Expanding Theme in *The Last Puritan*," *The Personalist*, XLV (Winter 1964) , 27–40.

46. David Riesman, *The Lonely Crowd* (New Haven, 1950), p. 288, sets his three "universal types" of personality—"the adjusted, the anomic, the autonomous"—over against his three "historical types"—"tradition-directed, inner-directed, and other-directed." "The autonomous among the other-directeds" is the theme of pp. 300–306.

47. Cf. H. L. Mencken, *Prejudices: First Series* (New York, 1919), pp. 20–21, on substitution of the term "catalytic criticism" for "creative criticism."

48. My use of "spiritually researching" and "researching" is in accord with the sense given "research" by Gabriel

Marcel, *The Existential Background of Human Dignity* (Cambridge, Mass., 1963), pp. 5–9, 12–15.

49. See ibid., pp. 169–70.

50. Richard Butler, O.P., "George Santayana: Catholic Agnostic," *Ramparts,* II (May 1963), 33–37; Cabell, *Jurgen,* Avon Library ed., p. 109; *Works,* VI, 136. Marcel's preference to be known as a "neo-Socratic" or a "Christian Socratic" rather than as an existentialist is commented on by Seymour Cain, *Gabriel Marcel* (New York, 1963), p. 114.

Irving Babbitt, Paul More, and Transcendentalism

By René Wellek

THE HUMANIST OR NEO-HUMANIST movement was an episode in the American debate about culture and literature which, one has the impression, is being forgotten today. Certainly, the issues then debated, though as unresolved as ever, are now discussed in other terms, rarely with reference to the slogans of the Humanists: one does not encounter the phrase "inner check" or the contrast between "humanism and humanitarianism," and even "classicism versus romanticism" is not an issue except in historical contexts. The public commotion around 1930, when Babbitt appeared at a large staged debate in New York and when two collective volumes—one Humanist, the other anti-Humanist—were published, was, after all, ephemeral in its effect. The polemics in the press seem from today's perspective to have been on a low level: they were often quite acrimonious and, as is usual in such cases, often reflected misunderstandings or misinterpretations of the opponents' tenets. There seems to be little point in rehearsing these debates. It would give them a false importance and distort the historical perspective.

1930 is not the year that matters for a proper understanding and interpretation of the thought of the two protagonists, Irving Babbitt and Paul Elmer More. Both belong to a much earlier time: to the 1890's, when they formed their basic convictions. Their main writings appeared in the first decade of the century: the first seven volumes of *Shelburne Essays* between 1904 and 1910,

Literature and the American College in 1908, *The New Laokoon* in 1910, *Masters of Modern French Criticism* in 1912.[1] More and Babbitt must be discussed in terms of the period in which they achieved maturity. It does not help their cause if we focus on the late years and thus on their reaction to their younger contemporaries after the first World War. Inevitably, we shall come to the conclusion that Babbitt indulged in an imperceptive wholesale condemnation of the whole modern world and modern literature and that More—while willing to discuss Proust, Joyce, Eliot, and the American naturalists—did so with little sympathy and understanding.

We might feel today that More's low opinion of many of the prominent figures of the twenties, pungently phrased in the essay "Modern Currents in American Literature" (*NSE*, I), was, after all, not so far from the truth, or what we believe today is our more considered judgment. But I remain unconvinced that these opinions were arrived at on the right grounds, that they were judgments of aesthetic sensibility and moral scrupulosity and not merely deductions from a generalized rejection of naturalistic determinism and a repugnance toward anything ugly and low. The article on "The Cleft Eliot" (in *The Saturday Review* of Nov. 12, 1932, reprinted in *Designed for Reading*, ed. H. S. Canby, New York, 1934, pp. 333–38) confirms this judgment: the dichotomy between the obscure poet, the "lyric prophet of chaos," and the solid critic causes only "perplexity over some unreconciled paradox." Similarly, the essay on Joyce (*NSE*, III) simply asserts the "dilemma" of explaining how the sound view of life expressed in "The Dead" could have changed into the "moral slough" of *Ulysses,* its "weary and ugly art," its "philosophy of the inane," the change in Joyce being in the opposite direction from Eliot's, of course. The more sympathetic essay on Proust (*NSE*, III), which at least recognizes some of his power, is also satisfied with disposing of him as a "naturalist"; More expressly objects to Edmund Wilson's view of "symbolism as a revolt from nineteenth century naturalism." Naturalism for More is so all-inclusive a term that it abolishes all distinctions; apparently a work has to afford "relief in the promise of a future existence" to be exempt from the pejorative label. More had in his last years some personal contacts with Eliot and briefly with Edmund Wilson (who described his visit vividly in *The Triple Thinkers*); he had some sense of the mental climate and the literary events of the twenties and early thirties.

One has the impression that Babbitt at Harvard was much more insulated from the new winds of doctrine. Possibly as a deliberate policy, in his published writings at least, Babbitt never tangled with recent or even "modern" literature—"modern" in the sense used, for example, by Charles Feidelson and Richard Ellmann in their recent *The Modern Tradition*—if one excepts some slighting allusions to the "advanced stage of psychic disintegration" marked by Joyce's *Ulysses* (*BC*, p. 132). Even the most prominent names of French twentieth-century literature are missing in the indices of Babbitt's works. When he discusses contemporaries, he singles out only ideologists: Pierre Lasserre, Julien Benda, the Baron Seillière of the French antiromantic polemics and the Abbé Bremond and Jacques Maritain, more casually, as representatives of Catholic opinion. Babbitt was apparently resolved to remain a historian or at least to draw mainly on historical evidence for his diagnosis of the ills of civilization, while More, possibly because of his long experience as a literary journalist in New York, was paradoxically far less "academic": much more aware of the world around him in spite of his later immersion in the history of the Platonic tradition and his semiretirement to the academic groves of Princeton.

Babbitt's studied silence on concrete works and figures of recent literature and More's somewhat baffled and condescending articles of his last years explain such extravagant judgments as Oscar Cargill's, who speaks of their "almost complete unfamiliarity with the major ideas of their time" (*Intellectual America*, New York, 1941, p. 530) and must justify Santayana's phrase "The Genteel

Tradition at Bay," though one could rather speak of a Humanist offensive at that time.

We should then ignore the attempt around 1930 to bring Humanism to the general public, to make it a movement and even a kind of religion. Instead, we should try to make the mental experiment of imagining that both Babbitt and More had ceased writing in 1920. By then all their positions had been arrived at long ago. After that date More changed in the direction of a more specific religious commitment, but Babbitt held his creed substantially unchanged all his adult life even though its formulation and documentation were to stretch over several decades. *Rousseau and Romanticism* (1919) and *Democracy and Leadership* (1924) are implicit in Babbitt's first book, *Literature and the American College* (1908), and that book is in part made up of much older articles: the oldest, "The Rational Study of the Classics," dates back to 1897. More and Babbitt had reached the age of forty in 1904 and 1905, respectively, and by that time most people's minds are made up, solidified and set in a mold. This is certainly true of them: we hear that Babbitt knew his mind perfectly when he met More in Professor Lanham's seminar at Harvard in 1892, and what More often later felt to be his own youthful gropings seemed so only in the perspective of the religious certainty of his last years. Actually, the intellectual position of the two friends was defined very early, and the positions differ as the two differ not only in temperament but in their relation to the intellectual past. The friction between the two came out in the open only late: More found the strongest terms of dissent from Babbitt when he criticized in letters Babbitt's last book, *On Being Creative,* and was upset about his treatment of Wordsworth, so "frightfully one-sided and warped and vindictive" (Arthur H. Dakin, *P. E. More,* Princeton, 1960, p. 317). It is best to discuss them separately, as their writings raise different questions and give different answers. They will be remembered as intellectual personalities and not as leaders of an abortive movement (More, we may recall, did not even contribute to the volume *Humanism and America,* edited by Norman Foerster, but merely allowed a section of "The Demon of the Absolute" to be reprinted).

"Brunetière speaks English," said J. E. Spingarn in epitomizing Babbitt's *Masters of Modern French Criticism* (*Journal of Philosophy,* X, 1913, 693); and from the perspective of a historian of criticism it might be simplest to describe Babbitt as a classicist of the French type. Babbitt wrote two essays on Brunetière which he used in the book; he translated an essay for the *Atlantic Monthly* in 1897 when Brunetière visited Harvard. He shares in general Brunetière's view of the French tradition, his detestation of naturalism, and he wholeheartedly agrees with his attack on critical impressionism. Babbitt as a teacher of French literature became more and more familiar with the classics of the seventeenth century. He admired Racine for "reason, exquisite measure, supreme clearness, delicate sensibility tempered by judgment," quoting Lemaître of all people (*SC,* p. 95). He defended Boileau vigorously against Saintsbury's denigration and, later in particular, Pascal became the exemplary figure for the conflict of religion and science and the view of the three levels of man: animal, human, and divine. Babbitt saw the immediate ancestry of Brunetière in Désiré Nisard, who was the first to diagnose French decadence and to exalt the French seventeenth century as the embodiment of the classical spirit and the permanent human mind, in contrast to the eighteenth century. Babbitt, of course, discussed the evolution of Sainte-Beuve's criticism as a happy emancipation from the shackles of Romanticism and a discovery or rediscovery of the truth of the classical tradition. The rise of this French nineteenth-century Classicism is actually the central theme of *The Masters of Modern French Criticism,* Babbitt's best book or at least his best organized and most equitable book. *The New Laokoon* assumes the classical doctrine of the pure genre, *le genre tranché,* as a starting point for its onslaught on the confusion of the modern arts and their subdivisions. *Rousseau and Romanticism* is intimately related to the French

polemics of the early twentieth century about Rousseau—
to Lasserre's attack in *Le Romantisme français,* 1907,
which Babbitt himself calls "very drastic" (*RR,* p. 409)—
and to the many writings of Seillière and Maurras. Babbitt's relationship is very close, but still it seems a mistake
to call Babbitt simply an American Brunetière.

Babbitt could not sympathize with the other side
of Brunetière: his evolutionary theory, his attempt to
draw an analogy between literary history and biological
change (see *NL,* p. 215). He did not agree with his return
to the Roman Catholic Church (*SC,* pp. 145–46 and *MC,*
pp. 330, 334), as he had a very different relation to tradition. Babbitt appeals to the wisdom of the ages because
he believes in the stability of human nature and its substantial rightness. He rejects the appeal to "some dogma
or outer authority" (*RR,* xi) and thinks of himself as a
"complete positivist"—positivism meaning here the critical
spirit and a recognition of all parts of human nature,
including the supernatural. Babbitt sees and rejects Brunetière's "naturalistic pessimism" and his "stoic bleakness"
(*MC,* pp. 333, 335).

In spite of all agreement with the antiromantic polemics of the French group around the *Action française,*
Babbitt finally shied away from their authoritarian implications and the political consequences of their arguments.
Though there was a moment in 1924 when Babbitt preferred a hypothetical "American equivalent of a Mussolini" to the "American equivalent of a Lenin" (*DL,* p.
312), he disapproved of the Fascist or proto-Fascist forms
the anti-Romanticism had taken in France. He tells us
in 1909 that "A year or so ago I chanced to be strolling
along one of the narrow streets that skirt the Quartier
Saint-Germain, and came on a bookshop entirely devoted
to reactionary literature; and there in the window, along
with books recommending the restoration of the monarchy, was the volume of M. Lasserre, and other anti-
romantic publications" (*SC,* p. 90). Marcus Selden Gold-
man recalls that, early in 1923 in Paris, he was surprised
to find "how deep-rooted was his [Babbitt's] objection to

the combination of political, religious, and literary aims in a single program like that of *L'Action française*" (*Irving Babbitt: Man and Teacher*, ed. Manchester and Shepard, New York, 1941, p. 235). Babbitt, one must conclude, remained an American Republican and a Protestant, however high may have been his regard for the role of the Roman Church in history, and however far he was from subscribing to any definite Protestant creed.

It will not do to reduce Babbitt to an echo of the French classical tradition. He always looks at it from the outside, welcoming it only as an ally. Something more can, however, be said in favor of seeing Babbitt as a part of the classical revival in English criticism, as a follower of Matthew Arnold. Arnold's early professed classicism, particularly the 1853 Preface to the *Poems*, with its appeal to Aristotle, and Arnold's criticism of the English romantic poets must have shaped Babbitt's outlook significantly. The admiration for Sainte-Beuve and Scherer, though variously motivated, is shared by both. Babbitt's strong interest in Joubert comes from Arnold and his model, Sainte-Beuve. Babbitt's concept of Goethe, which stresses the sage presented by Eckermann, has much in common with Arnold's view. Arnold's idea of culture, *paideia,* whatever its antecedents, and Arnold's ideal of the total man, with his "imaginative reason," were in Babbitt's mind when he formulated his pedagogical aims. The review Babbitt wrote of Stuart Sherman's rather elementary book on Arnold (1917 in *SC*) agrees with Arnold's recommendation of the "saving remnant," his qualitative democracy, but ignores the main issues of literary criticism and makes reservations against Arnold's "hope for poetry" as an eventual substitute for religion. Babbitt objects that Arnold does not rise "far enough above the naturalistic level, which in his case means the stoical level." He misses what he finds in Tennyson, "a suggestion, at least, of the pure supernatural light" (*SC*, p. 56).

This "pure supernatural light"—unimpeded by anything "medieval and narrowly theological" to which Babbitt objected in Pascal (*SC*, p. 88)—was offered to Babbitt most nearly in the tradition of American Transcendentalism. Transcendentalism was all around Babbitt in his youth: at Harvard he knew and admired Charles Eliot Norton, who had known Emerson and Carlyle. Norton, after the publication of *Literature and the American College,* sent the book to Horace H. Furness with a highly approving letter (*Letters,* Boston, 1913, II, 401). But, obviously, Babbitt cannot be described simply as a descendant of the American Transcendentalists, and he can only whimsically be described as a New England Saint. One could even argue that intellectually he represents an extreme revulsion against Transcendentalism. The obvious conflict between Babbitt and his father might support this view. Austin Warren called Edwin D. Babbitt "a physician with a mind open at both ends, a kind of naïve and belated Transcendentalist" (*New England Saints,* Ann Arbor, 1956, p. 144) and surmised that his son considered him a charlatan. Harry Levin described his practice "in the light of hypnotism, spiritualism, phrenology, clairvoyance, massages, sun-baths, electrical treatments, inhabited planets, and utopian socialism." Levin quotes the titles of his pamphlets—*Babbitt's Health Guide, Vital Magnetism, The Fountain of Life,* and *Marriage, with Sexual and Social Up-Building*—in *Irving Babbitt and the Teaching of Literature* (Cambridge, Mass., 1960, p. 13). One is tempted to think that Irving Babbitt rejected everything his father stood for, and even without benefit of Freud one could see Babbitt's early development not only as a "temperamental and intellectual hiatus between father and son" (Warren, p. 145) but as a verbal slaying of the father. But this appearance is deceptive. Austin Warren recognizes that Babbitt did not totally turn away from his father's views, but "retained always a qualified respect for Emerson" (p. 145). The relationship to Emerson is not merely respectful. It is certainly a continuity, even a conscious discipleship, if we think of the Conclusion to *Masters of Modern French Criticism,* in which Emerson is played up as the great counterweight to Sainte-

Beuve, the absolutist against the "doctor of relativity." The ideal critic is envisaged as the synthesis of Sainte-Beuve and Emerson.

No doubt Babbitt disapproved of what he must have considered the degeneracy of Transcendentalism in the facile optimism of Christian Science, the quackery of his father, and even the pragmatism of his formidable colleague, William James, who seemed to him a preacher of drift and flux, of passive surrender to motion, a glorifier of drunkenness—alcoholic and spiritual (*RR*, pp. 183–84). Babbitt is also uninterested in the minor Transcendentalists: he never discusses Thoreau or uses him as an example, though he must have known Lowell's essay on Thoreau with its anti-Rousseauistic points, and though More was deeply interested in Thoreau. But Emerson looms large on Babbitt's horizon: he drew from him not only some of his favorite slogans but, I think, much of his basic scheme of the mind and soul of man. The term "inner check" comes from Emerson, who in turn derived it from Colebrooke's *Essay on the Vedas* (see Warren, p. 162). It had been used before Babbitt emphasized it in *The New Laokoon* (p. 201) by More, but Babbitt, of course, had spoken before of "self-discipline" (*SC*, p. 145), which surely supplements and contrasts with Emerson's "self-reliance." The phrases "law for man" and "law for thing" from Emerson's "Ode: Inscribed to W. H. Channing" provide a key quotation in support of dualism. But, more than such catchwords, Emerson's general enterprise mattered to Babbitt: a reconciliation of the absolute and the relative, of permanence and change, of the One and the Many. Like Emerson, Babbitt assumes some kind of "model" of the human mind, a stratification in which perception is action and manifestation of the will and the individual is transformed into character and finally confronted with the supernatural. Babbitt upholds what could be called abstractly an "intuitive voluntarism." Insight is man's main tool and aim, insight into human nature, which is for Babbitt embodied in tradition, a tradition very similar to the Over-Soul. Babbitt, for instance, praises Emerson as having "a new sense of the unity of human nature—a unity founded, not on tradition, but on insight" (MC, p. 346). He approved of what he considered Emerson's genuinely Socratic interpretation of the idea that "man is the measure of all things," and he uses without irony Emerson's whimsical saying that all the books of the world are the work of "one all-seeing, all-hearing gentleman." "The individual man is the measure of all things only in so far as he has realized in himself this essential human nature" (MC, p. 346), that is, as he has understood the gentleman. Babbitt quotes and endorses Emerson's declaration of trust in the verdict of the ages: "The permanence of all books is fixed by no effort friendly or hostile, but by their own specific gravity or the intrinsic importance of their contents to the constant mind of man" (MC, p. 352). Babbitt thinks that "The oversoul Emerson perceives in his best moments is the true oversoul" (MC, p. 362), a realm, one assumes, of spiritual values and not merely the common soul of all men—an "undersoul" in Babbitt's parody of humanitarian identification. Emerson is called "spiritually perceptive," a "wise man," a "true sage" (MC, pp. 375, 361), because "he aids criticism in its search for inner standards" and "helps it to see in the present anarchy the potentialities of a higher order." Emerson has a "sense of unity" (MC, pp. 391–92), a sense of the absolute which Babbitt defined as "a purely spiritual perception of the light beyond the reason, entirely disassociated from the faith in creeds and formulas" (SC, p. 144). Babbitt sees this as an agreement with Indian philosophy. His own studies of Indian (mainly Buddhist) philosophy could hardly have been undertaken without the initial inspiration of the Orientalism of the American Transcendentalists and Emerson's own lifelong concern with the "Wisdom of the Brahmins."

Here is a central point of agreement, even though it is difficult to determine the precise nature of Babbitt's own "spiritual perception." At times he sounds simply like a Stoic or possibly a Kantian or even a simple Puritan who believes in the voice of conscience, which is, however, not simply an inner light but a superindividual obligation, the voice of tradition. But usually what for Emerson is "moral sense" is in Babbitt conceived of as a negative force, a *"frein vital"* as he punned in contrast to Bergson's *"élan vital."* It is recognition of standards and norms, of a "higher will," where "higher" seems to mean overriding individual desire, not the will of a higher being. Babbitt seems impatient with any attempt to anchor these standards or norms: the fruits of religion are assumed to be available through work, an inner work, an inner discipline whose purpose is inner satisfaction, even personal happiness. But at other times the "inner check" is identified with God and felt as giving access to the supernatural, the divine, the numinous. It is Babbitt's peculiar aim to combine what seems an ethical rigorism, even asceticism and renunciation, with a glimpse, a hesitant intuition of the realm of the divine beyond and above reason. But this combination is also at least one strand of Emerson's thought. Emerson too can be described as aiming at a perception of the law of the universe and of the mind of man through conscience, will, and character; one can also speak of Emerson's glimpses of the supernatural.

Yet Babbitt was strongly aware of his disagreements with Emerson. In all contexts he suspected him of Rousseauism, of undue optimism, unwarranted trust in the goodness of man and particularly of the common man. Babbitt calls him one of the "sycophants of human nature" (*MC*, p. 361). He suspects his "exaltation of genius" (*RR*, p. 67) and is entirely out of sympathy with his concept of "Compensation": he does not believe that spiritual laws parallel physical laws. Babbitt grew up in the atmosphere of mechanistic nineteenth-century science and simply dismissed as "absurd" the many traces in Emerson of *Naturphilosophie* or the even older idea of hieroglyphics of nature. Emerson's fondness for electricity, magnetism, geology, etc., struck him as merely quaint, for he disapproved of the fundamental romantic enterprise in question: the reconciliation of man and nature, the bridging of the gulf between subject and object. We see this in

Babbitt's harsh treatment of Coleridge and Wordsworth, who were, after all, among the most important teachers of Emerson. In these discussions Babbitt's inability, or rather reluctance, to see a poem as an aesthetic totality or, alternatively, as the expression of an assumed *persona* in a momentary mood leads him into disturbingly literal interpretations and interrogations. "One impulse from a vernal wood" is taken as a statement prescriptive for all mankind, as is Emerson's "The Humble-Bee," "Wiser far than human seer, / Yellow-breeched philosopher" (*BC*, p. 76). Babbitt charges Coleridge—alluding to the water-snakes in *The Ancient Mariner*—with obtaining "subrationally and unconsciously ('I blessed them *unaware*') the equivalent of Christian charity" (*BC*, p. 120). The same could be said, with more justice, of Emerson.

I realize that interpretations of Emerson diverge widely, that in recent years attempts have been made to "modernize" him. I will allude only to Stephen Whicher's *Freedom and Fate* (Philadelphia, 1953), which emphasizes the later, more "scientific" Emerson or the recent book of Jonathan Bishop, *Emerson on the Soul* (Cambridge, Mass., 1964), which rightly reverts to the early Emerson and expounds his doctrine of the gradations of the soul sympathetically. Mr. Bishop even tries to assimilate Emerson's moral sense to a socially derived rule or norm (p. 70). But I believe that such attempts can succeed only partially and that Babbitt and these recent expounders of Emerson mistake the main tenor of Emerson's philosophy. In my reading Emerson should be interpreted as a symbolist and a complete monist. Certainly, art is drawn completely into a monistic world view, in which it functions as a language of ciphers revealing in fluid transformations the essence of a nature that is divine and good and luminously beautiful. The poet is exalted as genius and prophet. In his identification of beauty, goodness, and truth, of the act of vision and creation with the act of reception, all attention is focused on what seems to him the one indispensable thing: the web of convertible symbols, the rhetoric of metamorphosis speaking of the divinity of nature and

Irving Babbitt and Paul More

man. One can believe the story reported by Warner G. Rice that late in his life Babbitt showed no interest in a newly acquired set of Emerson's *Works.* "Rereadings of Emerson had proved disappointing. The driving force of the man was an expansive—and really a shallow—optimism. He had lost himself in a mystical-transcendental mist, where it was impossible to follow him" (*Irving Babbitt: Man and Teacher,* p. 258). I would dissent from the value judgment but find it natural that Babbitt could not ultimately sympathize with Emerson's symbolic view of the world: he had himself nothing of the fervently mystical, whimsical tone of Emerson's mind. He did not share the same intellectual ancestry in the Neo-Platonists, Greek and English, Swedenborg, and the Swedenborgians. Babbitt simply did not understand the symbolic view of the world. He could not have made anything of Emerson's saying, "Every solid in the universe is ready to become fluid on the approach of the mind" (*Complete Works,* VI, 43).

An understanding of this view seems to me precisely the quality of More's mind. More said himself that in his youth he was "steeped in the rankest romantic literature of Germany" (Dakin, p. 313) and the essay on "Thoreau's Journal" (*SE,* V, 106–31) shows More's first-hand acquaintance with Fichte, Schelling, Novalis, Friedrich Schlegel and particularly with Schleiermacher's *Reden über Religion.* At that time (1908) he had long ago reacted against this early Romanticism. He criticizes the German Romantics largely in terms of a contrast between their *Gemüth* and the New England character or conscience. More in his earnestness seems often to misunderstand the Germans' romantic irony and the polemical context and terminology in which they were writing, but he shows a far more correct and more sympathetic understanding of the romantic tradition, and hence also of Emerson, than Babbitt does. More, speaking in later years of his intellectual development, said extravagantly that he had "changed as often as a chameleon" (Dakin, p. 323). The set of the *Shelburne Essays* gives him "the impression of a mind groping about

[*197*]

and not knowing whither it is bound. The field is too wide and the effect scattered. I seem not to be one intelligence but an unassimilated bundle of impulses and curiosities" (Dakin, p. 371). This may have seemed so to More from the vantage point of his final position, and is supported by the diversity of the topics handled in the *Shelburne Essays,* but it seems unjust to the coherence of the mind approaching all this variety of literature and thought. This is particularly true of More's view of the American tradition, which was recently traced perceptively by Daniel Aaron in the Introduction to his collection of *Shelburne Essays on American Literature* (New York, 1963). More's striking emphasis on what has been called "the power of blackness" in American literature, the "gloom, that habitual dwelling on the supernatural significance of life" as the "dominant intellectual tone of the country" (*SE*, I, 64), the emphasis on the continuity from the earliest New England versifiers through Jonathan Edwards to the Transcendentalists—all this shows an understanding of the American tradition which seems to me absent in Babbitt. The work of Emerson's generation is lauded by More as the highest and most homogeneous culture this country has yet produced (*SE*, XI, 105) in a sweeping commendation which—somewhat uncritically—extends even to Whittier, Longfellow, and Lowell. More had first been impressed by Emerson's essay on "Fate" in 1894. It "contains, he said, such 'wisdom and morality and power and consolation' that 'all the prophets and seers of the world' could hardly surpass it" (Francis X. Duggan quoting a letter in *American Literature*, XXXIV, 1963, 554). In the formal essay on Emerson, which comes as late as 1921, the judgment is hardly changed. Emerson "is the outstanding figure of American letters" (*SE*, XI, 69). His position is not incorrectly described as "romanticism rooted in Puritan divinity" (*SE*, XI, 83) and his philosophy as a "kind of vanishing dualism" (*SE*, XI, 87). Years before in the first volume of the *Shelburne Essays* (1904) More had rightly objected, in the essay "The Influence of Emerson," to the view that Emerson is self-contradictory and incoherent.

"His essays ripple and recoil on the surface, but underneath there is a current setting steadily to one point" (*SE*, I, 73).

More goes to great lengths to assert the unity of the American tradition. He sees its roots in the England of the seventeenth century: "out of it grew the intellectual life of our nation, and even to-day the poverty of our art and literature is partly due to the fact that our strongest colonists brought with them only one faction of the endless feud" (*SE*, I, 203) between truth and beauty, the Reformation and the Renaissance. The continuity of American literature includes also Poe, who appears as a kind of brother to Hawthorne. Hawthorne's and Poe's vision of evil, with its awe and terror, is—somewhat too easily if we think of E.T.A. Hoffmann and certain parts of Jean Paul—contrasted with the pleasant *Waldeinsamkeit* of the Germans, with the "forgotten weavers of moonlight and mysticism" (*SE*, I, 52, 57). Puritanism, in the teaching of Jonathan Edwards, gave "an extravagant sense of individual existence" (*SE*, I, 48) to the New England man and thus prepared for the utter solitude of Hawthorne. He had lost the Christian faith, and "overwhelming superstition" had changed into "shadowy haunting symbolism" (*SE*, I, 65). More quotes Hawthorne: " 'We are but shadows, and all that seems most real about us is but the thinnest substance of a dream,—till the heart be touched. That touch creates us,—then we begin to be,—thereby we are beings of reality and inheritors of eternity' " (*SE*, I, 34). Here More, through a quotation, formulates best his own basic experience, the illusion of the world and the ethical substance in man. This is also the main topic of the essays on Thoreau. Criticizing Santayana, More states bluntly that "no great poem was ever composed whose author did not have . . . faith in the reality of the ideal world" (*Harvard Graduates' Magazine*, IX, 1900, 21), and late in life he speaks of "all worthy art" as "mystical initiation" (*The Catholic Faith*, 1931, p. 215).

A close examination of More's many essays on English literature would confirm this conclusion, though More's interest in English literature was too diversified to be so clearly confined to this symbolist (in the old sense) tradition. He wrote much on eighteenth-century wits, on poets such as Crabbe and on Victorian novelists such as Gissing. But his deepest concern is, after all, with such figures as George Herbert and Henry Vaughan, whom he prefers to Thoreau, because "he never cut himself off from the Church and the State, but moved in the greater currents of tradition" (SE, V, 131), and Sir Thomas Browne, whom he commends for his "religious imagination . . . the faculty, that is, by which we unite the broken and dispersed images of the world into an harmonious poetic symbol" (SE, VI, 167). The Victorian writers who resume this spiritual tradition find his fervent approval: Tennyson for the vision in "The Holy Grail," which is "nothing else but a sudden and blinding sense of that dualism of the world and of the human soul beneath which the solid-seeming earth reels and dissolves away" (SE, VII, 90), and the now forgotten Richard S. Hawker, the vicar of Morwenstow (whom Tennyson visited in Cornwall) for his poem, another "Holy Grail," which More considers "the most purely spiritual poem in the language" (SE, IV, 33). The interest in Shorthouse's historical romance *John Inglesant* falls into the pattern and so does the admiration for the very different Carlyle, whose sense of the world's illusion makes him at once a "Hindu seer" and a "Hebrew prophet" (SE, I, 98, 101). The essay on Newman, which disapproves so strongly of his conversion as to speak of "failure in duty, a betrayal of the will" (SE, VIII, 77), starts with Newman's illusionism, quoting a very early letter, from 1828: " 'What a veil and curtain this world of sense is! beautiful but still a veil' " (SE, VIII, 45).

Even when More rejects an author he has the standard of a spiritual symbolism in mind. Browning's "theory of love," he says, for instance, "does not expand like Dante's into a great vision of life wherein symbol and reality are fused together" (SE, III, 160–61), while Arthur Symons' illusion, although attractive to More as any sense of illusion, seems to him a false illusion and a false dis-

illusion (*SE*, I, 127). More treats Walter Pater with un-
usual harshness, because he sees him as a hedonist ending
in "weariness, and satiety, and impotence" (*SE*, VIII, 114).
He must disapprove of Pater's interpretation of Plato and
consider *Marius the Epicurean* as "only another manifestation of that aestheticism which Pater sucked from the
romantic school of his century and disguised in the
phraseology of ancient faith" (*SE*, VIII, 96). But More
acknowledges that in the past "I could not dissociate his
Epicureanism from the intellectual and moral dissolution
which from the beginning had been so insidiously at work
in the romantic school, and from which, as I thought, I had
myself so barely escaped" (*SE*, VIII, 83). One feels that he
still senses the danger and wants to ward it off even at the
price of injustice. It seems to me false to say that "Pater
was in no proper sense of the word a critic" (*SE*, VIII, 99)
and to see him purely as the spiritual father of Oscar
Wilde and decadent aestheticism (cf. the chapter on Pater
in my *History of Modern Criticism*, Vol. IV, New Haven,
1965).

There are serious shortcomings in More's critical
writings: a certain tone of smugness and extreme "delic-
acy" in sexual matters most offends us today, but these
seem minor blemishes in what after all are collections of
occasional essays, often extended book reviews, which
achieve as a whole a definition of a specific taste and a
spiritual position. *Shelburne Essays* can easily be seen as
preparation for the later studies in the Platonic tradition,
which for More revives in seventeenth-century England in
the appealing figures of the Cambridge Platonists. He
praises them in reference to Newman because "these earlier theologians, notwithstanding their apparent dogmatism, were in reality akin to the mystics of all ages who
find their peace in a faith that needs no surrender [of their
mental integrity]" (*SE*, VIII, 76). On two occasions when
I called on Mr. More in Princeton in 1929, he lent me, I
remember, the *Sermons* of John Smith and *The Candle of
the Lord* by Nathaniel Calderwell. He was a Neo-Platonist
steeped in the symbolic tradition out of which Emerson

also grew. Babbitt could not have had a taste for this kind of rarefied spirituality. All his criticism shows that he rejected the symbolic view of the world, that he was a moralist who, ultimately, appealed to an immediate perception of supernatural truth.

Thus, we may conclude with a contrast in the relations of the two men to Emerson. More was a better reader of Emerson, as he was reared in the symbolist tradition of German romanticism and its Neo-Platonic ancestry; Babbitt, who was temperamentally and by education a classicist and even a rationalist, still felt the need of the "pure supernatural light" that he recognized in Transcendentalism but was unable to accept fully its implications. Babbitt's relation to Emerson remained ambiguous, but paradoxically More depended less on Emerson and took less from him than did Babbitt.

I realize that the method used in these reflections is substantially that of the history of ideas, a method of confrontations, of inquiring into sympathies and antipathies, placing a writer in relation to the large currents or the great figures of history. Inevitably, as Jonathan Bishop recently warned in regard to Emerson, the method can involve "an unconscious condescension, a diminishing of the object observed" (*Emerson on the Soul*, p. 3). The effect is a flattening out, a black and white technique. We must always keep in mind that a full characterization would want to add the third dimension and the colors. Jakob Grimm, the founder of Germanic philology, said wisely: "Der Gott ist im Detail." Only the details of Babbitt's and More's writings, the density of their quotations, the sharpness of their epigrams, can restore them to life. Critics—like poems—cannot be paraphrased.

NOTES

1. I refer to the original editions of Babbitt's writings as *BC: On Being Creative and Other Essays* (Boston, 1932); *DL: Democracy and Leadership* (Boston, 1924); *LC: Literature and the American College* (Boston, 1908); *MC: The Masters of Modern French Criticism* (Boston, 1912); *NL: The New Laokoon* (Boston, 1910); *RR: Rousseau and Romanticism* (Boston, 1919); and *SC: Spanish Character and Other Essays* (Boston, 1940).

More's *Shelburne Essays,* 11 volumes (Boston, 1904–21) are quoted as *SE;* and *New Shelburne Essays,* 3 volumes (Princeton, 1928–36); as *NSE.*

Eugene O'Neill, the Orient, and American Transcendentalism

By Frederic I. Carpenter

In this essay I shall not attempt to define Eugene O'Neill's "transcendentalism." Instead, I shall trace his attitude toward the historic American Transcendentalists, especially Thoreau. And I shall relate this to his life-long interest in the Orient—an interest which he shared with the earlier Transcendentalists. In one sense O'Neill was more of an Orientalist than Emerson or Thoreau had ever been.

I

Toward the American Transcendentalists, O'Neill's feelings were often ambivalent. The mixture of admiration and irony with which he regarded them suggests one of the many paradoxes of his nature. Whether he reacted as a member of the younger generation toward the literary tastes of his father, or as the son of an Irish immigrant toward the social idealism of an earlier New England, his feelings were mixed. The Transcendentalists had been rebels against the materialism of their times, but their idealism had also been the product of a Yankee and Puritan society.

In the New London house of James O'Neill, Sr., Emerson's books had been available on the library shelves, and the young Eugene probably read them there.[1] He later put some of the mysticism of Emerson's "Brahma" into the mouth of his own Lazarus, who proclaimed: "We are the Giver and the Gift!" But it is probable that he derived most of this "transcendentalism" from his favorite author, Nietzsche, whose "Zarathustra" had earlier been inspired by Emerson.

More ironically, O'Neill remembered the older Transcendentalism when he bought a country house at Ridgefield, Connecticut, named "Brook Farm," and composed there his famous *Desire Under the Elms*. The contrast of the naturalism of the modern play with the earlier idealism seems obvious; yet, more subtly, this modern *Desire* also translated the earlier irony suggested by the "Spirit of Nature" in Emerson's "Hamatreya": " 'Mine, not yours. / Earth endures.' " Both in the play and in the earlier poem, the true hero is Nature, who brings tragedy equally to the desires of the Cabots, and to the possessiveness of "Bulkeley, Hunt, Willard, Hosmer, Meriam, Flint."

As O'Neill grew older, his theme of possessiveness seemed to become increasingly obsessive, and gradually the idea of a cycle of plays about American history developed in his mind. The title should be: "A Tale of Possessors Self-Dispossessed." And the ironic contrast between his later pessimism and his earlier idealism was sharpened by the borrowing of a title from Oliver Wendell Holmes' "The Chambered Nautilus"—"Build thee more stately mansions, O my soul." Emphasizing only the materialistic drive of modern American civilization, O'Neill now sought to dramatize its continuing struggle to build "More Stately Mansions."

This contrast between an earlier idealism and a later pessimism is emphasized even more sharply by O'Neill's changing attitudes toward Thoreau. In *Lazarus Laughed* he had made his hero paraphrase Thoreau, in replying to the question: "What did you find beyond there, Lazarus?" Replying to a similar question on his death-bed, Thoreau is reported to have said: "One world at a time." Now Lazarus replies. "Is not one world in which you know not how to live enough for you?"

But after dramatizing the mystical idealism of Lazarus

in transcendental terms, O'Neill seems to have become increasingly skeptical of the practical aspects of Thoreau's Transcendentalism. And when he began work on his ambitious new "Cycle," which, he hoped, would progressively dramatize "the story of America," he imagined a strikingly Thoreauvian character as the founder of his projected "Irish-American family." But he imagined Simon Harford, the Thoreauvian hermit, as a disillusioned idealist, in process of abandoning his romantic and poetic dreams of "living the simple life" beside his pond. And now Simon's unillusioned mother, Deborah Harford, observes ironically to her future Irish daughter-in-law, Sara Melody, that: "evidently he has found a new romantic dream by way of recompense." *A Touch of the Poet* centers upon the hero's abandonment of his earlier "transcendental dream," for a "new romantic dream," which gradually turns into the wholly "material dream" of amassing a fortune and building "more stately mansions."

That Simon Harford, the "hero" of *A Touch of the Poet* and of *More Stately Mansions,* was partly modeled after the historic Thoreau, seems self-evident. But a recent article by Professor Mordecai Marcus[2] has argued that Deborah Harford, his mother, was also suggested by Thoreau's mother (who was not always too happy about her son's Transcendental individualism), and that Cornelius Melody, the Irish father-in-law, was himself suggested by an Irish tavern-keeper described vividly in Thoreau's *Journal*—a romantic but disreputable character who had known better days. O'Neill had pretty certainly been reading Thoreau's *Journal* while planning his famous "Cycle." But the remarkable fact is that he should have changed the character of his Thoreauvian hermit so radically. For the historic Thoreau, of course, had never been seduced by any conventionally romantic entanglement, and had never capitulated to American "materialism."

An explanation of O'Neill's distortion of the character of his hermit in *A Touch of the Poet* is suggested by Deborah Harford's repeated use of the word "dream" to describe her son's deluded idealism. His dream, like his father's and his grandfather's before him, was "fanatic" and Byronic. "I cannot imagine you taking that seriously," Deborah exclaims. Therefore, because it was wholly illusory, it soon became a "romantic dream," and then a "material dream." In an interview reported by Hamilton Basso about this time, O'Neill explained: "We talk about the American Dream, and want to tell the world about the American Dream, but what is that dream, in most cases, but the dream of material things? I sometimes think that the United States, for this reason, is the greatest failure the world has ever seen."[3] In other words, O'Neill believed that Thoreau's American Dream had been essentially a "pipe dream," like the delusions of the denizens of Harry Hope's saloon in *The Iceman Cometh*. It was a delusion whose failure inevitably led to "the dream of material things."

To O'Neill's mind, therefore, the failure of Thoreau's dream of "saving our souls by being content with little," led inevitably toward the symbolic disillusion of "Hope" in *The Iceman*. Historically, Emerson, Thoreau, and the Transcendentalists had all imaged the future realization of "the American Dream" in history. But now O'Neill dramatized the later disillusion of "the modern temper." And it seems that his later pessimism expressed his own progressive disillusion.

Nevertheless, it can be argued that O'Neill's denial of "Hope," and his rejection of Thoreau's "American Dream," should not be interpreted merely as "disillusion." His modern pessimism gave expression to another aspect of the historic Transcendental philosophy, and even suggested echoes of Emerson's own "Illusions." O'Neill's emphasis on the necessary defeat of all human illusions merely repeated the ancient Oriental philosophy which Emerson and Thoreau had also shared. But where the historic Transcendentalists had interpreted Oriental idealism in terms of pragmatic action, O'Neill rejected their pragmatism in favor of an older quietism. His disagreement with the American Transcendentalists lay in his total rejection of the American philosophy of pragmatism, and in his acceptance of a purer Orientalism.

II

O'Neill's Orientalism is—I think—the most important and distinctive aspect of his art, and yet the most difficult to define. I have tried to suggest its effect upon his dramas in a recent book.[4] This essay will describe the more specific evidences of his interest in the Orient and its philosophy.

From the beginning his dramas expressed a compelling—if often vague—fascination with the Orient. The hero of his first full-length play to be produced—Andrew Mayo in *Beyond the Horizon*—emphatically proclaimed his idealization of "the beauty of the far off and unknown, the mystery and spell of the East which lures me in the books I've read." And the later hero of *The Fountain*, Ponce de Leon, also described his mythical quest for "some far country of the East—Cathay, Cipango, who knows—a spot that Nature has set apart from men and blessed with peace."

At the height of his career, however, O'Neill wrote two dramas to describe more fully the meeting of East and West. And both used Eastern philosophy to comment upon the materialism of the West. In *Marco Millions* the hero travels through Persia and India to confront "the Great Kaan" of China. Then, after Marco has made his "millions" and departed, leaving tragedy behind him, the priests of the four great religions of the East seek to console the Great Kaan. Buddhism, Taoism, Confucianism, and Islam offer their wisdom in turn. But the medieval "Babbitt" from the West has proved too much for them.

Following *Marco Millions*, O'Neill wrote his most ambitious—and most imaginative—drama of ideas. In *Lazarus Laughed* he dramatized what he believed the essential message of all religions. His ideal Lazarus strove to realize the gospel of the resurrected Christ, and, in the second scene, visited Greece to suggest the similarity of his gospel to that of the Greek god Dionysus. But then, more subtly, he went on to identify his message with that of the religions of the Orient. In the third act, the Emperor Tiberius has crucified an Asiatic lion, adding the scornful comment: "From the East, land of false gods and superstition, this lion was brought to Rome to amuse Caesar." Now Lazarus befriends the lion, which licks his hand as a sign of sympathy. In an article on *"Lazarus Laughed* and Buddha"[5] Doris Alexander has shown that this action repeats a pattern common to Buddhist legend, and has suggested many parallels between the story of Lazarus and the legends and teachings of Buddhism.

In *Lazarus Laughed,* indeed, O'Neill may be said to have defined his Orientalism in terms of dramatic action. Because he explicitly compared his Lazarus to the Greek Dionysus, and because he always avowed his enthusiasm for Nietzsche's *Thus Spake Zarathustra* and *The Birth of Tragedy,* Lazarus has sometimes been said to preach the Nietzschean gospel of the superman. Yet O'Neill's Lazarus was no Occidental superman, performing victorious acts of the will. Rather, he became an Oriental superman, whose triumph was that he refused to act in opposition to evil. And his greatest triumph came when he refused to act to prevent the death of his wife, Miriam, at the hands of the Romans. His final victory was an inner victory over his own selfish attachment to life.

Not only *Marco Millions* and *Lazarus Laughed,* but all of O'Neill's dramas of this period show evidences of his interest in Oriental ideas. *The Great God Brown,* for instance, described Cybel with humorous incongruity: "She chews gum like a sacred cow forgetting time with an eternal end." And Dion Anthony remarked: "One must do something to pass away the time while one is waiting— for one's next incarnation." Similarly, the giant "Dynamo," which gives its name to the following play, is described as having "oil switches . . . their six cupped arms stretching upward . . . like queer Hindu idols tortured into scientific supplications."

In 1930, after having studied Emerson's reading and interpretation of Oriental ideas, I called attention to O'Neill's apparent Orientalism in the last chapter of a book on *Emerson and Asia*. And in 1932 I wrote to ask information of O'Neill. On June 24, 1932, he replied from Sea Island, Georgia:

> As for your question regarding Oriental ideas, I do not think they have influenced my plays at all. Certainly, not consciously. Many years ago I did considerable reading in Oriental philosophy and religion, however, although I never went in for an intensive study of it. I simply did it in order to have some sort of grasp of the subject as part of my philosophical background. The mysticism of Lao-tse and Chuang-Tzu probably interested me more than any other Oriental writing.[6]

O'Neill's emphatic disclaimer, asserting flatly that "I do not think Oriental ideas have influenced my plays at all," obviously must be discounted. Not only do his later remarks in this letter qualify it, but similar disclaimers of his suggest that he tended to minimize any "influences" from other authors or ideas, in order to assert his own creative originality. In discussing his debt to Freud and Jung, for instance, he made a similar disclaimer in a letter to Martha Sparrow.[7] Nevertheless, it is probable that he read Oriental literature less intensively—and less extensively—than might be supposed.

The original source of O'Neill's Orientalism has recently been discovered by Doris Alexander.[8] And this source was not so much literary as personal. A close friend of O'Neill's early days at "The Hell Hole" was Terry Carlin, an alcoholic philosopher who loved to discourse on the wisdom of the Orient to all who would listen. A worshiper of Dionysus both in practice and in theory, he also introduced the young O'Neill to a book of mystical theosophy entitled *Light on the Path*. And from this subliterary book, proclaimed by this hobo philosopher, O'Neill first learned of the Orient and its ideas.

Later, in 1928, after writing *Lazarus Laughed* and

Marco Millions, O'Neill left America on a voyage to the Orient. In the actual Orient, however, he found only disillusion with the desperate poverty and squalor which he saw; and in Shanghai he went on one last, desperate, alcoholic binge, which ended in a hospital. Cathay, the country of his early dreams, apparently destroyed his last illusions.

And yet, eight years later, when the O'Neills moved to California and built a new house there, they named it "Tao House." And the name invoked again the old mystical religion of Lao-tse, which he had read more than a decade before. Certain features of the house and grounds suggested Chinese ideas and superstitions: the garden paths, for instance, were laid in zigzags, remembering an old Chinese superstition that evil spirits could only travel in straight lines. And yet there is no evidence to support the assertion of Croswell Bowen that "Eugene O'Neill, like so many people who settle in the San Francisco area, quite suddenly took up Oriental philosophy."[9] Rather the opposite. The name of "Tao House" merely reaffirmed O'Neill's old fascination with Oriental ideas. Even his disillusion with the actual Orient could not destroy his life-long faith in Oriental mysticism.

III

The facts of O'Neill's lifelong interest in the Orient point toward some important conclusions. His Orientalism was much less literary than was Emerson's. It was more personal in origin, and more temperamental in expression. Moreover, it was much less concerned with facts and with actions, and it was more concerned with internal feelings and attitudes. But for this very reason, O'Neill's Orientalism seems more genuinely "Oriental" than Emerson's. For the Orient has always been less concerned with facts, and more concerned with internal feelings, than has the Occident.

O'Neill's lack of concern with the external realities of science and social action, and, indeed, his very hostility toward "material things," seems to set him apart from the mainstream of American literature and thought. It also helps to explain his differences with the historic American Transcendentalists. Although Emerson and Thoreau believed that "Things are in the saddle, / And ride mankind," they never scorned material things. Rather, they sought to ameliorate the actual situation, and they appealed to the future. But O'Neill disbelieved in the future, and in "Hope." He considered tragedy to be essential to the nature of things. Yet this belief made him, in a sense, even more "transcendental" than Emerson.

Historic Transcendentalism has, in fact, divided into two streams. The first has become active, scientific, and pragmatic. The second has become passive, mystical, and psychological. Emerson's thought flowed largely in the first stream, toward modern pragmatism. O'Neill's thought tended towards modern, nonrational psychology.

Early in his career, O'Neill had explained the general principles which were to guide his whole theory and practice of playwriting. "Our emotions are a better guide than our thoughts," he asserted in 1922. "Our emotions are instinctive. They are the result not only of our individual experiences but of the experiences of the whole human race, back through all the ages."[10] Like modern depth psychology, O'Neill's dramas always probed man's emotions, rather than his thoughts and actions.

Yet, in a sense, both O'Neill's dramas and modern depth psychology were melioristic, and "hopeful." In another statement made in 1922, O'Neill explained: "It seems to me that . . . man is much the same creature, with the same primal emotions and ambitions and motives, the same powers and the same weaknesses, as in the time when the Aryan race started toward Europe from the slopes of the Himalayas. He has become better acquainted with those powers and those weaknesses, and he is learning ever so slowly how to control them."[11] O'Neill's tragic dramas were directed toward the understanding of man's "primal emotions," rather than his pragmatic actions. This goal resembled that of the Oriental religion which originated on "the slopes of the Himalayas." Thus, O'Neill clung to one, last, melioristic illusion. He hoped that man, by means of the insight into human emotions suggested by tragic drama, might ultimately learn to "know himself," and through knowledge, "ever so slowly," control.

NOTES

1. Arthur and Barbara Gelb, *O'Neill* (New York, 1962), pp. 84, 88.

2. Mordecai Marcus, "Eugene O'Neill's Debt to Thoreau in *A Touch of the Poet,*" *JEGP,* LXII (April 1963), 270–79.

3. Hamilton Basso, "The Tragic Sense," *The New Yorker,* XXIV (March 13, 1948), 37–40.

4. Frederic I. Carpenter, *Eugene O'Neill* (New York, 1964).

5. Doris M. Alexander, "*Lazarus Laughed* and Buddha," *Modern Language Quarterly,* XVII (Dec. 1956), 357–65.

6. From a holograph letter to F. I. Carpenter. Quoted by permission.

7. Quoted in an article by Arthur H. Nethercot, "The Psychoanalyzing of Eugene O'Neill," *Modern Drama,* III (Dec. 1960), 242–56.

8. Doris M. Alexander, "Eugene O'Neill and *Light on the Path,*" *Modern Drama,* III (Dec. 1960), 260–67.

9. Croswell Bowen, *The Curse of the Misbegotten* (New York, 1959), p. 259.

10. Mary B. Mullett, "The Extraordinary Story of Eugene O'Neill," *American Magazine,* XCIV (Nov. 1922), 34, 112–20.

11. Oliver M. Sayler, "The Real Eugene O'Neill," *The Century Magazine,* CIII (Jan. 1922), 351–59.

American Transcendentalism's Escape From Phenomenology

By Herbert W. Schneider

I WISH TO RECONSIDER a question raised by George Santayana in 1911: "Have there been ... any successful efforts to escape from the genteel tradition, and to express something worth expressing behind its back?[1] Now that Santayana himself belongs to the genteel tradition it may be an appropriate time to make a reexamination of American escape mechanisms from Transcendentalism. It has now become evident that Santayana preferred the traditional modes of escape: a physical escape to Europe and an intellectual escape to phenomenology.[2] He hardened his spirit gradually to the bracketing of existence and to playing with essences. That he was tempted to do this even before he made his escape is clear from his own confession, made in the context of his famous California lecture, in which he raised the question of escape:

> As a method I regard it [Transcendentalism] as correct and, when once suggested, unforgettable. I regard it as the chief contribution made in modern times to speculation. But it is a method only, an attitude we may always assume if we like and that will always be legitimate. It is no answer, and involves no particular answer, to the question: What exists ... ?[3]

Increasingly, existence offered to Santayana "little digestible material" and in this lecture he read his starved attitude back into Emerson and New England Transcendentalism:

> The three American writers whose personal endowment was perhaps the finest—Poe, Hawthorne, and Emerson—had all a certain starved and abstract quality. They could not retail the genteel tradition. . . . life offered them little digestible material, nor were they naturally voracious. They were fastidious, and under the circumstances they were starved.[4]

He charged them with what later became a habit with him: they were "employed on a sort of inner play, or digestion of vacancy." This notion, that there is a void in the center of the American soul, has been made a stereotype of American culture by Europeans, notably by Jaspers and his disciples. It may serve a useful purpose to try to explain how the Americans have filled this phenomenological void, which may well continue to seem empty to those who still labor in the genteel tradition, but which takes on a different quality in the context of European existentialism.[5] It is now possible to present the trends in and after New England Transcendentalism as a Yankee straight and narrow path from idealism to existential habits of mind, which evades the agonies of the tortuous ways of phenomenology. In the long pages of European history, to say nothing of human evolution in general, this short story tells of a revolutionary transformation in the theory of human existence. As lived in America, however, it is the commonplace of daily experience; existentialist mentality is here not an ideology of crisis but a banality of progress. It is expressed less in philosophy and art than in the behavioral sciences, in politics, and in secularized religion. There was a genuine crisis in the middle of the nineteenth century which still afflicts the American conscience; but now, on the whole, existential thinking is definitely postrevolutionary and conventional. Having stated this theme, I am not inclined to embellish it with a series of historical variations which are too familiar to need repeating. I shall merely call attention to a few traits in American philosophical thinking which bear witness to this transformation of Transcendentalist faith into existential sciences and which may explain the absence of existentialism as a brand of philosophy, despite the prevalence of existential categories and modes of thought.

After a generation or two of pilgrimage in the wilderness of New England, our pioneers began to feel at home in the land of "the free and . . . the brave," and what began as an escape mechanism at Plymouth became a vast experiment in continental appropriation. The brave "new world" turned out to be a corollary of "the expansion of Europe." Within the short span of three centuries European exiles converted virgin forests into a comfortable home for an industrious, industrial, international community of European nationals. Under these circumstances the sharp dualism between nature and culture, between the external world of objects and the subjective world of mind, which these migrants brought with them and to which they had given a new, vigorous expression in early New England Puritanism, ceased to haunt their imaginations and theologies. In their new home "the free" and "the brave" lost the romantic form of these virtues and settled down in habits of liberty and courage to build vast enterprises of agriculture and industry, of slavery and democracy. In the American culture which has thus emerged, the European exiles have learned to look upon their natural resources and their cultural institutions as partners in a single environment; they have become accustomed and acculturated to an existential ambiguity which "comes natural" to them, but which in the European idealistic and phenomenalistic tradition appears to be "absurd" and unintelligible.

Ralph Waldo Emerson is the classic example of this philosophy. His interpretation of what he ambiguously called "Nature" was not a world of external objects but a world to be appropriated. Superficially, he may appear to be a perfect specimen of transcendental phenomenology, especially when he professes to become "a transparent eye-ball." But on closer examination one understands that his conception of the ego, though central, is not transcendental. It is the empirical focus of the world of intentions and final causes. His seeing of all things in personal perspective is not a mental structure that is imposed on an alien world; it is a thoroughly practical philosophy, the ideology of Emerson's self-reliance. His building of his own world in poetic imagination is at the same time his practical appropriation of the real world. He is not interested in the formal essence of objects; he is intent on the world's meaning for him. "To what end is nature?" Natural ends exist for any natural creature that can implement them by "discipline" for his own existence. "For you is the phenomenon perfect." This applies to any "you" and is the ultimate context for any humanly intelligible natural order. The whole effort of such an analysis of the world aims at making the individual at home in the world, well-disciplined for both thought and action, or rather for a type of reflection that integrates existential and mental relations.

From this point of view Walt Whitman's *Song of Myself* is merely an extension of Emersonian world-appropriation. To be sure, his "leaves of grass" were less genteel than Emerson's personal idealism, and he took the satisfactions of sense-experience more seriously (or at least more naturally) than did the New England Transcendentalists; but the "ego-centric predicament" and perspective obviously dominated, and were represented as inevitably natural and biological. It is significant that European existentialists like Nietzsche found in both Emerson and Whitman prophets for their revolt; whereas in the American tradition they represent the complacent wing of New England individualism.

Turning to the tragic exploration of man's situation in the world, we come at once upon Herman Melville, whose existentialism is closer to that of the twentieth-century Europe. These rebels from society, Thoreau and Melville, were not rebels against nature; on the contrary, they took respectively to the woods and to the sea as to their natural residences. The explorations of the actual world and its ambiguities were couched not as free judgments upon an alien or external world, but as the immediate environment of the human spirit and body. This world, which to Emerson and Whitman was full of infinite significance ("Whoever you are, to you endless announcements!"), was to Melville utterly unintelligible. It could not be "realized" rationally or imaginatively; it must be faced, accepted, lived with as brute fact and moral destiny.

> But let us not give ear to the superstitious, gundeck gossip about whither we may be gliding, for, as yet, not a soul on board of us knows—not even the commodore himself: assuredly not the chaplain; even our professor's scientific surmisings are vain.... And believe not the hypochondriac dwellers below hatches, who will tell you, with a sneer, that our world-frigate is bound to no final harbor whatever.... For how can this world-frigate prove our eventual abiding place, when, upon our first embarkation, as infants in arms, her violent rolling—in after life unperceived—makes every soul of us sea-sick?
>
> . . . .
>
> Yet the worst of our evils we blindly inflict upon ourselves.... From the last ills no being can save another; therein each man must be his own saviour. For the rest ... let us not mutiny....[6]

It is not necessary to point out the similarity of this expression of nausea and absurdity to Sartre's existentialism. But it is important to note the contrast between Melville's consciousness of being caught in "a moving world" and the phenomenologist's stance of observing objective essences from the standpoint of a transcendental ego.[7]

This blind faith or sheer will, inherited from both New England and Schopenhauer, led another American idealist and tragedian, Edwin Arlington Robinson, to interpret man's energies and animal intelligence as the substance of man's existence, enabling man to stand against the sky, his existence dominating his essence. To Robinson this did not mean a surrender to materialism, which he despised and feared, but an assertion of the moral will. It enabled him to endure the degradations of human culture and institutions, and also to enjoy with sardonic humor, rather than pity, his poetry of scorn and condemnation. He referred to this attitude as the survival of his "New England conscience."

Now that "E. A. R." is coming to be regarded as a fine monument to an antiquated philosophy, Victorian romantic pessimism, it may be worthwhile to call attention to the following self-portrait, expressed in very plain language which even the present generation understands, since the language bears a close resemblance to the contemporary European existentialist emphasis on anxiety, care, and crisis.

> We have acquired a great deal of material knowledge in recent years, but so far as knowledge of the truth itself is concerned, I cannot see that we are any nearer to it now than our less imaginative ancestors were when they cracked each others' skulls with stone hatchets, or that we know any more than they knew of what happened to the soul that escaped in the process. ... If a man is a materialist, or a mechanist, or whatever he likes to call himself, I can see for him no escape from belief in a futility so prolonged and complicated and diabolical and preposterous as to be worse than absurd; and as I do not know that such a tragic absurdity is not a fact, I can only know my native inability to believe that it is one. ... If life is only what it appears to be, no amount of improvement or enlightenment will ever compensate or atone for what it has inflicted and endured in ages past, or for what it is inflicting and enduring today. ... Our teleological endowment spares most of us from worrying over such matters to any great extent, or from disturbing ourselves unduly over the freedom of the will. There is apparently not

much that anyone can do about it except to follow his own light.[8]

My poetry is not pessimistic, nothing of an infinite nature can be proven or disproven in finite
terms—meaning words—and the rest is probably a
matter of one's individual ways of seeing and feeling things. There is no sense in saying that this
world is not a pretty difficult place, but that
isn't pessimism. The real pessimist sees too much
of one thing, and the optimist is too likely to
see only what he wishes to see—or perhaps not
to see at all beyond the end of his famous nose.[9]

Of course I am never really bitter, or anything
but cheerful and full of metaphysical joy and
hope, but people don't seem to understand that
and so call me all sorts of names which also they
don't understand. So far as I can make out, most
people are so afraid of life that when they see it
coming their first impulse is to get behind a tree
and shut their eyes. And for some odd reason
they call that impulse optimism—which has always seemed funny to me.[10]

The Christian ethics might have done some good
if they had ever been tried, or understood, but
I'm afraid it's too late now. There's a non-theo-
logical religion on the way, probably to be revealed by science when science comes definitely
to the jumping-off place. It is really there now,
but isn't quite ready to say so.[11]

The passage of American idealism into scepticism and
emptiness has become by this time a familiar story. It is
commonly interpreted not as a crisis for American culture but as the transformation of Transcendentalism into
realism. It is important to note, however, that this realism
or existentialism is not based on the "spectator theory"
of experience, as in phenomenalism and orthodox phenomenology, but on the consciousness of man's involvement actively in a moving world of action and reaction.
In the language of Schopenhauer, who exerted a marked

influence on this kind of idealism in America, human existence is dependent for its substantial element and real knowledge on "the world as will," not on "the world as idea."

A good example of such realism in nonacademic circles is afforded us by those realistic theorists of the Law who attempt to define Law for lawyers in terms of its actual operation: Law is the systematic ability to predict how a judge will decide. The "obiter dicta" in terms of which a conventional judge tries to justify his decision are extralegal "transcendental nonsense." Such a definition and methodology are adopted not in the spirit of cynicism or revolt, but in the attempt to understand law as it actually exists in the context of pressures and powers.

The emergence of similar doctrines among academic philosophers is a complicated story, but it culminates in the same general acceptance of what are now called "the behavioral sciences." Noteworthy, first of all, is the work of Charles S. Peirce, because he was the first to play seriously with phenomenology. Like Husserl, he arrived at his own "phaneroscopy" through a critical study of Kant's *Critiques*. As early as the 1860's he dismissed Berkeley's empiricist dictum that *esse est percipi* together with the idealist contrast between the world of spirit and the world of objects. In place of the traditional idea that man is an observer of phenomena, he assumed that man is himself a factor in the objective world. The experienced world is linked "triadically." Man is an observer, to be sure, and science is essentially "scopy," but observation implies experimentation: the kind of selective activity that goes on in a laboratory. Phenomena are not merely given or seen but taken and manipulated; the mind is not merely an eye but an operator; all science is "normative." In the spirit of Hegel and Schelling, he conceived of a phenomenology of the spirit as part of the analysis of human history and experience; the real world is a continuity of phenomena and "noumena," a cosmic relativity. The outcome of his philosophical "coenoscopy" (that is, of a general or common observation of the world, as distinguished from the "idioscopy" of the specialized sciences) is a doctrine of categories—categories that are both of experience and of existence—which divide the "phaneron" or world into three kinds of beings: particulars or individuals, relations or "relatives," and generals or interpretings. These factors of Being he respectively called Firstness, Secondness, and Thirdness. The world is not merely a causal order among phenomena but a generalizing process. There is a built-in structure and process of interpretation which transforms things-physically-related into signs-socially-interpreted. Observation when scientific, therefore, is not external to objective existence (as it is in the phenomenological model) but is a triadic, social process in which "relatives" interpret each other. This analysis shifts the problem of knowledge from the seeing of essences to the art of interpretation and communication, from vision to operation. All this is to an orthodox phenomenologist a bad case of "psychologitis," but the infection did not trouble American minds when it became evident that it is simpler to begin with a single world than to arrive at it laboriously through the logical implications of meeting "other subjects" as the phenomenologists, starting with their "Cartesian meditations," were obliged to do. It seemed simpler and more "natural" to begin with human beings not as "transcendental egos" but as clever workers among other animals.

With this basic methodology achieved, it was possible for Royce and James at Harvard, both working with Peirce, to develop a distinctive doctrine of "intentionality" of the mind. Logical meanings, as they developed psychologically, are related, according to both Royce and James, to the intentions which guide purposive activity in general. But James went a bit further than Royce in conceiving of psychology as "a natural science." James opened his treatise on *Psychology* by defining mind as "the pursuit of ends." He showed how the so-called "essences" of objects are put into the context of conscious manipulation of things-under-observation. The behavioral psychology of conscious action led to a "radical empiricism" for

James, which, when combined with Peirce's ontology of the three categories, carried both Harvard idealism and Harvard pragmatism over the elaborate hurdles of phenomenology to a neo-realism and humanistic naturalism.

Meanwhile, another development in American idealism took place in the West, less familiar to laymen, but very important for the revision of phenomenology. This movement, as it spread, had St. Louis, Michigan, Chicago, and Cornell as its headquarters. Both the Eastern and the Western movements owed much of their first impetus to England: the New England movement to Coleridge, and the Western movement to Oxford idealism. The former was predominantly neo-Kantian and the latter neo-Hegelian. It was the latter, the so-called "objective idealism," that made the most incisive attack on the "spectator theory" of knowledge. The Western movement, less individualist, derived its social theory of mind in part from the Oxford idealists who had undermined the extreme individualism of the utilitarians, and in part from an Aristotelian interpretation of Hegel's logic and historical dialectic, which was imported directly from German revisionists among Hegel's disciples. These American Hegelians conceived historical dialectic, or the creative meeting of opposites, less as a dialectic of reason, more as a biological struggle of intelligence from potentiality to actuality. The objective or institutional realization of mind meant to them the creative course of social conflicts (not necessarily or primarily class struggles, as for the left-wing among the Hegelians). The conflict of ideals, they explained, is a process of *mediation* which is at once logical and social. Their interpretation of what Hegel had called the *Phenomenology of the Spirit* emphasized the categories of "activity" and "purpose" as both primary forms of experience and as natural powers. This revival of Aristotle in Hegelian garb was an important factor in transforming the idealistic phenomenology into a theory of community or cooperative inquiry.

The meeting of these two types of American transcendentalism at the Concord Summer Schools and at

Escape From Phenomenology

Thomas Davidson's summer institutes in the Adirondacks during the 1870's and 1880's was a dramatic event, or, as Europeans would say, a crisis in the course of American philosophical thought. It provided the immediate background and stimulation for the development of four centers of existential idealism (St. Louis, Michigan, Chicago, and Cornell) in addition to the center at Harvard. The meeting of minds at these summer schools, and later at the meetings of the American Philosophical Association, promoted rapidly the transformation of traditional romantic idealism into a social theory of mind. This in turn contributed notably to the development of the behavioral sciences and to a philosophical methodology for them.

By 1910, and increasingly thereafter, there was a general effort to get away from "the ego-centric predicament" and to get down to existential work. Despite differences of philosophic backgrounds and schools, despite a wide variety of -isms and idioms, there has developed among American philosophers and social scientists a detailed analysis of the mind and its diverse interests which can best be conceived as behavioral studies. Philosophers from the growing number of academic centers for such studies—notably John Dewey, James E. Creighton, George Mead, Ralph Barton Perry, William P. Montague, F. J. E. Woodbridge, William Ernest Hocking, E. B. McGilvary, Arthur Bentley, E. Jordan, Morris R. Cohen, and C. I. Lewis—developed their analyses of human experience into more or less explicitly behavioral patterns. Gradually the "psychologitis" of the early "how we think" period expanded into a socialized "radical empiricism" and a not-so-naïve realism, which may well be said to constitute America's contribution to contemporary existential thinking, and which has its own methodology.

In view of these developments in American thought and social science, it is somewhat amusing to refer back to Santayana's California lecture of 1911 on "The Genteel Tradition in American Philosophy." Philosophy has now lost practically all of its gentility and most of its phenomenology in America. But Santayana's lecture is still worth reading and taking seriously. It is also worth noting as a very genteel performance. At that time Santayana had not yet succumbed to the temptation which later carried him into phenomenology. His lecture was full of enthusiasm for William James and other liberators from the genteel tradition, but in the closing sentence he returns, perhaps ironically, to the genteel tradition as something needed, at least in California. After portraying existence in California as an open-air emancipation by communion with nature, he closed as follows, no doubt with his characteristic smile:

> The peculiarity of man is that his machinery for reaction on external things has involved an imaginative transcript of these things, which is preserved and suspended in his fancy; and the interest and beauty of this inward landscape, rather than any fortunes that may await his body in the outer world, constitute his proper happiness. By their mind, its scope, quality, and temper, we estimate men, for by the mind only do we exist as men, and are more than so many storage-batteries for material energy. Let us therefore be frankly human. Let us be content to live in the mind.

NOTES

1. *Winds of Doctrine* (New York, 1913), pp. 186–215.

2. "Phenomenology," in the strict sense of Husserl, signifies a kind of knowledge acquired by observing an object with "the mind's eye," logically, in order to discover the object's essence. Existential involvements are here irrelevant.

3. *Winds of Doctrine,* p. 194.

4. *Winds of Doctrine,* p. 192.

5. Existentialism, in its European development, is a movement of revolt: (1) against Husserl's dictum that in phenomenological analysis existence is "transcendental" and not observable or objective; (2) against Hegel's faith that historical dialectic is a purely logical development. German existentialism has emphasized human existence as an object of phenomenological analysis and dialectic, while French existentialism emphasizes social crises and psychological anxieties as objective factors in human existence and essence.

6. *White Jacket* (New York, 1963), pp. 502, 504.

7. The supposed parallel between Gide and Melville which Charles Feidelson draws (pp. 187–207 of his *Symbolism and American Literature*) is instructive. Gide is caught in the "paradoxes" of the phenomenological approach: the chasm between objectivity and subjectivity, the irrationality of "external data" and "eternal forms." But Melville's problem is different: it is the existential frustration of trying to grasp a world in motion, a world whose movement condemns the movement of mind to "the everlasting elusiveness of truth." There is nothing subjective about this problem. It is the existential correlativity *in the same world* of absolute and relative perspectives (as expounded by Plinlimmon in *Pierre*) that creates the ambiguities of moral life. Pierre is not "a

sovereign nature" as is the ego of transcendentalism for Gide. For Pierre, "As soon as you say *Me,* a *God,* a *Nature,* so soon you jump off from your stool and hang from the beam." It is the inherent involvement of all three in the moving world that creates the tragedy of human existence. There is no world of appearances here, nor is there freedom except in death.

8. Letter to Will Durant, Sept. 18, 1931. Published in *Selected Letters of Edwin Arlington Robinson,* ed. Ridgely Torrence (New York, 1940), pp. 163–64.

9. *Selected Letters,* pp. 165–66.

10. *Selected Letters,* p. 168.

11. *Selected Letters,* p. 169.